Philos.

IN THE MINDS OF MEN

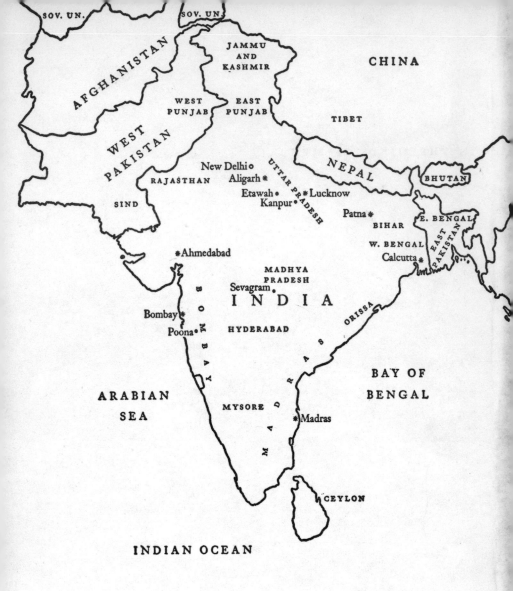

SOV. UN.
SOV. UN.
AFGHANISTAN
JAMMU AND KASHMIR
CHINA
WEST PUNJAB
EAST PUNJAB
WEST PAKISTAN
TIBET
RAJASTHAN
NEPAL
BHUTAN
New Delhi
Aligarh *
UTTAR PRADESH
Etawah •
* Lucknow
Kanpur •
Patna *
E. BENGAL
SIND
BIHAR
W. BENGAL
EAST PAKISTAN
Calcutta *
* Ahmedabad
MADHYA PRADESH
Sevagram •
I N D I A
Bombay *
Poona •
HYDERABAD
ORISSA
B O M B A Y
ARABIAN SEA
M A D R A S
BAY OF BENGAL
MYSORE
* Madras
CEYLON
INDIAN OCEAN

*Locations of UNESCO Teams of Social Scientists

In the Minds of Men

THE STUDY OF HUMAN BEHAVIOR AND
SOCIAL TENSIONS IN INDIA

GARDNER MURPHY

BASED ON THE UNESCO STUDIES BY SOCIAL
SCIENTISTS CONDUCTED AT THE REQUEST OF
THE GOVERNMENT OF INDIA

Basic Books, Inc. Publishers
NEW YORK

TO THE MEMORY OF PARS RAM

Since wars begin in the minds of men, it is in the minds of men that the defenses of peace must be constructed . . .

From the Preamble to the Constitution of the United Nations Educational, Scientific and Cultural Organization.

Contents

III

SOCIAL TENSIONS IN TODAY'S INDIA

Foreword

In 1949 the Ministry of Education, Government of India, asked UNESCO to make available to it a consultant who would spend six months in India organizing research teams to explore the reasons for "social tensions." UNESCO sent me to India for this purpose in 1950. The technical reports of the research teams which were set up have been submitted to the Government of India, and some or all of them will be published.

It was, however, felt both by the Ministry of Education and by Mrs. Alva Myrdal, Director of the Social Sciences Department of UNESCO, that there was also a need for a nontechnical report of my impressions regarding social tensions in India and regarding the many constructive forces working for national unity. The present volume is my attempt to respond to this request. I do so on the understanding that the reader will at every point recall that I went to India simply as a technical consultant on research methods; that I am *not* an expert on India; and that I offer my observations and recommendations for whatever little they are worth, hoping that those better informed than I can develop them into something useful to India.

It is well to keep in mind that in India 1950 was a rather bad year. On account of the exodus from East Pakistan in February to April of that year, Hindu-Muslim tensions had been greatly accentuated. Moreover, from the very nature of the whole study, I had to concentrate on areas, such as Aligarh and Kalyan, where tension was high, rather than in regions in which a relation of stable accommodation between Hindus and Muslims was maintained.

My chief debt of gratitude is to Dr. Otto Klineberg and Dr. Robert C. Angell, formerly of the UNESCO staff; Dr. Tara Chand, Professor Humayun Kabir, and Mr. P. N. Kirpal of the Ministry of Education; Professor Pars Ram, whose tragic death occurred while serving as Director of the Department of Child Welfare of the Gujarat University and while this book was being written; Professor C. N. Vakil and Dr. A. R. Desai of the School of Economics and Sociology, Bombay University; Dr. Zakir Husain, Vice-Chancellor of the Muslim University at Aligarh; Professors Kali Prasad and Radhakamal Mukerjee of Lucknow University; Professor H. P. Maiti, Institute of Psychological Research and Service, Patna; Professor B. Kuppuswamy of Presidency College, Madras; Dr. Kamla Chowdhry and Dr. Vikram Sarabhai of the Ahmedabad Textile Industry Research Association; Mr. Gautam Sarabhai of the Calico Mill, Ahmedabad; Dr. B. S. Guha, Department of Anthropology, Government of India; Professor W. Norman Brown and Dr. Richard Lambert, South Asia Regional Studies Center, of the University of Pennsylvania, whose reading of the manuscript freed it of many errors; and above all, to my fellow observer, Lois Barclay Murphy, who often opened my gaze to the world of Indian women and children—a world screened from many Western eyes.

Gardner Murphy

Birchlea,
Ashland, New Hampshire.
August, 1952

I

AN INTERNATIONAL "TENSION PROJECT"

I

World dislocation and social science

International disorders call for international remedies. The confusions and miseries of recent years are conceived more and more as problems which no single nation can solve. They are problems of humanity, problems calling for a method to which humanity has more and more given its allegiance in recent decades, the method of science. It is important to feel deeply, to share in the sufferings of our fellows; it is also important to seek the most complete and accurate sources of information as to the ways in which such sufferings can be removed.

It has been the function of many world organizations, such as the World Health Organization and the World Federation for Mental Health, to think in terms of recruiting an international membership consecrated to the conception of an international rather than a national solution of problems which bedevil the men and women of any one country. UNESCO[1] is one of these world-organized federations of human beings concerned with the attempt to discover a way of writing a prescription against social disorders like intergroup suspicion and prejudice, not merely against local manifestations of the disease. The very fact that we share with the people of other lands the conception that intergroup hostility destroys the worth of living means that we regard
. . . .
[1] United Nations Educational, Scientific and Cultural Organization.

3

the problems of India or the Philippines or Chile or Japan as essentially common universal human problems. All over the world there is not only physical disorder such as malnutrition and disease; there is likewise social disorder such as group hostility and prejudice. Variations in degree are indeed to be found, and variations in the level of technical competency in dealing with such ills. Essentially, however, it is because we are human beings in an imperfect society that these things exist.

The social sciences are of course called upon today far more than ever before to play their part in the clarification of these world disorders. Some of the social sciences are more effectively utilized than others. The technical resources of economics have long been understood to some degree by administrators and by the public. More recently sociology has played its part, as, for example, in the study of race relations and immigration. Still more recently cultural anthropology has added powerfully to our understanding of the collective viewpoint and outlook, and the capacity for group cohesion, which each human group may manifest. Sociology and anthropology are everywhere useful to the administrator who seeks to understand the suspicions and hostilities between human groups living near to one another and between such groups and those whose administrative task it is to gear them into effective living with one another.

More recently still psychology and psychiatry have been called upon to make their contribution. Erik Erikson, David Levy, and others have studied the role which childhood experience played in preparing for Hitler's regime. In the same way, attempts have been made to understand the special personality traits which have led to the successful ascendancy of despots or oligarchs of one sort or another. But it is not only the *leaders* whose personalities are studied in terms of psychology and psychiatry. More and more our attention has been drawn to the psychological factors, whether conscious or unconscious, which lie behind prejudice, suspicion, authoritarianism, and other failures of human beings to understand one another and devise means of working toward group ends.

Unfortunately, however, the use of these various social sciences has been somewhat like mounting a staircase; first one uses, let us say, the historical approach, then the economic, then the sociological; and one may pride oneself on having superseded all earlier approaches when one reaches the psychological or even the psychoanalytic domain. The aim of the most useful types of investigation, however, is not the step-by-step accumulation of data from various disciplines; rather it is the attempt to see social relations in the light of *all* these disciplines at once jointly utilized in relation to a common problem. We cannot compartmentalize human life, separating that which is economic, that which is sociological, that which is psychological or psychiatric.

ECONOMIC WASTE AND PSYCHOLOGICAL FAILURE

It is in connection with this last point that we must answer as honestly as we can the question constantly put to us: "Are not these difficulties all basically economic?" The answer depends on what one means by economic. From one viewpoint they are; from another, they are not. The point is that the word "economic" has proved in many cases to be too slippery to be helpful in this type of analysis. Two men hate each other so violently that neither can accept the resources or the labor of the other; is this an economic fact? It certainly is. If we shift the scene from two men to two *groups*, so that we have two human groups unable to trade or exchange commodities with one another because they hate each other's guts, is this an economic fact? Certainly it is. At the same time it is a psychological fact. In India, as our volume will try to show—and this is true of most countries—there are countless instances in which the suspicion and hatred which have developed make impossible the mutual gain which ordinary trade or other economic exchange might permit. There are countless instances in which the psychological attributes of human beings prevent the rational economic operations which classical economics tell us should occur. This is by no means a claim that psychology takes precedence over economics. This would be utterly fatuous. On the contrary, it is an attempt to show that the organic wholeness of human personality makes absurd that kind of cliché in which we would speak of the economic factor. We shall look at human beings, as far as we may, in terms of the integration which their own lives have achieved, as they respond to the soil, the climate, the technology that affects the growth and development of plants and animals, the accumulated resources of capital and labor which make possible the production and distribution of commodities worked into finished and consumable form. There will be a large place here for the cooperation of experts such as economists, sociologists, and psychologists, but in the last analysis we shall be dealing simply with social tensions expressing the frustrations which humanity encounters at present through the fact that it does not utilize the available resources for bettering its own lot. We must stress the fact that all over the world there is huge economic waste through psychological failure as well as psychological failure through economic waste.

THE UNTRIED APPROACH THROUGH RESEARCH

In general the approach of modern man to the dislocations and hatreds which prevail group by group, nation by nation, over the face of the globe is the method of exhortation. By and large, our political leaders, our clergy, our educators, our journalists, our artists plead with us to be less stupid, to be more humane, to develop a rational "one world" in which cooperative endeavor will meet the needs of all. Whether we think of that portion of the world which believes that a forced authoritarian state control of production and distribution is the only way of coping with the human tendency to conflict, or whether we cling to the ideal of the West in believing that somehow without such a central authority at the top we can find our way toward group integration and cooperation, we shall practically all agree that the method of exhortation has failed. As a matter of fact, the method of exhortation is ordinarily followed at once by the method of force, simply because exhortation will not by itself do the job. This is what has happened in the portions of the world to which we are likely to apply the term "iron curtain." The use of force by the United States is not only very evident through the mounting defense budget, but through the no longer concealed assumption that it is only by force that the pressure of the Soviet system can be contained.

A third approach might, however, be found useful here: Can we not add to our strength by making strong all that we have of democracy by devising techniques for the actual utilization of the social sciences and by finding fresh ways of developing the social sciences? Indeed, cannot democracy itself be made the subject of social science research? Can we not, in the spirit of Kurt Lewin, study the psychological structure of democracy; investigate democratic and authoritarian groups; find ways of casting direct light upon the dynamics of democracy and autocracy; and above all find ways of maintaining and deepening the satisfactions which come from democratic living? If indeed we can, through psychological and social research, understand more fully the satisfactions which democracy yields and the practical ends which it can serve if more fully understood, we may find a way of enormously strengthening the democratic forces of the world without thereby adding a cent to the defense budget and, indeed, without incurring the enormous psychological losses which the unlimited reliance upon force entails.

The conception that all the social sciences are dealing with the same human beings but merely from different angles is one which has been developing in recent decades. Take, for example, the work of the Social Science Research Council in New York, in which social scientists representing economics, government, history, sociology, psychology, anthropology, and statistics have merged their research efforts; and the long series of interdisciplinary researches, such as those on cooperation and competition, with which they have been identified.

INTERNATIONAL RESEARCH

Another obvious step in merging our social science knowledge is to preface with the word "inter" the word "national." When interdisciplinary research exists in one country, the question arises: "Why should a nationalistic frame of reference be applied to interdisciplinary research?"

When UNESCO has agreed that "war begins in the minds of men," it is not by way of any reduction of emphasis upon factors other than the psychological which bring them in conflict; rather, it is an attempt to make clear that all the forces from which war springs are ultimately passed through the filter of human thought, feeling, and impulse before they lead to the decisions from which war follows.

During and after the UNESCO deliberations in Paris in 1946, there seemed to be some agreement as to a few central factors which could be discovered in the dozens of contemporary research problems which are concerned with the reduction of the threat of war. It was finally determined that the word "tensions," so often used in psychiatry to describe a state of suspense, uneasiness, or readiness for violent action, might be chosen as typifying many different kinds of distress from which the preparations for war spring. In time the phrase "tensions project" was established to describe a group of interrelated branches of inquiry. A few of these are relevant as background for our present endeavor. One of them relates to the development of a new kind of history, a history which shall be an account not of the grandeurs and glories of the country represented by the historian, but rather an attempt to show what each country owes to its neighbors. Thus French historians are engaged in a study of the French nation from the point of view of the interdependence of France and its neighbors, and the gains which France has received from them. A second line of inquiry deals with the ideas which children of school age develop regarding the people of other countries. This is called the "stereotypes" study. In Norway, for example, schedules of questions have been administered to children to find what ideas they hold regarding Swedes and Danes, Frenchmen and Englishmen, Chinese and Argentinians. The stereotypes study is closely related to a wider study of prejudice in the school system to which some English educators are devoting their attention. A third line of work relates to the effects of industrialization. Four countries—France, Sweden, Australia, and India—have agreed upon a uniform method of research on the effects of industrialization in producing social tension. In a "planning conference" held in Paris in 1949, leaders of social science in these four countries met together and underwent a short training course to prepare them for the types of field work and psychological investigation which would be carried out in their respective countries by a uniform plan. The industrialization study is a pioneering endeavor to get the same common plan of human investigation operating in very different cultural conditions under international auspices.

Among the many aims of UNESCO is the training of a social science personnel which will ultimately be international in outlook. One will find in the course of the present study many of the difficulties and the joys of working at the same time as a typical member of one's own national group and as a servant of an international organization.

2

Our UNESCO mission to India

As soon as the new government of India assumed power in August, 1947, it began to orient itself toward the problem of its relations with the Western world. It had always dealt with the United States and the other powers of the West as a part of the British Empire; now it must learn to make its own contacts. One of the first things in the new era was to learn how to deal with the new international agencies: the World Health Organization, the World Federation for Mental Health, and above all the United Nations and UNESCO. It had to learn on what terms it could participate as a full member in such international planning bodies as directed the policies of these groups, and what benefits could be derived from such bodies.

We shall attempt here to sketch the steps by which the Indian government determined upon the program of action, involving the support of UNESCO, which is the subject of this book. The reader who is interested only in the facts and impressions gleaned from the author's six months in India and the detail of the research program, and not in the arrangements with UNESCO and with the government of India, may skip directly to Chapter 3. The reader who is thinking, however, about the broad question of ways in which an American can obtain opportunities to observe in India, and the social and technical conditions surrounding such work, may find something in this chapter that will apply to his own problem.

In October, 1948, the Ministry of Education at New

11

Delhi sent to the Vice-Chancellors[1] of all Indian universities a systematic and vigorously phrased account of the problem of social tensions and intergroup hostilities in India. An appeal was made for systematic study by the universities of the problems of social tension as related to religion, caste, language groupings, economic class, etc. No budget or research timetable was suggested. Rather, it was urged that each Vice-Chancellor should establish a council or committee within his own university which would represent the various interested social sciences and would develop an interpretation of social tensions within the area of the university, submitting a report on its findings to the Ministry of Education.

THE APPEAL TO UNESCO

Documents of this sort are of course not likely to produce vigorous action, even when some preliminary statement about facilities and budget is provided. It is not surprising that the action which resulted from this appeal was quite limited. Consequently, during the months of February and March some members of the Ministry gave thought to the question of obtaining more vigorous action and definite implementation of the proposal for interuniversity research studies of social tensions. The occasion finally developed for a specific request to UNESCO in this matter. This was a visit by Mr. P. N. Kirpal, of the Ministry, to the UNESCO office in Paris at the end of March, 1949. He stated the general contours of the interuniversity project in social tensions and asked the aid of UNESCO. Dr. Otto Klineberg, Acting Head of the Department of Social Sciences of UNESCO, pointed out that one primary requisite was a system of intercommuni-

. . . .

[1] The governor of a state in the Republic is often *ex officio* the Chancellor. The effective "President" of the university is entitled the Vice-Chancellor.

cation between the universities in their studies, a method of coordinating their research program, and a way of drawing together uniform types of information into a coherent general scheme relevant to the problems of India as a whole. On these terms Dr. Klineberg felt that UNESCO might be able to give some support in India's social tensions problem.

This proposal was gladly accepted and, after due consideration, official action and a budget of $20,000 were provided. It was understood that this sum would make possible the designation of an American research consultant, providing him with a round trip by air and six months' residence in India, with facilities for extensive interuniversity travel, and at the same time providing a research budget which would take care of a series of research investigations which would be set up by the Indian universities during the period of incumbency of this consultant.

Dr. Klineberg asked the writer in April, 1949, if he would be willing to consider this assignment. The only possible reply was that this could not be done at the time, but might be considered at a future date. During the next six months attempts were made to find someone else with a background in social psychology or related fields who might be interested in this particular UNESCO assignment. Success did not attend these expectations and the invitation to the writer was renewed in November, 1949. It was then gratefully accepted on condition that the next few months would be spent in preparing for the Indian trip and that the journey to India would occur in June or July, 1950. In this period, the Social Sciences Department of UNESCO was in the hands of Dr. Robert C. Angell, and it was through his help that the final arrangements were made.

Actually one of the most salutary things about the whole project from the writer's point of view was the fact that this arrangement made possible some months of careful preparation. During this time correspondence was carried on with about a hundred Indian scholars, in all parts of India, representing the various social sciences, as well as with university Vice-Chancellors and other educational leaders. It made possible a great deal of communication with the Ministry of Education and the clarification of plans. It made possible the exchange of ideas with UNESCO, and some degree of integration between what UNESCO wanted and what the Ministry of Education wanted. It permitted the gathering of ideas as to the sorts of research which Indian scholars felt to be important, and the types of methods which they thought to be feasible.

Most important of all, however, the period of six months of preparation made possible many long and intimate interviews with Indian scholars and other informed persons. Contact was made with some forty experts on India, both Indian and American, some of them teaching on the Eastern seaboard or on their way to the West, some of them on periods of furlough prior to return to duties in India. It would be impossible to do justice to the continuous and generous assistance offered by these many friends. From these conversations the planning of the study emerged.

It is, however, necessary to single out two individuals who during this period played a pre-eminent part in planning the Indian studies of social tensions and without whose aid the plan as a whole could not have achieved very much.

First we must mention Pars Ram. Pars Ram was a psychologist trained at the University of Calcutta, long interested in child psychology, a lay psychoanalyst who had been deeply concerned with problems of Indian character structure and of the capacity of India to understand and control her own development with respect to the pressing forces of industrialism and westernization. Pars Ram, a Hindu (and a Brahmin), had been teaching for some twenty years at the Forman Christian College in Lahore. Here he had been in continuous contact with Western science, technology, psy-

chology, and the social sciences, and had been using the
methods of progressive education: discussion techniques, in-
dividualization of instruction, democratization of the teaching atmosphere. At the same time, as one closely in touch
with Indian nationalism and as a follower of Gandhi, he had
foreseen the era in which India would control her own desti-
nies. When the partition of India brought a direct challenge to
every Hindu who remained on Pakistan soil, it was Pars
Ram's thought simply to stay at Lahore where he had
worked so long. This privilege was not, however, accorded
him, and he and his wife and family made their hasty journey, under compulsion, to Delhi, where he became head of
the Department of Psychology at the East Punjab University
and lecturer in the Delhi School of Social Work. Here, during the years 1947-48, he had been thinking deeply about
the problem of social tensions and of the use of social sciences
in clarifying India's social problems; when the writer went
through the sheaf of documents on social tensions collected
by UNESCO, he found three documents by Pars Ram dealing with these problems. Pars Ram had become a UNESCO
Fellow to the United States in the autumn months of 1949.
Nothing was more obvious therefore than for the writer to
rejoice at the opportunity to meet him in January, 1950,
when he was in New York. From this meeting followed a
series of interviews looking forward to types of all-Indian
collaboration which became one of the most fruitful parts
of the whole venture in India.[2]

Of the greatest importance is the conception which Pars
Ram developed of a kind of planning activity which would
bring all Indian scholars into the field of social science research related to social tensions. It would not be enough,
he said, for us to select able scholars and ask them to share

. . . .

[2] Professor Pars Ram's death in the summer of 1952 was not only a
great loss to these investigations but a deep personal loss to us as well.

our interest. Rather, the effective thing would be to write a very large number of letters to specific individuals who might possibly be interested, individuals representing not only psychology and the social sciences but also literature, the arts, journalism, administration, educational policy-making, and all the various aspects of public life in India which are colored by the fact of social tensions, or which permit a special vantage point for their understanding. In the spirit of his suggestion letters were drawn up to reach individuals from these various groups.

A primary aspect of Pars Ram's thought was the conception that those who were invited to take part in such study should meet together for a long and leisurely *planning conference*, at which they would think through the question of coordinating their efforts, drawing up uniform research plans and reporting the results in a form permitting practical action. Finally, from discussion between Pars Ram and the writer, a scheme was devised for a four-day conference in New Delhi as soon as Mrs. Murphy and I arrived in that city, at which the various leaders of Indian thought relating to the problem would meet together and discuss the philosophy of the research attack. From what follows the reader will see that whatever success the venture achieved was due in very large part to this planning conference which had been to such a large degree the result of Pars Ram's thinking.

The other individual to be specially mentioned here is Professor C. N. Vakil, Director of the School of Economics and Sociology at the University of Bombay. Professor Vakil, an economist trained in the London School of Economics, is very widely known as an educator and administrator of a powerful modern training center for economists and sociologists; as a man who has directed and integrated a great deal of research in pure and applied economics; and as a man who in contact with the Planning Commission of the Government has been directly concerned with the practicalities of the new government's action with reference to agricultural and business economics.

I had written to Vakil at his Bombay address. Immediately came an airmail reply from Mrs. Vakil indicating that Professor Vakil was in Puerto Rico but would be in New York in a few days before returning to India. I was lucky enough to catch him at his hotel, and to go through a rapid-fire exchange of ideas which actually gave substance within thirty minutes to all of the rather indistinct and vague ideas which I had been hoping to broach with him in the course of several hours. He seized instantly the importance of the problem, the value of UNESCO's assistance, the desirability of the planning conference. He went on from that to foresee what could be done in the city of Bombay. As the story unfolds, the reader will see that Vakil had foreseen most of the practicalities of the situation, and had ready for us at the time we reached Bombay a research team of great power and competence, ready to go to work within the framework later established at the New Delhi Planning Conference.

One other phase of our preparation should be noted here. Through the generous assistance of the Social Science Research Council of New York City, a conference was held at the South Asia Regional Studies Center of the University of Pennsylvania in May, 1950, at which the Chairman, Professor W. Norman Brown, and most of the members of his staff sat with us for two days, going over preliminary questions which we formulated regarding the nature of the social tensions problem in India and giving us their very practical advice as to how to proceed. This planning conference at Philadelphia served to throw into relief some of the issues which we later presented to the New Delhi Planning Conference in August.

THE UNESCO MANDATE TO ITS CONSULTANT

This is the appropriate place to discuss the general orientation of the UNESCO consultant before he set out on his way. What exactly was he expected to do? According to the mandate received from the UNESCO office, he was to assist the universities in the integration of their research plans. At that time, however (March, 1949), the universities had not yet drawn up research plans. The only research plans were those broached in a vague preliminary form by Professor Pars Ram in some of his papers submitted to UNESCO. Actually it was the exchange of letters, the many personal interviews, and the New Delhi Planning Conference in August, 1950 (immediately upon our arrival in India), that led to the formulation of plans. In other words, the making of the separate university plans was a result of the planning conference in New Delhi rather than a precursor to them. It had become evident that the business of the UNESCO consultant was to find out what kinds of research the Indian universities were capable of and interested in doing, and to use the UNESCO funds which were available to bring them together in the first place, and then to assist them in setting up the projects in which they had interest.

In the second place, the question naturally arose whether pure research on social tensions was the thing which India most needed. From the very beginning I thought a great deal about the question whether fact-finding, and fact-finding alone, was to be the center of this study. I spent some time talking with people who had had experience in the practical mediation between conflicting groups, people with an interest in creating understanding and good will across the chasm of utter failures of communication. Indeed, people were considered as possible members of our research team whose skills lay not at all in the areas of research but in the area of practical leadership in the development of coworking groups. These plans, however, were ultimately abandoned, partly because the first-class personnel with such training were not found, partly because it was felt that after all UNESCO was asking for a fact-finding study; and partly because it was felt that any group of Western scholars arriving on Indian soil and trying to show Indians how to do practical inter-group adjustment work would inevitably run into the general response: "Look, we know our own problems and our own difficulties; look at the dozens of consecrated individuals who are themselves working on such problems." Indeed, intergroup harmony was a major factor in Gandhi's whole program during the last decades of his life; the Prime Minister and a huge number of leaders of the Congress Party had made it practically their life work to develop closer understanding between communities and between castes; was it likely that a few technicians from the West in a "barn-storming" study involving a few months would have something practical, something to be received gratefully, something actually likely to be applied to Indian conditions?

Rightly or wrongly, it was decided to concentrate our study upon fact-finding as such, with later discussion of implementation and application of the facts in so far as facts of an unexpected sort or pointing a new direction might be unearthed. Indeed, there were no "barn-storming experts" available for this assignment. The reasons why UNESCO acted as it did were defined by the spirit of the request of the Ministry of Education itself, namely, a request for pure research as such; and it was in these terms that the request was accepted.

THE PLANNERS AND THE PLANNING:
NEW DELHI, AUGUST, 1950

On July 20, 1950 we took off. We had two days for UNESCO contacts in Paris, a short stopover in Rome, a week in Israel, and arrived in Karachi on August 3. The visit to that bedraggled yet booming new capital was chiefly of importance in giving us a sense of the gentleness, the warmth, the sweetness, the relaxation of the general life pattern in South Asia, despite the incredible misery to which both time and the recent partition of the country had led, and despite the universal and acute anguish, loneliness, and despair written on the faces of tens of thousands of refugees. Regarding Pakistan, however, we are not equipped to say anything whatever.

We flew on when a plane was available, arriving in New Delhi on the sixth, and on the following morning began our contacts with the Ministry of Education. Here Dr. Tara Chand, Secretary of the Ministry, together with Professor Humayun Kabir and Mr. P. N. Kirpal, assisted us at once to get a broad view of our problem. We also had long talks with Professor B. S. Guha, of Calcutta, Director of the Department of Anthropology of the government of India, already engaged in carrying out a UNESCO study of the effects of industrialization upon India, and Professor H. P. Maiti, of the Institute of Psychological Research and Service of Patna University, both of whom had come on for our planning conference. Likewise, we saw again our friends Pars Ram and C. N. Vakil, who had helped us so much in our preparations. Then our conference was formally inaugurated on Wednesday morning, to run through the rest of the week.

The meeting was opened by Dr. Tara Chand, and was followed by my own brief report of what UNESCO had asked me to do. Then came reports from several of the Indian social scientists who had something to say about what their universities might contribute to social tensions research. After each of the leaders who was ready to undertake research in India had been heard from, time was given to the question of the most acute problems facing India, and upon the suggestion of Dr. Tara Chand it was agreed that the problem of Hindu-Muslim relations would be central and fundamental. Attention would also be given to caste, language, economic, and regional hostilities.

Discussion turned then to the question of methods of research. It was agreed that the historical background of tension in each region in which a university was working would be considered, and that the general sociological and economic picture would be brought into relation to the current dynamics of personal attitudes of friendliness or hostility. The primary method would have to be the interview. The interview would not be a polling sheet of yes-no questions, but would be a free or conversational approach, emphasizing primarily "nondirective" or "open-ended" questions, lasting perhaps an hour or two. The questions would be carefully prepared, in the native tongues, and some uniformity from one university to another be guaranteed by mutual exchange of preliminary forms of questions.

The investigators in all cases were to be young staff members or graduate students working as assistants to the "team captain" or leader at each university. The data were to take a form which would permit uniform statistical treatment. Where possible the data could be random samples of the populations to be represented, but this would depend upon the problem, the resources, and the method being followed. It was agreed that the data would all be interchanged from team to team so that each would know what the others were doing, and that it would be my own responsibility to get the technical reports of these various team captains, in integrated edited form, to the Central Government when the studies were completed.

ESTABLISHMENT OF THE RESEARCH TEAMS

Six teams were constituted at the New Delhi Conference on the basis of the interests expressed and the agreement just reached. Most of these teams had been, as it were, foreseen; the possibility of their participation had been discussed in correspondence. A definite agreement was reached and entered in the minutes that the following six teams should be constituted:

Professor C. N. Vakil of Bombay was to make a study dealing with the three-cornered hostility pattern which had developed in that area between the Hindu residents, the Hindu refugees, and the Muslims. He would make use of graduate students trained for interview work in his school, would make use of a sample adequate to represent the three primary groups discussed, and would apply statistical treatment which would show which aspects in the life history and the economic and social situation of each respondent were most directly related to his feeling of acceptance or rejection of the other community groups. At the same time the attitudes of all three groups toward the government were to be carefully studied, as to what was good and what was bad in the government's handling of the refugee and Muslim problems.

Professor Kali Prasad of Lucknow University was interested in a somewhat similar approach, but from the point of view of the fact that Lucknow has for centuries been a relatively low tension area. The problem of intergroup hostility might well be illuminated by studying a city in which relatively little such hostility has been manifest.

Professor H. P. Maiti of Patna University indicated that there was a considerable number of regional problems of interest, including the problem of the relations of the Hindus to the aboriginal population and including problems of relations between refugees and resident Hindus. He indicated a willingness to set going a series of minor interrelated projects, but did not wish at the time to commit himself to a single project.

Professor Pars Ram indicated his interest in the general historical-cultural background of Hindus and Muslims. In order to understand at a deep level the basic assumptions and outlooks which characterize these two groups with respect to one another, the economic factors would be brought into the picture, but the primary problem would be the difficulty of mutual understanding which prevails between the two groups. He indicated his willingness to give up all other work and to stay on the job for the whole year, while the captains of the other teams just mentioned were to direct the work in their spare time, and complete the studies in six months. Pars Ram also indicated his readiness to leave the Delhi area, and expressed a desire to carry out his investigation in a region in which Muslim influences are very well defined. Soon thereafter he established himself at the Muslim University in Aligarh.

The four teams just described were to be financed solely and directly from UNESCO funds. The fifth team to be described, the team to be led by Dr. B. S. Guha at the Government Department of Anthropology at Calcutta, was to receive UNESCO funds but was to use as its research staff men and women who were already members of the research staff of the Government Department of Anthropology, so that their salaries would be paid for by the government of India. Dr. Guha's interest lay largely in the problem of the plight of the refugees from East Pakistan and the nature of the refugee camps to which they had been assigned, as factors producing antigovernment or anti-Muslim attitudes among refugees. More broadly this was a part of the question of good and bad morale among refugee groups. He pointed out that he had already compiled extensive material on physical anthropology, personality dynamics through projective tests, and general cultural information regarding the villages in which he was doing his industrialization study (page 9), and he felt ready to use the same interdisciplinary approach in the tensions investigation. He would, in other words, look at the problem in terms of its anthropological as well as its psychological dimensions.

The basis of operations of the sixth team is quite different from that which is evident for the first five. In the great textile city of Ahmedabad, on the west coast, a city to which Gandhi gave much of his life and love, the huge development of textiles during World War II had led to a surprising opportunity for social science research. The fact is that the industry made so much money in the production of cloth and other necessities during World War II that its tax payments were huge. It was felt to be sound business practice, therefore, to turn a large part of the earnings into pure research, which in view of the government's need for research facts, would be entirely tax-exempt. The government agreed to the value of such a large-scale research enterprise, remitting the taxes on this basis, and even itself offered some direct assistance to the research association which was thus set up. Accordingly the industry established the Ahmedabad Textile Industry Research Association (ATIRA). The Sarabhai family, long prominent in the mills and in many philanthropic and educational enterprises in the city, played a considerable part in the establishment of this research association and the young cosmic ray scientist, Dr. Vikram Sarabhai, became its Executive Secretary. Sections were established for research respectively in physics, chemistry, economics, psychology, and other aspects of textile production.

From the very beginning it was conceived to be fundamental to the industry to understand the attitudes and outlooks of those taking part in mill production. After searching India for available personnel which might be suitable for the psychological division, the Director finally, upon interview, selected Dr. Kamla Chowdhry, a young social psychologist with a Ph.D. from the University of Michigan, who had made industrial psychology one of her primary interests. She expressed the willingness of the ATIRA, fully supported by the leaders of the Ahmedabad textile unions, to embark upon a study of the attitudes of workers, especially the attitudes of workers toward their immediate supervisors, as a concrete embodiment of a plan for dealing with something practical within the social psychology of the mill situation. The investigation became an official part of the sixfold UNESCO project launched at New Delhi, but it was financed by the ATIRA, except for the fact that after the original arrangements had been made, Mr. Ishwar Dayal, a young psychologist trained at the Educational Clinic at City College, New York, who had been employed by UNESCO as a technical assistant, was made available for some months to assist Dr. Chowdhry in her work in Ahmedabad.

We thus have the picture of six research teams following some degree of uniformity of method, and embarking upon a timetable involving some six months of work, except that in the case of Pars Ram an additional six months' work was to be done, lasting to August, 1951. It was fully understood that other teams might be added to these six at a later time.

About thirty-five people attended the conference. The six team captains mentioned were in several cases accompanied by their colleagues or research associates. There were several representatives from the Ministry of Education and from other ministries in the government. Dr. Sohan Lal of the Ministry of Defense reported on psychological research techniques used in the Army; Dr. L. C. Bhandari commented on the uses that might be made of psychotherapeutic (and especially psychoanalytic) techniques in gaining insights; Dr. Richard Lambert of the University of Pennsylvania reported on his extensive studies of communal riots; Dr. Dorothy Spencer represented the Department of State; and Mr. P. Bandyopadhyay represented the UNESCO Field Office at Delhi University. There were in addition several other social scientists who were interested in these problems.

At the end of four days of conference, we felt fully clear as to the main problem of orientation, procedure, and personnel.

Some weeks later we lunched with the Prime Minister and his daughter, described to them the main steps in our tension studies, and asked that the government of India make its own contribution to such research. He listened closely and courteously, but there were few smiles in his tightly drawn face. A keen, intense, closely analytical—and very skeptical—response. A feeling, "I hope you succeed, but it looks like a large order, and a very academic order, to me." The next day he phoned the Ministry, saying, "Put it in the budget and let's see what it looks like." [3]

. . . .

[3] This item of 100,000 rupees from the government of India is currently (1952) being used for the continuation of the social tensions research.

II

SOURCES OF SOLIDARITY AND CLEAVAGE IN INDIAN LIFE AND HISTORY

3

Village life as source of security and solidarity

Before we report our investigations, we must describe the background from which those factors emerged which long tended to preserve solidarity and provide security, but have nevertheless played a part in the production of cleavage and social tensions. While the present chapter concentrates upon the basic causes of cohesion and security in Indian society, and the fifth chapter emphasizes the modern factors leading to tensions, the chapter between the two traces some roots of both tendencies in Indian child development.

Over a period of more than two thousand years of India's known history, the village, as an economic and cultural unit, represented the basis of Indian life. An attempt will be made to derive from the nature and institutions of Indian village life some of the causes of the fundamentally cohesive nature of human relations in India.

THE FAMILY SYSTEM PROVIDES PROTECTION

First of all, attention must be given to the functional unit within the village, namely, the joint family. By this is meant a household of persons comprising the sons of a given pair of parents, together with their wives, children, and unmarried sisters, and all those (e.g., aged parents) who are dependent upon them; the oldest of these sons is ordinarily the head of the family. Typically, as the children grow up, the eldest male, if mentally and physically competent, will be regarded as destined to become the ultimate head of the family. As the sons marry, usually by an arrangement which the parents themselves work out with the bride's parents, a domicile is expanded if necessary, or gradually adapted in minor respects to the needs of the new couple. On these terms younger brothers have somewhat less independence than the older brother; and the womenfolk, being brought in from other families and frequently from other villages, are inevitably subordinate to the eldest male's wife's general sovereignty. The surviving father or mother, or both, of the male who becomes dominant in the picture continues to receive respect, but with their superannuation the old people step aside as far as the primary wielding of power is concerned.

One discovers everywhere in India the enormous importance of the burden which the eldest male carries. A typical tragedy upon which we stumbled was the issue confronting a brilliant young graduate student of psychology, a man with a magnificent future in research and application, who through the death of his father became the head of the family long before he was through with his training, and who under family pressures left the fascinations of the life to which he had looked forward to take a business position, simply because the income made possible many comforts and opportunities for his brothers and brothers' wives, and nieces and nephews, and the joint family as a whole. Another young acquaintance of ours was a man of great intellectual power and social promise who decided to spend his life in a petty clerical position in a mill town. This utterly "unintelligible" decision—that is, unintelligible from a Western point of view—was owing simply to the fact that to take two or three years off for advanced training would have meant jeopardizing the family fortunes; that was not the kind of decision which the head of the family could make. This sort of constraint upon the individual by virtue of his relation to the group reflects a system of joint responsibility widely known to the human race. The somewhat similar system of China and Japan is well known. Nor is it utterly unknown in the West, as we read of Greek and Roman family life. The industrialized Western societies, however, have in general forgotten it.

The term "family" has many meanings in India which it does not have for us. There is not only the formal structure of the joint family already mentioned: a family system in which brothers hold together, their wives and children constituting a part of one joint household, with economic unity of control; there is, no less important, a very rich emotional interpenetration of all their relationships. In many parts of India, for example, the child may be nearly as close to its aunts as to its mother. In the same way, older sisters and all females of the group may be thought of by the small child as essentially similar or even identical in function. The child is not disciplined by and responsible to a single individual. There are of course cases in which a domineering mother of the head of a joint family may feel herself to be charged with special responsibility for the children's upbringing, and one finds the usual mother-in-law—daughter-in-law battles. In general, however, the joint family is an emotional nexus of profoundly unifying value. One finds one's being in the family constellation. In effect this means terrific pressure upon the individual if in any way he breaks away from the tissued structure of the village life; but for the most part he does not, or if he does, he comes back.

Closely related to this matter of family closeness is the whole attitude toward women. A woman is in the first instance a mother who holds to herself all those who share not only in the tissue of her own body but in the blood of the group of which she is the symbol.

In the same way, the feeling about the joint family colors the attitude toward children. Children are not individuals only—individuals to be prized, magnified, pushed forward, warned, threatened, rebuked, idealized, fancied in grandiose terms of future achievement. Children are the stuff of one's being. It is warmth and closeness to them that makes life important, meaningful, and continuous. The continuity of Indian life, without which one's own momentary existence is meaningless, is conceived naturally in terms of fruitfulness, in terms of the health, welfare, reproductive capacity, long life of all the individuals who issue from one's own body.

This attitude toward children is perhaps at times overlooked in the West by those who say simply that India's great problem is overpopulation and her great need, birth control. There is not the slightest doubt that there *is* everywhere in India a great readiness for all sorts of revolutionary changes, including readiness for family limitation. The villages, necessarily the archetypes of traditionalism, are the last places anywhere in the world in which doctrines of family limitation or any other fundamental change could be expected to make headway. But there has actually been almost no articulate resistance to the idea of family limitation in India, whether in villages or cities. The Indian family, however, even when limited, would be large. Family limitation generally means decrease from perhaps eight or nine births down to five or four. (The "rhythm" method is being taught.) The Indian is not automatically accepting in and for itself the reduction of the number of children without further thought. Moreover, he is not prepared to give up the closeness of contact with those children whom he does have.

THE CASTE SYSTEM SECURES A PLACE FOR EVERYONE

Second to the joint family in the organization of village life is the fact of caste. No one knows the exact origin of Indian caste. It is, however, evident that the so-called "Aryan" invaders, the creators of the magnificent Vedic hymns, were a vigorous and dominant people. As they came into India from the northwest and established themselves, they of course regarded themselves as superior to the native population. Their own social stratification and that of the native population gradually evolved into the caste rigidities which we know.

The caste situation has never been completely rigid. It represents a historically moving scene based originally upon the social class distinctions within the conquering Aryan group and upon the differentiation of occupation or function, among the conquerors, among the conquered, and among that later hierarchical structure in which conquerors and conquered were integrated. As the system became relatively rigid, marked out by nonintermarriage of those identified with a different caste, the time came when the economic life of the village depended upon the fixity of the occupational distinctions and upon the transmission from father to son of special tasks, skills, and responsibilities which marked caste status.

This process, however, has never been finished. The aboriginals from hills or forest have moved and still are moving into the lower echelons of the Hindu caste system. They come in for the most part as landless laborers and as laborers with almost no special skills.

Another feature indicating some aspects of fluidity in the scheme is the changing status of castes which enjoy a specially favorable or specially unfavorable position in the hierarchy. The Brahmins, for example, have been undergoing a considerable amount of economic pressure in some regions through the loss of land and through the necessity of migrating to the cities in search of work. Among the Brahmin caste there are also variations in status to be noted, for example, the Brahmins dealing with the funeral activities along the banks of the Ganges being looked down upon by the traditional village Brahmins whose functions are priestly in the traditional sense, involving largely the ceremonial contact with the deities. It is with these, and many other exceptions and transitional states, in mind that we venture on the following very rough classification of the castes of India.

Hierarchy of castes

First, in accordance with universally recognized patterns of dignity and authority, come the Brahmins, originally the priesthood of the Aryan Vedic peoples. Recognized by their learning, by their clothing, by their manner, by their names, they are universally revered, and while frequently likewise resented, as in Madras, for their power, they represent the bluebloods, the aristocrats, the apex of Indian society. This does not of course mean that they are always wealthy nor even that they always hold local power. Their position of superiority is somewhat like that of the very old families in some British or New England towns where, though they have come down in the world, they are still after all the group to whom everyone defers.

Other high caste groups are easily recognized. In parts of India they are the Rajputs; in other parts the dominant upper caste group are the Kayasthas. The original military caste which came second only to the Brahmin in Vedic times, known as the Kshatriyas, have broken up into various splinter groups and in many parts of India are hard to recognize. These and a few others are upper castes or higher castes in any region. The castes represented may be many or few in a village or region, but their power and status are almost everywhere recognized, with practically the same general deference from those socially beneath them.

Next we have a rather well-defined group known as "intermediate castes," who are for the most part skilled artisans in the broad sense of the term. They are those who deal with material the acquisition of which takes time, or with skills the training in which takes time. There is a certain capital, so to speak, behind their very existence. Their skills may be very simple, as in the case of the cultivator, or more complex, as in the case of the goldsmith. We should be tempted to call the group as a whole by the term "artisan," were it not for the fact that it includes many moneylenders and landlords. Those who in the Western world enjoy high prestige through dealing with money itself, in the form of banking or moneylending, are in India among the intermediate castes. Within these intermediate castes there are of course definite distinctions from high to low, just as there are among the upper castes. It is in general agreed, however, that a line between upper and intermediate castes can be drawn.

We come then to the lower castes, whose skills and possessions are at a lower level, regarding whom we shall later quote considerable material from Professor Radhakamal Mukerjee.

Lower still, and sharply marked off from them, are the "untouchables" or "Harijans" (Gandhi's name for them, meaning "God's people"). Though some of the untouchable castes have skills which seem to us of the West to be comparable in complexity with those of the intermediate castes—take, for example, the case of tanning and leatherworking—these groups are regarded as unclean; both dirt and degradation tend to be associated with their labor. In general, contact with dead bodies, scavenging, the removal of filth are characteristic of the duties assigned to them.

The caste system serves definite functions, maintains definite opportunities for *solidarity* and mutual support, and at the same times serves as a *status* system interfering in some ways with the development of the egalitarian spirit in Indian life. The first and most fundamental fact about caste is that with only a few well-defined exceptions the system prohibits marriage between castes. From this viewpoint one even encounters the curious paradox that the Muslims in Indian society are often regarded as a caste.

In addition to the matter of limiting marriage to within the caste, there are many other aspects of cleavage between caste groups. There are limitations upon interdining; that is, meals are not shared across caste lines. Castes have their own distinctive ways of preparing and serving food. To eat with a man means social equality, as it usually does with us. On closer inspection, however, all sorts of gradations must be recognized. In a general way, castes which are relatively close to one another in the hierarchy may give to and accept food from one another. Raw (unprepared) food can be shared by people considerably above or below one, whereas cooked food betokens somewhat closer relationships. The barrier against interdining is everywhere breaking down much more rapidly than the barrier against intermarriage.

The West still often refers to the "untouchable" as if the untouchables were a sharply defined group. From the point of view of the Brahmin, a man of lower caste may either come to the door, or enter the house, or sit on the floor, or sit on the foot of the bed, or sit higher up on the bed, depending upon the caste level to which he belongs. And in the same way not only the Brahmins but people of all the higher and middle castes have their own status system and allow those lower than themselves varying degrees of contact with them.

Exchange of economic functions

Traditionally, in the Indian village, the economic tasks to be done were distributed by caste. In a religious society, the Brahmins as priests claimed the highest rank (think of Egypt, and of medieval Christendom). The warriors could enforce their prestige over the commons. Among these last were the cultivators of the soil, at a relatively high status level; there were those who cared for cattle, who stood somewhat lower; next there were those who were concerned with simple crafts such as those of the blacksmith and the carpenter; lower down there were the weavers and laundrymen; then scavengers and those who removed the dead bodies of animals which had died in the field, or those who prepared their hides for the tannery.

In a general way, one can see that a social group with a higher technological level of production, using more tools and requiring more capital, has a higher status. Those who are utterly dependent upon the simplest skills, or no skill at all, are the lowest.

Because each caste had in theory its own economic task, there was of course a well-integrated and stable system of exchange of functions, in the villages a system which usually permitted some degree of personal fulfillment by enabling each man to carry out the task required of members of his caste and by providing the community as a whole with the necessary things for a self-sufficient economy. In a literal sense, therefore, there is membership in the *whole* village community as a primary basis for personal living. One does not go and find a job. One does not make a brilliant original contribution. One does not carry out a pioneering investigation nor exploratory function in some other part of the land. For the most part Indian boys grow up to carry out in the village economy the tasks in which the family is involved, and

Indian girls are married to boys of their own caste, usually remaining within an orbit of some miles from the place where they were born.

The fact that people of a given caste have had their own kind of work means that they may have some or a great deal of pride in it, and at least a sense of identification with it. There is no uncertainty in the small child's mind as to whether he will be able to find work or to support himself. His future is clear. The destiny of the boy is to be ultimately employed in the way of his fathers and the destiny of the girl is to be married to one of the same caste.

Caste means, however, very much more than occupation. There are caste traditions, caste modes of greeting, caste ways of preparing food, caste ceremonial and ritual. Caste indicates a definite place in the social system.

Another aspect of caste cohesion appears in the economic problem of finding jobs under the new industrial system in which the men of a caste move together and those already in cities send back to the villages to bring in more members of their own castes. These new arrivals typically live in the quarters, the slums, in which their predecessors are established. In Professor Mukerjee's investigation in the great industrial city of Kanpur (page 99), we find a typical block-by-block arrangement with castes establishing themselves in huge areas; and insofar as there is infiltration or admixture of other caste groups, these will mostly be castes of approximately the same status. This is not solely on an economic basis—it is governed partly by the degree of proximity which one caste may enjoy toward another of higher station as developed in the whole discussion of village caste arrangement. In other words, the caste hierarchy and the caste distances are essentially preserved in the cities, though the rigors are increasingly lessened.

Arrangement of marriage

The greatest vehicle embodying the caste tradition is the arrangement of marriage for sons and daughters. This varies considerably from caste to caste and from region to region, but it is still characteristic of most Indians to initiate very early in their children's lives a preliminary reconnaissance with regard to future wife or husband. Although the age of marriage and the age of consent have been constantly pushed forward by various types of legislation supported by Indian and earlier by British reformers, marriages are still relatively early by Western standards and arrangements for marriage are earlier still. The parents of the girl have very strong economic motivation to marry her off as early as is feasible; thus poverty holds back a social transition which would otherwise be much easier to make. While in recent decades the age of marriage in the United States has been decreasing (a third of American women now marry before twenty), the age in India has been increasing; and while there is still a considerable difference, it is important to note that the conception of "child marriage" throws the whole picture into false perspective.

Let us take a rather common example: the arrangement on behalf of a preadolescent of a marriage which is to be carried through some years later. Typically one scours the countryside for a distance of fifteen or twenty or twenty-five miles in all directions, looking for a husband for one's daughter, going to those villages in which there are members of one's own caste and considering the general desirability and the economic competence of the family into which marriage is contemplated. There is of course exchange of gifts; and there are of course enormous individual differences in the degree to which the personal happiness and the compatability in marriage of the individuals concerned are brought into consideration. Under these conditions, we may ask, does not one occasionally step aside and consider a member of another caste? This question indicates the degree to which the West may fail to grasp the absolute chasm which separates the castes.

One may spend anywhere from the savings of two or three years up to the whole amount of savings, and of course very commonly one may bind oneself by a debt for many years to come, or in perpetuity, for the sake of an adequate marriage contract. Even so, there are some males so unfortunate that arrangements are never adequately worked out; there is no way to get them a wife. Even more rarely, one finds the mishap of the unmarried girl. Practically always, however, by one method or another, some sort of a marriage arrangement is made.

The typical arrangements are the ceremonial performance of the marriage and then the immediate return of the wife to her parents' home for a visit. This may be a period of months or in some cases a period of years. After the establishment of the man and woman as a married couple, the wife may regard herself as to a very large degree still a member of her original family, and the fact that she may appeal to them if she regards herself as maltreated is apparently an important protection. Although she is in the home of her husband, and in many cases one may marry outside rather than inside one's own village, her own people are, nevertheless, not as a rule more than a few miles away and they are in communication with her. The joint family, then, although it absorbs all to its central structure, nevertheless allows all the in-marrying females to keep some sort of contact with their own families.

So far it may appear that we are thinking of caste as a restrictive system. This would not at all do justice to the facts if left by itself. Caste members support one another; they carry one another through difficult times; they guide one another through economic and other difficulties; they stand together in crisis; and in this period of political realignment they become extremely articulate and vocal in planning their own election activities, choosing those who, whether in provincial or in federal bodies, will stand for the interests of the caste group. Of course this does not mean that every representative must himself in all cases be a member of the caste involved. We find much that reminds us of what we find in our own cities: a certain white man is voted for by Negroes because he has committed himself to defend Negroes' rights and is thought to be reliable in this respect. In the same way, one finds in the India of today all sorts of cross-caste representation which is nevertheless very well understood to be a device for centering upon a few candidates who are actually serving the interests of the caste.

Some authors stress the religious meanings of caste, in particular the fact that present caste status reflects what one has earned by one's deeds (Karma) in another life. This system of religious ideas is based upon a grand cosmology and a sense of the huge span of time through which each individual passes in reincarnation after reincarnation. It emphasizes the ultimate responsibility of each individual for his present status, and his power to make a new status for himself in another life. These ideas have today come into full-scale conflict with the scientific and technological ideas of the West. But as far as the social system is concerned, the castes remain bound together as representing phases of immediate earthly obligation, phases of interrelated joint tasks which support the Hindu community. The failure of any caste for any reason whatever in carrying out its economic obligations would tend to undermine the economic success of the community as a whole. From economic solidarity to the unity of piety and philosophy, Hinduism constitutes a vast and coherent social and religious system. The higher a caste, the greater its obligations; the conception of *noblesse oblige* runs throughout the system.

It may well be asked how the lower strata in the caste hierarchy can accept their inferior position. The reply is that traditionally they did so in the same way in which the lowest strata of European society accepted their inferior position, but that today there is much protest; and insofar as Western ideas have been imported there is much discussion of individualism, economic and social equality, the freedom of thought and expression, the rights of women, and all the panoply of Western liberalism and humanitarianism.

Under these conditions, one is frequently asked to answer in a simple phrase the question: "What is actually happening to caste in India?" I think the reply is that it is submitting to one hammer blow after another as far as ideological analysis is concerned. It is also being subjected to great stress through changes in the economic structure of society. But it has such a long history and is so deeply embedded in the social structure that as far as manifest social patterns of behavior are concerned the observer will have to wait a good many years to see the new ideas permeate all strata of society. The reasons are not difficult to spell out. First, as to ideology, caste has involved an arbitrary assignment of a person from birth to death to a particular category. Often the category is far above his intrinsic qualities or any qualities which he could use to prove to his fellows that he is entitled to any such superiority. On the other hand, a very large number of Indians are condemned by their birth to positions of low social and economic status or even of untouchability or misery and social oppression. The great body of educated Indians in whose tradition much that is vigorously democratic is to be found, and who have been influenced during the nineteenth and twentieth centuries by Western liberalism, are with considerable unanimity moving in some degree against the caste system.

HINDUISM AND RELIGIOUS TOLERATION

What can be said here about religion as a factor making for cleavage between Hindus and Muslims will have to be very inadequate indeed. I can only refer the reader to the huge literature on the conflict of Hinduism and Islam in theological, moral, liturgical, cultural, and many other aspects.

Hinduism is a religion of very great complexity, with highly abstract philosophical ideas, exquisite tenderness in interpersonal feeling, a multiplicity of supernatural forces, asceticism, gross popular superstition, and an agelessness of outlook that make for conservatism. It is also a social system, and the transition from caste to community, that is, to religious group, must be conceived as involving no basic change of logic. Hinduism is a system of ideas and practices many of which date essentially from the Vedic period. While perfectly clear as to the hierarchy of priest, warrior, etc., it has never been a proselytizing religion, and it has never shown any disposition to doctrinal intolerance of the faith of other men. Religious minorities are not, as such, subject to majority pressure; minority groups need not as such be suspect, or receive bad treatment.

Though historically the Muslims came to North India as conquerors in the medieval period, and most of the Indian Muslims of today are descendants of those voluntarily or forcibly converted to Islam, the Muslim group long ago became "wedded" to the land and found an accepted place for itself. A large proportion of the Muslims of India have their own economic functions. Take, for example, the weavers and locksmiths of today. These are tasks which traditionally call for some degree of skill, and tasks to which the Muslim community has long been adapted. In the same way the Sikhs, who broke off a few centuries ago from Hinduism, have for the most part lived with Hindu or with Muslim

* cf. Nirad Chaudhury - Autobiography of an Unknown Indian, Macmillan 1953

neighbors, carrying out a division of labor (usually as farmers, sometimes as soldiers) which all accepted. The Sikhs usually enjoy high status; a Hindu family may at times arrange that one of its boys shall become a Sikh. ?

Some other smaller religious groups, each with its own economic tasks, are more likely to be found in the cities, such for example as the Parsees, mainly businessmen. Parsees, Christians, and other smaller groups are not automatically subject to any particular exclusion or discrimination. Religious groups in India are often referred to as "communities," and interreligious problems as "communal" problems.

We might indeed go much further. We might point out that the whole conception of "exclusion" in Indian society is a functional one based upon the hierarchical position of groups, i.e., one is "excluded" from the privilege of higher groups; it is *not* based upon hatred or upon what would be called "prejudice" from the Western point of view. Moreover, broadly considered, Hinduism is intellectually tolerant, in the sense that all sorts of different religious and personal philosophies of life are accepted. Hindu worship is largely an individual and family matter, and persons who do not accept and practice the religion which is current at a particular place are not thereby subjected to suspicion. There are also sects of Hinduism which vary in strength in different parts of India, but one sect is not intolerant of another sect.

Taking all this together, it is not surprising to find in general that over long periods and throughout large regions caste and religion have been relatively free of the phenomena to which we would today apply the word "tension." There must always have been some jealousies of those who enjoyed a more favorable station, but this is an entirely different thing from the seething unrest and bitterness which often characterize the relationships of caste and of religious groups in recent years. We might put the matter very simply by saying that at the village level Hindus, Muslims, Sikhs and others have typically worked together without friction in economic and in other ways; tension based upon such divisive factors is to a very considerable extent a modern factor.

This is not meant in any way to deny that military conquest of a large part of north and central India by Muslims helped to create a sense of superiority among the victors, and that the Hindu feeling that the Muslims were vigorous or even ruthless conquerors has played a considerable part in the history of intergroup antagonisms in India.

4

Roots of tolerance and tensions in Indian child development

BY LOIS BARCLAY MURPHY*

In order to get some basis for tentative conclusions about the life and needs of children, Lois Murphy visited over thirty schools, orphanages, and other institutions for children, and spent some time—from a few hours to over a week each—in over thirty homes, at all levels from the home of a farmer to homes of professors and factory owners, as well as visiting villages along the west coast and across the provinces of north central India.

The children of India are the friendliest children I have ever seen. They trust people; their smile is wholehearted, warm, and gay. They have more than just passive friendliness; they are ingenious in finding ways of getting acquainted with anyone who does not speak their language, and they are perceptive and intuitively quick to understand how to make a genuine contact and establish a relationship. These things were discoveries to me, yet they were familiar to the dozens of Americans who had lived many years in India and knew these Indian children far better than I did.

. . . .

* Lois Barclay Murphy, the wife of the author, spent much of her time in India surveying the life and needs of children, as a background for recommendations and plans for the B. M. Institute of Child Development at the Gujarat University.

Since crying is so taken for granted in the children of the western world that it is even thought by some people that "it is good for babies to cry for a while each day," I have hesitated to remark that babies are almost never heard to cry in many sections of India. Lucy Sprague Mitchell, who stayed longer and is an experienced observer of children, commented that during a whole year in India she never heard a baby cry. Since they are put to the breast as soon as they get restless, they don't have much chance to practice "crying for what they want."

With all their spontaneity and gaiety, they are responsible too. Children take care of each other, moving about in mixed age groups, as well as caring for the flocks of goats, sheep, cows, and buffalo that one sees on the roads and in the fields. They are skillful in handling the everyday problems of reality. Young boys are quite as apt to care for the baby or small child as are girls of five years and over. There seems to be no feeling at all that it is unmasculine for boys or men to carry babies or small children, or to care for them; males may be almost as nurturing as females.

And while they are realistic and down to earth, they are also artistic; children from villages of rich tradition, and children of remote aboriginal tribes, children in most of the modern "basic education" schools, all showed a wonderful sensitivity to color and form. In the rigid schools this is channeled into traditional designs, but in the freer schools the children are doing very original paintings, often expressing their feelings for and observation of animals and the landscape familiar to them in sensitive, original ways, full of empathy and free movement.

I had been told that the children are veteran beggars, and this may be true in the cities, but since I was observing chiefly in villages I did not find it to be true; on the contrary, they were very giving—they run off to collect flowers to stuff in your pockets or put in your hair; they make wreaths and garlands like Hawaiian leis to put around your neck; and with the hospitality of their elders they offer you food and drink from whatever they have.

They like to communicate and to share—both passively and actively. I discovered the passive side of this a few times when I visited villages with a group of university people who occasionally pursued discussions with village representatives longer than I wanted to. I would go back to the car sometimes alone; the children would follow me, clinging to the car, laughing, chattering, especially if I started to sing American folk songs with simple, vigorous rhythms.

The active part appeared over and over again as I visited schools. Through an interpreter they loved to ask questions.

These are some of the things I saw in young children, up to the age of eight or nine. I did not see so much of the adolescents, but they did not appear so trusting, spontaneous, and friendly. A gloom settles down on adolescents like a fog and the warmth goes out of their faces. We also heard complaints about the lack of initiative and leadership in young people from professional and political leaders, although where they were encouraged we found the kind of zest and energy in university groups that we expect here. On the whole it seemed clear that Indian children did not have the stimulus to problem-solving or the practice in cooperative thinking and planning that would match the spontaneity and capacity for relationships with people which we saw so often. And on the whole it seemed clear that the early freedom and independence of the years under ten were not matched by opportunities to use initiative and freedom during adolescence and young adult years.

What kinds of early experiences might be related to these strengths and weaknesses, in our eyes, and what might be the backgrounds of these experiences?

ROOTS OF TOGETHERNESS

Indian children in the villages still do grow up in the large joint family, where the married sons and unmarried daughters have rooms or apartments in the house of their parents; children feel accepted by, and at home with, a large number of people. There is no need for strange baby-sitters; a baby is always with someone familiar.

But the feeling of trust and acceptance is due, probably, to more than just the experience of being close to dependably familiar people during the early years; there are many other respects in which children in India are given a comfortable, satisfying start in life which would contribute to a feeling of being able to count on people. Infants are nursed for two years or longer and in fact often wean themselves after they have become sufficiently used to adult food and are on their feet, so that nursing is no longer so attractive. There is little systematic toilet training; few children are forced; they seldom receive bewildering punishments for something their bodies needed to do. When small children are old enough to observe and learn where to go by watching adults, they do as older people do. Until that time, they may be treated much as we would treat a young kitten not yet old enough to train.

Infants and young children are not left at home, but accompany the family on visits, on the older children's wanderings about the village, even to the movies; they are not shut out or isolated. Their experience is predominantly an experience of being *with* the rest of the family. They are carried easily, first in cradled arms which do not grasp them possessively, do not poke, inspect, tease, or in other ways manipulate them; later they straddle a hip of sister or brother, father or mother, balancing comfortably, and following the movements of the parent's or sibling's body as the carrier goes about her way or about her work.

This constant togetherness and participation may mean that the small child is rarely exposed to new experiences without the support of a trusted person; it also provides an experience of kinesthetic and empathic richness which children brought up in cribs, play pens, carriages, and other articles of furniture could not possibly have. The child comes to know and to feel and intuitively to understand people with a depth grown from the time he is close to the muscles and bodies, the movements and the feelings of people, just as our children learn to understand the mechanics of objects through the hours and days they spend playing with, taking apart, and putting together the objects which are their toys and their vehicles.

This same empathy extends to the world of animals and the world of nature generally, for the same reason; this is the world of the child's experience. He learns to understand growth, and change, and continuity, cause and effect through his closeness to the processes of nature, not through changes he causes himself in mechanical things.

The artistic abilities of Indian children probably have several bases. First, the children of the villages live in a world where bad taste is unknown—the forms and colors and designs around them were originally and still are absorbed from the colors and forms of nature. In addition, it is normal to be an artist; artists are not set apart or regarded as people with special gifts not possessed by everyone. Almost every girl or woman is able to make beautiful decorative designs in honor of a guest, a festival, or a birthday; almost any village will have craftsmen making things of exquisite charm. In one little village I visited the homes of a goldsmith, a potter, and a carver almost side by side; in each of them beautiful things were being made, and each home was beautiful. Just as the children absorb the moods and feelings of people through their constant contact with them, they absorb artistic forms and techniques because these are part of their everyday life.

What I have described so far was summarized for me by P. N. Kirpal, of the Ministry of Education in the central government in New Delhi: "You bring up your children, we live with ours," he remarked, as he agreed that my observations of Indian child life seemed accurate in the light of his experience.

Since babies are carried about and nursed until two or later, there is no place for the kind of stimulation to achievement and to motor activity which our babies commonly experience. An American baby is greeted with cheers when he sits up after much coaxing, practice, and encouragement by his parents, who pull him up by his arms, hold him when he cannot support himself completely, and in other ways urge him on. When he stands alone and walks after additional stimulation—being "walked" with a parent or sibling holding both his hands, then with the support of one—he himself often feels triumphant; one baby laughed until she cried after she discovered that she could walk alone. In this way, accomplishment, skill, become deeply felt as values by our children.

Since an enormous proportion of the population has no property, little children are not exposed to the anxious, tense no-no's that are heard dozens of times a day by toddlers in our middle-class families when they are being taught not to touch breakable ash trays and other bric-a-brac, not to pull table cloths off the dining table, not to tear up magazines and books, not to get into mother's bureau drawers or knitting bag or sewing basket.

This means that Indian children are not exposed to so much frustration, pressure from adults, conflict with authority; anger and aggression are not stimulated, there is little or no evidence of the "resistance," temper tantrums, and hitting back at the world common among our two- to four-year-olds. By the same token, aggression does not have a chance to be patterned and shaped as happens with us. Typically,

we expect a child to use physical expressions of aggression
until the age of four and gradually to substitute verbal methods of standing up for his rights, getting what he wants, or
letting off steam. Nor does the older child go through the
stages of learning "fairness" in group play, good sportsman-
ship, how to "fight like a man" without using unfair methods (like biting, scratching, punching in vulnerable parts of
the body) as our children do.

Aggression is thus not elicited, nor is it patterned within
limits as it is with us. With us there are extremes of juvenile
delinquency, crime, race violence, at one end of the scale,
and highly structured outlets for aggressive activity like
baseball and competitive sports at the other end. When aggression is aroused (under pressure of economic and political
stress) in Indian adults, then, it may burst out in primitive
chaotic ways exactly because of the lack of the long slow experiences of patterning that we know.

Since before independence only a small proportion of
children went to school, education in the formal sense has
not played a serious role in character formation. But with increasing numbers of children attending school, this will no
longer be true, and it is important to look at the patterns of
education which are emerging and their probable effects.
Here we find several main roots:

The ancient tradition of the *guru,* the guide and teacher who
   works entirely with his pupil, imparting basic wisdom of
   living along with intellectual skills.
The British academic tradition, with an emphasis on verbal
   proficiency. Many of the civil service and government
   workers and businessmen come from schools of the British type. Graduates of these schools generally spurn
   village life and do not care to return to it from professional work.

The Montessori system, which trains sensory alertness and skills.

The tradition of Tagore, who believed that all the arts—painting, poetry, music, dance, crafts, and closeness to nature—were important to the education of the young.

These different educational traditions produce as varied results as the traditions are varied. All over India, wherever I found teachers especially sensitive to children's individual talents and creative abilities, most often those teachers came from the school Tagore founded at Santiniketan.

The "Basic Education" tradition, founded by Zakir Husain, advocated by Gandhi, is now given assistance by the government of India. This approach emphasizes the importance of making children self-sufficient through helping them to learn all the essentials of good living. In Basic Education schools children acquire the regular academic skills and develop some abilities in arts and crafts, but also learn gardening, animal husbandry, spinning and weaving, preparation of food, the elements of sanitation and healthy life. The Basic Education schools are training teachers and village workers; more than any other group they are the ones who can be counted on to raise the physical and spiritual level of village life.

The questions children from schools of different traditions asked were revealing. For instance, children in a large school of the British type asked me, "What is the schedule of American boys at school?" "What are the punishments given?" Children in the Basic Education schools asked, "What tools do farmers use in America?" "Why is there so much race conflict in America?" "Why did America drop atom bombs on Asia?"

Both the Tagore schools and all Basic Education schools are intercaste, and are an active force for better acceptance between different groups. Several "basic" schools that I visited had portraits of different religious leaders—Moses, Buddha, Confucius, Jesus, Mohammed, Gandhi. Since there is no color line anywhere in India, this means a degree of representativeness that we seldom find in any American schools, except a few progressive schools like Fieldston in New York and Putney in Vermont, attended largely by children of well-to-do liberals and professional people who are especially concerned with intercultural education.

Along with all of the strengths I have mentioned, there were some striking lacks in the growing-up experience of children, as judged from the American point of view. None of the schools I visited gave an opportunity for groups to think together, solving problems, planning work or entertainment. Individual autonomy was respected in the tradition of Tagore, Montessori, and Basic Education, in different ways. But group thinking, which is something else and needs its own stage setting, seemed nonexistent.

When we put this alongside of the fact that most Indian children do not have the toys or equipment to stimulate group activity in play—such as building an airport or fire station or boat—we see how consistent the absence of group thinking actually is.

It will probably be obvious that the deep acceptance which is a part of the Indian philosophy, which we ordinarily hear discussed in relation to India's hospitality to different religions, her absence of a color line, her capacity to endure through disasters which would destroy other cultures, is expressed also, and learned, through the earliest experience of children who learn acceptance through being accepted, and through sharing the attitude of acceptance with the adults to whom they are close.

Less familiar perhaps is the Indian sense of man as part of the cosmos, more intimate than our feeling of belonging to nature with the tendency to place man at the top of an evolutionary ladder in opposition to the "inhuman" or "subhuman" world. For the Indian of the Upanishads, "thou" (that is, personality) and "that" (the impersonal world) are close together, part of one whole, if not indeed ultimately the same. This intimate feeling of closeness to nature, reflected in the children's empathically sensitive pictures of animals and landscape, belongs to this generation as much as to the philosophers of three thousand years ago in India.

ROOTS OF TENSIONS

In any culture the weaknesses and strengths are apt to be opposite sides of one coin and this is true in India. The joint family which gives so much security, such a firm base of emotional strength and trust, to the small child can become very coercive and limiting to the adolescent and young adult. More than once as I talked with young college people about their plans for the future, they would say, automatically, without bitterness, and often patiently as if I should know this by now, "No, I can't go on to study for a Ph.D., which would make it possible for me to go into professional work, because I have to contribute to the support of our joint family right now."

It is still quite general to expect young people to accept an arranged marriage and to fit into the jobs dictated by caste. In other words, after childhood years of freedom the adolescent confronts an impenetrable wall which permits no choice, no way to use the freedom he has enjoyed and taken for granted. The frustration for many is intense and bitter, and generates conflicts which are solved in some cases by stolid resignation, in other cases by a struggle for independence attended by suffering rarely experienced even in the most acute struggles of our adolescents.

If we ask further what connections there may be between those aspects of child development and the social tensions we shall be discussing, we must consider the following possibilities:

The role of dependence in accentuating the sense of need, of expectation, of being cared for. Indians find it natural both to take care of others (as they take care of the members of the joint family, and of children generally) *and* to expect to be cared for. This is fostered at a deep level by the long period of infancy, and later by the governmental system under British rule; thus it is deeply frustrating and probably confusing when problems are not taken care of by some authority, as was true at the time of independence—there were too many problems for any new government to handle all at once.

The role of caste structure in accentuating the sense of "rights to have" status, property, etc. and the reliance on fixed order.

The role of early freedom from frustration in the later absence of habits controlling aggression.

The role of lack of opportunities in childhood for group thinking and planning in the later lack of methods of resolving conflicts between groups.

The children-who-used-to-be, the adults of today in India, grew up under a hierarchical authoritative system where the dominance of the British was at least a shadow in the background, and the caste system and joint family gave the design for living—the pattern and shape of things. The authorities set the limits, established the routine, took care of everyone, settled problems. Without this authority and this pattern, individuals might easily be at sea, rudderless, lost, even disintegrated. And if panicked by failure in satisfying basic needs to be cared for, and deep feelings of "because I am a member of ———— caste I have a right to. . . ," and by the flood of feelings that must have attended the deprivations and struggles of independence and partition, they gave way to primitive violent aggressive feelings and impulses. They did not have the resources of values (civil rights ideals deeply rooted) nor of techniques (group discussion) to deal with these feelings.

Without tools, toys, or objects of any sort other than kitchen utensils and the few simple implements of agriculture, it is no wonder the children learn little of the mechanics of problem-solving in general. It will be a temptation to Westerners, working on Point 4 programs and other missionary efforts, to carry our Western ingenuities to the East. They need some of it, but as we do this it will be important to keep a sharp eye on the values which are lost in the process, or which may be lost if we do not give attention to the ways in which they can be encouraged while new values are developed. Agricultural production can be increased a hundredfold, and the relation to nature lost. Literacy, in the sense of ability to read and write, may be increased from 20 per cent to 90 per cent in a generation, but will the deeper literacy of understanding remain? Industrialization may bring more clothes to a large population, but will it destroy the taste and artistic values which people with few clothes still have? Encouragement to individual achievement and fulfillment will come with exposure to Western ambition and Western ideas of love; will these mean the loss of loyalty, responsibility, and devotion which have been the fruit of Indian institutions, including the joint family and regional and caste loyalties as well as the religious sense of oneness of people and the cosmos?

At this time of concern from both sides of the world with the question of what East-West relationships can mean, it is not enough to guard against destroying important values in cultures like that of India. We have much to learn as well as something to give. We speak of security and the child's need for love; yet our children are more troubled and tense and uncertain than those of some of the "backward" nations. Some of the deep trust and sense of at-homeness in the universe which they have might be possible for children here also if we can be receptive to the values and ways of life which contribute to these qualities. We cannot imitate them. We cannot transplant their philosophy, their climate, their patterns of living to our soil.

But some of the flexibility, the acceptance of children in the everyday pattern of family living, the easy participation of people of any age in the activities of the rest might be possible. We talk about standards of living, and what we teach the rest of the world, we believe, can improve their "standard of living." But their acceptance of children, and of differences in ages as well as differences in religions and color can teach us something about standards of living together.

5

The rise of tensions

Up to this point we have viewed village life, and
the religious and caste systems, as providing a base for orderly and relatively tensionless social organization. In the
following chapters we shall seek in the village, in religion,
and in the caste system some of the factors which in modern
times are associated with the rise of social tensions. Most
of the data of this chapter come from a UNESCO research
team established by Professor R. K. Mukerjee when we were
in Lucknow in October, 1950.

THE DIVIDED VILLAGE

The term "village" is used in the Census of India to describe
a settlement of less than 5,000 people, and is often loosely
used to include also small "towns," as we should call
them, of several thousand or even up to 20,000 population.
Using the term as the Census does, there are about 600,-
000 villages in India. This staggering figure can be kept in
mind with the aid of this device: Imagine India as ruled
off with vertical lines a mile apart, and with horizontal lines
a mile apart. On the average there is one village in each of
the little cells, or each of the little square miles, which you
will create in this way. Often villages are in only limited
communication with one another. Even today it is common
to find only a footpath connecting adjacent villages; if economic or other motives warrant it, it is possible to broaden
this so that a bullock cart can pass. Dirt roads lead from

small village to larger village, and horse-drawn or bullock-drawn vehicles deliver goods to market, and even at times for the world market.

The typical mentality of the mass of people, however, is the rural mentality which we well know from the premotor-car era of American and European life, a mentality still found in those parts of the Western world where communication is poor. Into this relatively isolated village life there has emerged recently the kind of communication which goes with the spread of newspaper-reading habits. Excitement greets the return of a villager who has gone to a neighboring town and picked up some news, or the word of some literate person who has read the newspaper and can pass around among his eager listeners reports and gossip regarding national or world events. The death of Gandhi apparently reached most of the people of India within a few hours, by a network of communication based partly in the first instance upon radio and press, but very largely upon the fact that each person who received the news managed to radiate it out through many channels with incredible rapidity.

This fact is of very great importance with regard to social cohesion and social hostility. The channels of communication are inevitably established to a large degree along the lines of language and along the lines of community (religion) and caste. Since the Muslim press is independent of the Hindu press, it is not surprising that stories related to Hindu-Muslim strife take on two essentially different forms, one of which is circulated through Hindu sources and the other through Muslim sources. Supposedly authentic and factually well-documented news therefore becomes "a matter of course" to all members of one religious group but not to the other. The basic facts and interpretations are unknown to the other group which through its own system of communication provides a different approach.

We see something of this sort in our own country. But

after all, Roman Catholics and Jews do see something of what is in a press that is read primarily by Protestants, and even the newspapers and magazines aimed at one religious group are likely to be restrained somewhat by the fact that any sectarian view will be subject to some criticism in a nonsectarian press. People do mingle and move about in exposure to a common language and ideology filtered through the radio. Often one can hear political discussion for a considerable period before knowing the sources through which the speaker has drawn his information. All of this is very hard indeed to duplicate in India.

While we may use the word "village," as noted above, for collections of habitations comprising a few hundred or even some thousands of people, huge importance attaches in India to the few great cities, mostly the courts of the great potentates, which have always been the centers of culture and progress. These cities were developed by the British regime, were emphasized by the British a hundred years ago, and became fundamental nerve centers in the military, economic, and political unification of India. These cities today are of enormous importance in regard to problems of social integration or disintegration. In countless instances the cities have been the focal points within which movements toward either unification or dissension were carried forward. The great riots in Calcutta in 1946 had a typical effect in crystallizing Hindu-Muslim hostility. Large-scale group hostilities are often quickly aroused in cities, as in the race riots (Detroit) and outrages (Miami) of recent history in the United States.

Another very obvious reason for emphasis on Indian cities is the fact that the *new* in almost every type of institutional practice makes its appearance first in the cities. Scientific and engineering enterprises, new ideas in the arts, religion, and philosophy are typically city products. In the city is the money which makes possible the development of productive enterprises such as the mills of recent decades. The village is inevitably conservative, inevitably the bastion of traditional stability, poise, reverence for the past. It follows that the movement of the village population into the cities, in response to industrial opportunities or by economic forces which have driven them off of their land, are among the factors making for the most rapid social change and at the same time making for bitterness, hostility, and intergroup tension.

THE CASTE SYSTEM IS CHALLENGED

Under the impact of economic forces, Western ideas, and specific historic events, the caste system, so important in the cohesion of social groups, has played a role in setting the stage for modern tensions. So rapid is the change today that the reader is reminded of the date—1950—in which most of our data were gathered.

As we saw earlier, practically everyone in India is governed to some extent by the caste hierarchy. Awareness of a man's background and of the duties and status associated with that background is an elementary form of "placing" the man in conversation or other social dealings. In general one knows the caste of a person by his name. There may be some mistakes made, but there are other clues: clothing, appearance, cultivation, manner of speech, evidence of education, all play some part, just as we likewise use many clues in placing a man. Some of our Indian friends went rather far in emphasizing the ease of identifying people by caste without even knowledge of the name. Others went far in the other direction. In the Madras study one of the questions dealt directly with the problem of whether one can carry on a conversation with a person without knowing his caste. The replies indicate that in general about half of the South Indian respondents can get along very well without knowledge of caste and do not demand to know it, while the other half require such knowledge. This may be partially colored by the great tension of recent years between Brahmins and non-Brahmins, and may be related to the desire to nullify the existence of caste as far as feasible. In general it may probably be safely said that in India most people know the castes not only of their own village-mates but those of neighboring villagers, which makes up the social world of most persons, and that even in large villages and cities one can often identify caste without much difficulty by the clues given above or by the appearance of the individual in a group which can easily be identified.

In emphasizing the hierarchical position of the castes from top to bottom, we have emphasized primarily the problem of status or prestige. There are, however, more specific ways in which the acceptance or rejection of members of other castes may be defined. This has led Professor R. K. Mukerjee to develop the conception of social distance, initiated at the University of Chicago and beautifully formulated in a test of social distance by E. S. Bogardus. Social distance between castes is represented not only by nonintermarriage or the rejection of others from a seat at the same table at dinner, but by numerous other types of restriction, as in the use of public water supply, spring, well, or whatnot; the adoption of distinctive titles, sobriquets which have deferential or depreciative tone; the mode of greeting, varying in the degree of deference or intimacy; the sharing of the common tobacco pipe which is passed around only among those who are socially close to one another; the seating arrangement, the adoption of restrictions in regard to the use of shoes, umbrellas, and so on, involving physical contact of an indirect sort.

In religious services, one does not make the sharp distinction between those who may share intimately in temple services and those who are altogether excluded. Some of the caste groups cannot enter the temple at all; some can enter the temple but cannot go near the Deity; some can touch the Deity. The same conception of *degree* comes up when the matter of approach to a high-caste-man's living quarters is involved.

Regarding untouchability as a matter of degree, the study of Mukerjee reveals the following ascending scale of social avoidance (from small to large social distance): one, against sitting on a common floor; two, against interdining; three, against admittance into the kitchen; four, against touching metal pots; five, against touching earthen pots; six, against mixing in social festivals; seven, against admittance into the interior of a house; eight, against any kind of physical contact. Such arrangements sound strange to those who organize human status relationships in a different way; but any social arrangement—the army hierarchy, the academic hierarchy, or the class system of a small American town—likewise sounds strange to those who encounter it for the first time.

These differentiations are generally understood throughout the village, and learned early by the children: thus the Chamars learn that they are excluded from the interior of the Brahmin's house, while others, like the Doms (scavengers) learn that they may make no physical contact whatever. The hierarchical status of the whole system is clear to everyone: "The scavenging castes are absolutely segregated even by the Chamar group which itself is avoided by the rest of the community."

Naturally the proximity of living quarters is another very good indicator of the degree of intercaste acceptance. Typically the lower castes live on the fringe or outskirts of the village or in some cases at a distance from it (there are some villages entirely made up of untouchables, as we noted). The same sort of problem appears, as we shall see, in the cities.

It may be worth while to spell out in more detail the specific content of this conception of degrees of admission to group ceremonial. In view of the enormous importance of religion among Hindus, the following figures on the admission of the various castes to worship, as reported by Mukerjee, may be of some significance: in the U. P. villages which were studied, four of the untouchable groups are still totally excluded from entry into temples or places of worship. Among the Chamars and Pasis less than 10 per cent reported that there were no caste barriers against them in this respect, whereas an overwhelming majority cannot enter places of common worship, or even if some of them sometimes can do so, they must (unlike the upper-caste members) keep a respectful distance from the Deity. On the whole, barriers to temple entry are giving way today; the Constitution, 1950, forbids such barriers. As usual, progress is faster in the cities than in the villages.

Another fundamental sign of exclusion relates to the use of the water supply. Professor Mukerjee's report highlights the fact that a scavenger cannot take water from a common source along with the rest; he must have his own independent well or stand at a distance for someone else to give him water. Not only does this limit the water supply for him whose requirements for personal hygiene may perhaps be the greatest, but he is sometimes compelled to satisfy his water need from a stagnant pool or even a drain, or may share the filthy and contaminated water with cattle. Here again the 1950 Constitution forbids such exclusion, and the whole pattern is due for a change. But we are reporting the 1950 situation as found by Mukerjee's research team. Many other castes against which prejudice is not so deep as to exclude them altogether from a common water supply suffer through caste priority in the drawing of water or discrimination in the type of vessel or the access to the common platform from which water is drawn. In many cases individuals of intermediate caste cannot draw water from a well in an earthen pot as do those of the highest castes. Sometimes they must wait until members of other castes have satisfied their needs and must not put their buckets down into a well as long as any member of an upper caste is drawing water. Muslims, while admitted to common sources of water supply, are in a considerable number of cases excluded from the common platforms of the wells. The extent to which barriers in this respect operate in the villages studied appears in the fact that all of the lowest castes, including the Muslims, are subject to exclusion or restriction of one sort or another in their access to the village's common water supply.

The rigidity of this system does not, however, mean that the system as a whole is absolutely intolerable in all respects for the lower castes. One has definite duties and a definite place in society. There is complete autonomy within the caste or occupation. The clientele of the craftsmen is well defined; no one may cut in upon their monopoly or challenge their basic right to make a living, such as it is. The caste councils (Panchayats) firmly defend the caste against encroachments by other castes. The caste has some reason for pride and self-satisfaction. It has, for example, its own code of etiquette and manners, worship and ceremonial. Finally, although the degree of importance to be attached to religion in these matters is always subject to argument, it is the impression of some careful observers that the doctrine of Karma, according to which each individual reaps the cumulative fruit of his good and evil deeds through a long succession of births and rebirths, gives some degree of feeling of reconciliation to one's caste and status in this life.

This, then, is the traditional situation, a situation which can be maintained as long as economic specialization exists at the village level; as long as each caste group has a clear idea of its position and is not altogether frustrated in that position, and as long as disturbing practices and ideas are not introduced from outside. But the last of these conditions can no longer be maintained in modern India. There has been under the British regime a long series of economic and political changes directly or indirectly affecting the positions of the castes; and with the independence of India there have come many vigorous challenges to the traditional privileges enjoyed by many and aiming in the long run towards the amelioration of the lot of the lower economic and social strata. Some of the changes in recent years and the types of tension which are associated with them can be listed, following Professor Mukerjee's classification of the facts.

1. Changes in the distribution of land rights and in the pattern of income distribution have been following directly upon the passage of legislation giving permanent rights in land to those who previously were employed as landless laborers. In India one must distinguish between ownership of land and tenancy. A very large group of tillers of the soil, while not owning the land, have permanent tenant rights. These rights not being enjoyed by the landless laborers, we find a three-cornered struggle among those who own, those who have permanent tenancy, and those who have no rights whatever. This three-cornered situation is being altered both by the struggle to give absolute ownership to tenants and by the struggle to give either tenancy or absolute land rights to those who have been landless.

2. There is also a relative increase in the numbers of the lowest castes, many of whom of course are landless, in such fashion as to force them in effect off the land. The land which they cultivate may be relatively barren and the share of the crop which falls to their lot may be insufficient to keep them alive. Under such conditions they may wander in quest of a livelihood, and some of them appear among the migrants who seek employment in the cities.

In this period of economic stress, much importance attaches to the new ideology which has come from the whole Congress Party campaign in recent decades, and from the

Harijan uplift movement: specifically, the constitutional guarantees of the right to labor, unaffected by caste or religion.

Immediately the question arises: "Why then does the system persist?" To answer this one must go back to the problem of joint family and arranged marriages, as already noted. It is one thing for the individual to be dissatisfied with an institution, an entirely different thing for that individual to act as if the institution had already come to an end. What normal father or mother, looking forward to the welfare of his son or daughter, could possibly act as if no such system existed?

As students have repeatedly told us, they hope that India will have changed enough when their children are of marriageable age to permit the children free choice. No such conditions existed while these students themselves were preparing for adulthood. There is not only the exchange of property; there is not only the time-honored system of guarantees in systems of mutual protection which both young husband and young wife enjoy; there is also the stark fact that marriage outside of the caste system means reducing oneself immediately and completely to an outcast status. We ourselves ran into a few cases of outcasts, men and women who were respected but who were relatively isolated in the social life of their cities, not having the support which normal members of the community enjoy.

Perhaps enough has been said to indicate some of the preliminary reasons why caste is a major source of tension in India today, and why there is every reason to believe that it will become more and more a center of tension in the next ten or twenty years. In general, the entire struggle of the lower castes to improve their lot has led to virtually the same pattern with which we are familiar in Europe and the United States. The privileged groups feel that these people "do not know their place"; "these upstarts" are demanding things which are "too good for them." Just as the gentlemen of England put up a heroic rear-guard action against the struggle of the factory population for improved conditions, shorter hours, higher wages, even the elimination of the labor of women and children, just as a similar campaign had to be fought through in the United States, today the economic struggle gathers momentum in India. The tensions are essentially the tensions arising from those who demand the rapid and dramatic improvement in their lot and those who find that too much is being demanded too fast.

THE BARRIER OF LANGUAGE

Over a dozen major languages besides English are spoken in India today. They have their own folklore and literature, and these have great value to those who share them. But they tend to cause isolation, and, at times, suspicion based on failure of communication.

One Indian political leader asked me in a friendly conversation, "So the Americans agreed upon English as a language, did they?" The question dramatically and amusingly throws into relief the problem of a unified language. The question almost asks us to visualize "the Americans" who at first spoke, let us say, French, Spanish, German, Dutch, Swedish, and English, sitting at a conference table deciding to talk English henceforth. Actually, India is up against exactly this kind of problem of making a resolution determining a plan for the development of a common tongue. We might look for a moment at the background of the present difficult issue which faces India in the determination of a common language.

When the makers of the Vedic hymns entered India from the Iranian plateau upwards of 3,000 years ago, they established themselves in the northwest, and very slowly spread south and east. They spoke an Indo-European or Aryan tongue very closely related to Greek and Latin. This tongue, developed as a literary medium, chiefly as the vehicle of the great religious and philosophical literature, is called Sanskrit. As the civilization spread to cover the whole Indian peninsula, many of the religious and cultural ideas spread further than the language itself did. Thus in South India today Hinduism as a religious system is as solidly entrenched as it is in the north, but Sanskrit and the languages derived from it did not make their way so far south. In South India a hundred million people more or less still speak the Dravidian languages which antedate the Aryan invasion of India. These languages include the Tamil and Telugu of the Madras area and south, and the Kannada and Malayalam of the country to the west and northwest of Madras. The Dravidian-speaking peoples think of themselves as separated in deep cultural respects from North Indians. To them, North India, with her greater economic development, represents today a relatively aggressive and dominating influence.

But however their opposition to the North may be expressed, the Tamil-speaking and Telugu-speaking people are themselves in constant suspicion of one another's power. Whenever there is competition for jobs and opportunities, whenever there are economic dislocations and sufferings, one begins to notice the lines of cleavage within the group and to attribute to those across such a line of cleavage a specially successful quest for power or an unfair advantage in the struggle for economic gain. Those on opposite sides of the fence always find the grass a little greener on the other side. Thus the Tamil and the Telugu, both from our point of view relatively handicapped peoples facing serious economic difficulties, watch with jealousy whatever struggle for political or economic power the other group may undertake.

A newspaper in Madras is published for Brahmin Telugus, in which the issue of Brahmins versus non-Brahmins and the issue of Tamils versus Telugus is necessarily jointly presented. An Indian friend put it to me with a wistful smile:

"Monday, Wednesday, and Friday the issue is the diabolical things the non-Brahmins are doing against the Brahmins; Tuesday, Thursday, and Saturday the great question is the injustices perpetrated by the Tamils on the Telugus."

Though, as we have noted, the general economic backwardness of South India as compared with the North has been a factor leading to general suspicion and sense of insecurity in the South, the factor of language is probably responsible for inflating this economic suspicion to an importance which it would not otherwise assume. We can only say, as matters stand, that South India feels cut off from the rest of India both in language and in economic terms.

Turning now to the language problems of the North, we have through the whole span from the Gujarat country on the west to Bengal on the east languages which are related to Sanskrit. They are all basically alike in structure and vocabulary, but they differ more or less as the different languages derived from Latin differ, in the sense that a Frenchman cannot necessarily understand an Italian or a Romanian. In the same way the Gujarati cannot necessarily understand the Bengali unless an effort is made on both sides to choose words and forms of expression which are rather close together.

The major tongues from west to east are these: On the west coast, Gujarati and Marathi are spoken. Towns or regions are dominated by the one or the other, but here and there there is overlapping, as in the city of Bombay, in which both tongues are spoken by large numbers of people. Marathi is spoken in the southern part of Madhya Pradesh (formerly Central Provinces); more and more as one goes north and east one finds the predominance of Hindi. Hindi is spoken all the way across central India until it finally encounters in the extreme east the use of Bengali, while in the west it merges into Rajasthan, and in the northwest it encounters Punjabi.

But what about Hindustani, sometimes spoken of as the "common language" or "lingua franca" of India? This is based upon a form of Hindi current in and near Delhi during the period of Muslim power. It seems to have been a bazaar or trade language. During the Muslim period it acquired many Arabic and Persian words. More and more these words became an accepted part of the common speech. The Muslim armies used it as they went to different parts of India. In the Muslim court of Hyderabad in the Deccan it acquired literary usage. This tongue ultimately became known as Hindustani. In much of North India, despite the attempt of Hindi-speaking purists to exclude Arabic and Persian elements, Hindustani is the current colloquial speech of cities and towns. The same spoken language, Hindustani, is naturally spoken by the Muslims in towns and cities of north central and northwestern India.

In writing, however, Hindustani has two forms. One is Hindi and is used by Hindus. The other is Urdu and is used mostly by Muslims. These two literary languages are completely different scripts. Hindi uses Devanagari, which originated in India and reads from left to right. Urdu uses the Perso-Arabic script which reads from right to left. Strictly speaking, Urdu and Hindi when spoken are the same tongue, Hindustani, but when written appear as two languages. If a man says he reads an Urdu newspaper, it ordinarily means that he is a Muslim. If he reads a Hindi newspaper, it ordinarily means that he is a Hindu. If the two men are talking together, however, they are to all intents and purposes talking the same language. The Constitution of India says that Hindi is to become the national language. Many Hindus tend to want "pure" Hindi as their tongue, that is, they wish to purge from it the words of Arabic and Persian origin and substitute words from Sanskrit. Muslims bitterly resent this, partly because Urdu is their own distinctive literary language, and partly because it contains much beautiful poetry and prose precious to the Muslim world. A very concrete daily example is the tendency of the All India Radio to move in the direction of a purified Hindi. This means to the Muslims not a fulfillment of the constitutional effort toward the development of a unitary national language, but a quite unnecessary affront, as if our radio networks tried to purify English of its rich borrowings from Spanish or French.

In the face of this situation the Indian government at the time of the framing of the constitution determined that Hindi should ultimately be made the national tongue, but provided that a number of years should elapse before any attempt would be made to implement this in practice. One sees in the meantime examples of some of the consequences of this action. The boys in the central provinces whose native tongue is Marathi can choose, as they take the competitive examination for the Navy, whether they will take it in English or in Hindi. This sounds fair enough because English has been the universal language in higher instruction, and Hindi is destined to become the national tongue. But suppose that among the competitors there are many boys whose native tongue is Hindi. These latter will be taking the competitive examination in their own tongue instead of in a tongue which has merely been acquired in a school. The Marathi community feels that the attempt to make Hindi a national tongue should not be pushed to the point where it has this kind of discriminatory value against other language groups.

Traditionally, of course, English was imposed from above upon the civil servants throughout the whole administration, and under the influence of the trend towards Anglicizing of all education, as represented by Macaulay, it became central and dominant in the entire educational system of India. English is very well spoken all over India not only by university people but by business people, doctors, lawyers, men of affairs. It *has to be* well spoken. The complicated adjustments with which India is concerned require a correct, smooth, rapid, and subtle use of the medium of communication and Indian English is equal to this occasion. To my ear, at least, it is well structured literary English based on good traditions, tastefully used and beautifully pronounced.

Since this is the case, a question may occur to the observer which is probably not very realistic or practical today but may be worth keeping in the back of one's mind: Why cannot English remain the central medium of communication beyond the level of the local village speech which may survive for a while, like the French *patois?* Why can it not become a universal language, which as literacy mounts, can spread down, so to speak, so that ultimately English will be the medium of communication of all?

The first difficulty here is, of course, the issue of national feeling. The same sort of question can be asked regarding dozens of language groups. One might ask the Dutch why they cannot agree to drop their language and talk German, or the Welsh why they cannot use only English. The inconvenience of talking Welsh as compared with English or the necessity of a double language system are serious enough, but we do not encounter the abdication of languages; we find them only with difficulty extirpated and often dying a lingering death, or refusing to die.

In India the shoe is on the other foot. Instead of finding the Indian languages dying slowly under the pressure of the domineering force of English, we find that the local language groups in India, proud of their own tradition, devoted to their own local customs, confident of their future, are by no means willing to sign an instrument of abdication. It would be utterly alien to the feeling of Gujaratis, Marathis, Tamils, or Telugus to throw up the sponge and accept English. On the contrary, there has been a considerable increase in what might be called "nationalistic" language feeling, not in the sense of Indian nationalism, but in the sense of essentially nationalistic pressure exerted by the language groups against one another. In many instances there has been very strong political pressure to constitute "language states" (i. e., states within the Indian union based on language as such). Thus Madras State might actually be carved into Tamil or Telugu states, etc. While this pressure has not actually proved sufficient to produce its intended result, it has led to the establishment of language universities (using the local language), e.g., at Ahmedabad, the new Gujarat University. There are not enough well-equipped universities in India, and those that do exist cry pitifully for more support, but the pressures are such as to require new, albeit inadequately equipped, language universities, universities in which the instruction will be given in the tongue native to the villagers of the region.

There is certainly a serious dilemma here. India can hardly afford the luxury of localisms, subdivisions, cutting across her many loyalties; caste is already enough of a subdivision. If one bears in mind that the caste subdivision and the language subdivision are usually "at right angles," that is, that there are all castes present in a language group and all language groups of a certain region present within a certain caste, one realizes the degree to which the fractionation of national effort may be drawn. Think of it, for example, in economic or in political terms. Suppose one prefers to give a job to a person who belongs to one's caste and to one's language group. Suppose one decides to seek employment where one is welcome both in caste terms and in language terms. Suppose those who represent us in a provincial or central legislative post must be right on both scores. The whole machinery is just made more complicated. In the meantime, truly functional groupings such as those offered by occupation or by other economic needs are likely to be somewhat impaired.

A very gross illustration is offered by the factory workers in Kanpur already mentioned. In Kanpur, trade unionism has made very little progress, largely because the different castes cannot pull together. In the same way in Ahmedabad, in spite of its effective union supported and developed by Gandhi and by some members of the Sarabhai family, there is such poor cohesion that we find strong anti-Harijan feeling on the part of caste Hindus.

THE PARTITION OF INDIA AND ITS AFTERMATH

There is scant justification for the conception that religious strife is more characteristic of India than of other lands. In parts of India the Muslim group has been dominant and there has certainly been some resentment on the part of the subjugated Hindus. In other parts of India the dominant Hindus have at times been accused of oppressing their Muslim tenants or employees. Considering the face of history and the regularity with which groups under the economic, military or political tutelage of others have felt themselves to be oppressed, one could not characterize India as a particularly strife-ridden land. Neither can it be said with any great confidence that this is due to an essential passivity or quietism on the part of the Indian population. Resentment against despots or dominating landlords is a universal human phenomenon. At the same time, resentment against one's neighbors who at times seem to make the best of economic inequalities is so highly standardized a human phenomenon that it would not make much sense for the Western observer to regard India as a land of especially acute suspicion or violence.

The role of the British

One must note certain facts, however, regarding the background of Hindu-Muslim relations which are pertinent to the present situation. The British entered the country from the sea. Though it was often from the Muslims that power was seized, the British dealt for the most part with the upper crust in Indian society: Hindu rulers, landlords, men of culture and erudition. Civil service posts, which were the primary means by which able and promising young men could achieve some status in their own country, went to Hindu rather than to Muslim lads. Over a period of time the British regime spread its way toward the center and north, and encountered regions where Muslims predominated. In the meantime Hindu resentment under British rule became more and more acute, and despite the role played by Muslims in the mutiny of 1857, it later appeared advantageous to the British regime to offer opportunities to young Muslims far beyond those previously enjoyed. Despite the fact that the Hindu majority was necessarily the chief instrument through which to work, there was a tendency to favor the Muslims as against the Hindus. The Muslims began toward the end of the century to receive their share and perhaps more than their proportional share of administrative posts carrying a degree of security and importance.

The Muslims began to be caught between the appeals of two opposing ways of responding to the British. On the one hand, some shared the general spirit of *nationalism*, as expressed in the Indian Congress; and we find some leaders of the Muslim group sharing in the new movement toward the freeing of India. At the same time others were drawn into the temptation to work with the British as against the nationalist elements in the Hindu majority. Early in the present century a serious additional wedge was driven between the Hindus and Muslims through the fact that the British Government initiated the "separate electorates." This meant that each religious group would elect political representatives from among its own number. It is just as if when you went to the polls you would vote for a Catholic if you were Catholic, vote for a Jew if you were Jewish, vote for a Lutheran if you were Lutheran, etc. This phenomenon, providing a certain amount of representation of each group, may seem at first to suggest democracy. Actually it reminded people of religious and other nonpolitical bases for their national life, and immediately poisoned the first springs of unity in nationalism which had become evident. In fact, from the first years of this century, one finds factors of this sort gradually splitting the bulk of the Muslims off from the general movement toward self-sufficiency and autonomy.

The Hindu-Muslim riots

The general Muslim feeling against the full participation with the Hindus in their anti-British movement had become especially evident in 1906 in the founding of the Muslim League. At the same time, many educational institutions serving Muslims began to nurture the conception of a non-Hindu autonomous Muslim state within India. In the thirties the Muslim University at Aligarh became actively identified with the development of a separatist movement, young scholars and their students thinking more and more in terms of the desirability of splitting off from India a powerful Muslim State, which indeed came in time to be realized in the new state of Pakistan. As Hindu-Muslim relations deteriorated, one heard more and more about "riots." The word "riot" is not to be understood in the Western sense as sporadic violence, throwing of brickbats, and the like, but rather a mass attack by an incensed group against the available members of the opposing group. There are records of violent riots stretching back over many decades. The riots of the period between the two world wars were, however, not out of proportion to the general seething confusion and vigorous experimentation of the period, and by themselves betokened in no way the inevitability of a political split between Hindus and Muslims.

But the leadership of the Muslim League, particularly

Mr. Jinnah, succeeded more and more in unifying the more powerful and articulate elements among the Muslims in favor of complete separation from India. The outbreak of riots, often due to trivial causes, contributed to the estrangement and strengthened the separatist tendencies.

We cannot here recapitulate the whole story of the Indian achievement of independence. Most Indian leaders, not only through the period of the World War I, but into the period of the twenties, continued to work for dominion status or for a partnership with Britain; the economic and political struggle ultimately took more and more radical forms. Led by Gandhi, the Indian National Congress declared for independence in 1930, and that party, which included men and women of every caste and community, pursued this goal, despite the mass arrest of leaders, through the thirties and the period of World War II.

Hindu-Muslim relations were deteriorating during this period. Disputes grew more heated between the Congress Party and the Muslim League, and the latter declared for Pakistan in 1940. After World War II, relations became worse still, especially when Mr. Jinnah's call for "direct action" in Calcutta in August, 1946, led to widespread rioting and much carnage.

During World War II British efforts to secure some sort of reconciliation between India and Britain failed, and by the conclusion of the war, it was evident that the British would leave India. The question was when and in what manner.

The economic and other factors which were slowly but surely eroding the British control of India would inevitably have had to lead to complete Indian independence within a generation or two, but there was no clear economic necessity that the end of World War II should bring such independence. Rather, it was the three-cornered struggle of the British interests, the Muslim League, and the Indian National Congress that led to the curious execution of a document which at the same time (August 15, 1947) rent India asunder and gave the remaining portions their independence. The two portions which appear on the map as East and West Pakistan gained and retain the status of a dominion within the Commonwealth, while India became a republic in 1950, although remaining within the Commonwealth and thus retaining some slight economic and administrative ties with London. With the economics of partition we are not here concerned, except to note that the social tensions were in many ways enormously increased by the separation of lands producing raw materials from the factories which processed them; notably in the case of jute, where India had the mills with which to process the Pakistan-grown jute. Similarly, the great rivers watering the farm lands of West Pakistan flow first through or beside Kashmir, whose ruler accedes to India. Instead of dealing in detail with economic consequences, we shall content ourselves with the fact that most Indians felt revolted and outraged by the partition of the country, whereas those Muslim leaders who had been identified with the movement for the establishment of Pakistan were jubilant at the fulfillment of their hopes and at the opportunity to develop the fifth most populous nation in the world.

Many Indians of the period 1946-47, both Hindu and Muslim, resented the fact that rapid three-cornered deliberations had to be conducted and that the partition of India was the price demanded by the Muslim leaders. There were nevertheless many Muslim leaders who were fully identified with the conception of a new state, and many in fact who thereupon became functionaries at all levels in the establishment of the new regime.

Trapped by partition

The drawing of the partition line between India and Pakistan (see the map) inevitably caused hundreds of thousands of persons to find themselves almost instantly in the role of refugees; in a great many cases people who had always lived quietly with their neighbors found themselves forced off their land and with no place to go, often forced to sell the family jewelry or odds and ends of possessions at a loss, and to get out with such cattle or conveyances as they could command. A great many of them suffered violence. Many were killed or lost in the wave of hostility and bitterness which accompanied this forced exodus.

What happened in India and Pakistan was that people set out to join those of their own religious faith at a great distance, sometimes joining members of the family who had gone on before, and sometimes without a very clear picture of a destination except in terms of some large city or region. Travel by foot or by bullock cart in a long caravan under military protection, though painful and difficult, was not by itself necessarily very dangerous. A great many, however, attempted to escape by rail and here the worst phases of the rioting occurred. In fact the word "rioting" becomes less and less appropriate as one notes that tens of thousands of people were cut down by the violent, in fact fanatical, attack of those who barred the refugees' escape. It was a common thing for about three months for Muslims and Sikhs to slay each other by the thousands as each group tried to make its way to its forced settlement in a new country. Many of India's leaders, notably Mahatma Gandhi and the Prime Minister, worked heroically and at great personal danger to try to interfere with this fanaticism. In relation to events on the Indian side of the new boundary, we are sometimes reminded of the fact that most of the Muslim police as well as the British police had of course been withdrawn by the very process of partition of India, and it would have taken long training and great discipline to make possible the control of the infuriated populace by the inadequate Indian police which remained. In the end, Gandhi was killed by a fanatic who resented his powerful advocacy of toleration and good will between Hindus, Muslims, and Sikhs.

The reader must not, however, infer that the outbreaks were themselves altogether spontaneous or that they represented something totally new. Hostility, as we saw, had been expressed at a gradually rising pitch since the beginning of the century. It had at times been encouraged by the Muslim League and by the counterreaction of vigorously nationalist Hindu groups. The Muslim and Hindu newspapers had been working up feeling against the opposite community year after year. Stories of injustice and barbarous maltreatment were generally accepted by each group with reference to the sufferings of its own kind at the hands of the opposing group.

The new India found her hands more than full with the tremendous economic problem of helping the refugees to get settled, and if at times the job was badly done, the fact must nevertheless be remembered that several millions of refugees from West Pakistan were actually established and cared for somehow or other during 1947-48. Transportation was often supplied and loans made available to get the refugees started. During a similar though not quite so severe upsurge of feeling in 1949-50, millions from East Pakistan were similarly cared for.

The problem of the refugees

This will serve to bring into focus the fact that care of the uprooted refugees constituted a major problem. The refugees were frightened, frustrated, dislocated, and confused, with no idea of the future. They had lost all they had and had been cut off frequently from their own family members without knowledge of what had become of them (or knowledge only that the worst had befallen them).

It will also make clear why in the story that follows one will find a good deal of emphasis upon the psychology of the relations between refugees and resident Hindus. The refugee everywhere in the modern world has found at first what seems to him to be a warm and accepting response from those among whom he is placed; almost everywhere, however, he finds after a few weeks that he does not really get what he had counted upon. People do not fully understand his sufferings, are not really ready to share with him all that they have. This has been very evident in terms of the whole history of the DPs and other refugees from Europe. Even in the incredibly hospitable State of Israel, which has taken the position that any man or woman in the world who is a Jew must be received with open arms regardless of problems of economic and cultural assimilation, one finds nevertheless serious problems of adjustment. Those already established must find a way, often with great difficulty, to harbor and give equality to those who came later and have an utterly different cultural point of view.

In India, it must moreover be remembered that those established in a given region have usually no economic margin with which to work. In the cities, for example, their tiny little shops may line some of the main streets and they may eke out a precarious existence by selling a few items a day for a profit amounting to thirty or forty cents in American money year in and year out, taking care of the interest on debts, marrying off their daughters, and providing little if anything for their old age. Among these conditions now appear a considerable number of refugees with a tiny bit of capital of their own, whatever they have been able to scrape together and glean from selling the women's jewelry or have gotten from the government, and they start little competitive shops along the same street, often attempting to undersell. One can read beween the lines the inevitability of a very deep sense of hostility and effective barriers against understanding.

Most of the refugees have come a long way. They come quite often from the very far West of the old India, from Sind. They arrive, let us say, in Ahmedabad or Bombay, where the language spoken is different; their different caste practices, their traditions, their family structure, and above all their language, make it hard for the people of Bombay or Ahmedabad to accept them without some feeling. The feeling of the refugees themselves in the camps to which they are assigned is often one of utter and abject misery, and at times, if their backbones are still unbroken, there is violent and inarticulate expostulation against the authorities and imprecations upon all to whose control they must submit.

To illustrate, there was much apparent demoralization among the group of sixty refugees whom I was asked to talk to at the great Kalyan Camp outside of Bombay. These were apparently perfectly normal human beings who had as a matter of fact been small landlords and self-sufficient pillars of society in their own world. Forced into barracks and the goldfish-bowl type of living in a place with no homes of their own, forced to eke out their existence with pitiful and often submarginal activities, these men had become more and more deeply disturbed, more and more confused, inarticulate, verbally striking out madly and without self-control at those who day by day administered the operations of feeding, housing, and caring for them. From their point of view, the Muslims in the new area to which the refugees had come were evidently still being taken care of, provided with jobs, allowed to go about their way; here were they, the refugees, the victims of Muslims, treated to the utmost human indignity. Why should not the Muslims be turned out, and they, the native sons of the soil, be given a chance to support themselves and their families?

The black market

In the period before the British came, the villages in some parts of India were self-sufficient economic units, and, moreover, they held the village land in common. There was, in other words, no transferable family title or personal title in the land. The cultivator paid over a portion of his crop to the village artisans and a portion to the state. Everywhere, however, as the British spread through the land, they maintained their system by revenue collected through money taxation. They succeeded in introducing in one form or another a system of private property in land. By their network of railroads they were able to transport raw materials for a world market; and their Lancashire and Yorkshire mills, through the same transportation systems, supplied cloth to the people of India in place of the traditional local manufactured product.

This general invasion of India by a system of private property must not be understood as an equivalent to what we call the "free enterprise system." For one thing, people inevitably depended upon local loans to carry them through until the harvest; and the moneylender, both traditionally and under the British regime, was a person of major economic importance. The moneylender is satisfied with the revolving fund which his own money supplies and is in no need of investing his money in capital goods. By and large, the British came with capital goods as represented, for example, in the rolling stock of the railroads, while Indians for the most part continued to derive their income from economic operations based on little or no capital except insofar as the money itself be regarded as capital. Even to this day, despite the development of the industrial system by the Brit-

ish, and despite the development of large Indian holdings in
industry, the habit of the small moneylender to rely upon
his obvious source of return has prevented the development
of what we should call a capitalist system, and in particular a
competitive system of productive enterprise. If one remembers that at the same time the landlord has seldom put much
capital into the land and has been content to derive a rather
large share of the produce simply because he held title in
the land, we realize that India has not been ripe for industrialization in the Western sense.

The few very wealthy industrial families such as the great
Parsee family, the Tatas in the Bombay region, the enormous
jute and textile operators, the Birlas in North India, and a
few others give to the Westerner a rather misleading conception of the state of economic enterprise in India. For the
most part it is a poor land, a land where few people have
much margin and those who do have a margin are likely to
use it in the traditional ways without embarking upon large-
scale economic development of their country. Naturally the
Indian leaders, fully aware of the problems of industrialization as they saw them in the West, have been struggling
for decades, and particularly since the independence of
India, to establish a system of true capitalist industrial expansion in the whole country.

This is by way of attempting to give a factual and non-
moral picture of one of the most serious difficulties which India has faced: the problem of the black market. The term
"black market" as applied to the West may mean essentially
the irresponsible evasion of social controls by those who have
the ingenuity and the complacency, the lack of moral sensitivity to the needs of others, and the habit of embarking
upon operations in buying and selling which evade social
control. The term "black market" as applied to India must,
however, be brought into relation to the general assumption
on the part of those who have a little money at their dis-

posal that the normal and proper thing is to use this money
for as safe a return for one's family as is possible. This is not
in itself conceived to be immoral but a necessary process of
living. Now if one bears in mind the fact that in recent years,
and particularly since the partition of India, it has been absolutely essential for the government to control the distribution of food, clothing, and other necessities which will keep
the population as a whole alive and able to function, one
realizes that there is no more fundamental source of social
tension than the automatic, continuous, and widespread per-
sistence of the traditional view that the thing to do is to get
what one can from one's money.

Take, for example, the operation of textiles. Here one has
typically the very normal desire of the government to see
that cheap but good cloth reaches the whole public. There
is consequently a quota system and a system of prices which
are established for cloths of different grades. About a third,
probably, of all the cloth in India is actually sold through
the open government channels. Remember that those who
deal in cloth include large numbers of refugees who are entirely dependent for their living upon by-passing the strict
system of government controls. Remember also that there is
a considerable Muslim population which can only exist if it
sells to those with whom it can safely deal, which in many
cases will be members of its own community group. There is
nothing particularly surprising about the fact that about two
thirds of all the cloth which is sold at retail in India is sold
in the black market, sold at prices very much higher than
those which officially prevail.[1] Likewise there is nothing very
surprising about the fact that widespread suffering and hos-

. . . .

[1] We have let this passage stand, to represent the findings as of 1950.
The decontrol of cloth has practically abolished the black market:
an illustration of the fluid character of generalizations about modern
India.

tility result; that in many parts of India the bitterness against the government on the part of refugees who can hardly make a living selling cloth must be great; that bitterness among Muslims, who feel that they are unable to get their share of the cloth, should likewise be great; and that in general the atmosphere should be one of cynicism and hostility. Nothing is accomplished to clarify the situation by referring here to the "low moral tone" of Indian economic operations. The great bulk of the Indian public struggles as best it can day by day against a situation which it cannot understand, a situation in fact created largely by recent developments, and in particular by the system of events attending the partition and independence of India in August, 1947. This is one of countless instances in which the dispassionate observer from the West is likely to come to the conclusion that there is sufficient basis in India for an enormous amount of social tension.

III

SOCIAL TENSIONS IN TODAY'S INDIA

6

The crumbling patterns of social distance

Earlier we have viewed the caste system in its cohesive and its divisive aspects; we shall now discuss in the light of our UNESCO studies the way in which it contributes to today's social tensions.

We were so fortunate as to be able to gather a considerable number of small units of data regarding the psychology of the caste situation, particularly as it undergoes present-day transitions.[1] Using these and other data, I shall present here my own outlook on the present situation as regards caste in India, insofar as this bears on the problem of social tensions. I shall make no pretense, however, that I am surveying the whole problem of caste in present-day India. Rather, my purpose is to show where a specific quest for facts may clarify details, may give better perspective on the whole, and may introduce quantitative measurements to show the *degree* of intercaste tension or the *degree* of effectiveness of conciliatory moves.

. . . .

[1] The caste problem appears in connection with the Bombay and Ahmedabad studies dealing with the interrelations between resident Hindus, refugee Hindus, and Muslims, and incidental data on caste also come from the Etawah study, from the Lucknow study of Professor Kali Prasad, and from the Calcutta study of Dr. B. S. Guha. But caste is the primary center of interest in the studies by Professor R. K. Mukerjee at Lucknow and by Professor B. Kuppuswamy at Madras.

In the first part of my account, I shall draw mainly upon the work of Professor Radhakamal Mukerjee and his colleagues,[2] but instead of keeping these data sharply separate from the rest, I shall attempt to interweave with them the materials from certain other studies which will take a larger and larger place in the total as we move forward.

As to the whole question of whether the caste situation is leading to acute tension at the present time, we quote Mukerjee's cautious phrase: "The lower castes seem to be somewhat dissatisfied with their present position, social and economic." They are becoming aware that their situation is not inevitable. They observe many aspects of the new economic and social scene, and they know they have powerful friends. Gandhi gave enormous emphasis to the Harijan (untouchable) uplift movement. It was his preoccupation during the last years of his life to live among Harijans, to help to improve their lot, to remove the stigma against acceptance and employment of them, and to prepare the way for the constitutional guarantees of equality which did so much to rectify the legal and moral position of the Harijans in Indian society.

It is of course one thing to legislate and another to implement such legislation. It is true that one may not now legally discriminate against Harijans in employment. The fact remains that they live for the most part as they have traditionally lived, carrying out the dirtiest and most menial forms of agricultural labor, almost always being without their own land, and being required by their poverty to carry out tasks of scavenging, sweeping, the removal of the carcasses of animals that die in the fields, the acceptance of the lowest status on all occasions, the exclusion from most public ceremonials to which all other Hindus throng. Very few Harijans indeed

. . . .

[2] Dr. Baljit Singh, Dr. Shridhar Misra, Mr. Basuder Narayan, and others.

are found in schools or colleges (just as there are comparatively few Negroes in American colleges);[3] here and there a few are found, either mixed with other children or in their own special schools or colleges.

While the word has gone forth everywhere that their lot is to be improved, it does not move anywhere near fast enough to satisfy them. They struggle at times, protest at times, carry out primitive forms of sit-down striking, seek allies among others who would like to protest, and in general mill about, needing the help and direction of those with more education and perspective. Doctor Ambedkar, long their leader and long a prominent member of the government, has repeatedly indicated that the government is not moving fast enough and has constantly threatened and used one pressure or another to try to get more action.

TROUBLE ON THE VILLAGE LEVEL

In one village we had the opportunity to observe a somewhat more concrete example of present-day caste tensions. This was in the village of Sonwarsa in the Uttar Pradesh, not far from Etawah, and a part of the Pilot Development Project mentioned on pages 260ff. In the course of the agricultural rehabilitation, the development of roads and schools described there, acute issues arose relating to the political power of the Brahmins on the one hand, the lower castes on the other. To quote Mukerjee: "There are two wells in the Chamar group and a number of wells in the Brahmin's area. An old sweeper draws his water from a small well at a distance from the village. In this village of 150 households the Brahmins are about 70 families strong and the Chamars have between 40 and 50 families. The intermediate castes are

. . . .

[3] A comparison of the situation of the Harijans with that which faces American Negroes will be found on pages 215ff.

each represented for the most part by two or three up to
10 families each. Interviews were held with some 50 individuals from among the 500 in the village as a whole, ranging
from the Brahmins down through the intermediate to the
Chamars and the Dhobies and the sweeper. There was a
good deal of tension due to caste friction. This has not taken
the form of a riot as might have happened in the city. The
old traditions and time-honored sentiments of amity and
fellow-feeling towards one another have been successful
in keeping the various castes together, presenting a semblance of the harmonious pattern of life. But the old patterns
are crumbling and disruptive forces are making themselves
very evident. The era is one of struggle for new economic and
political power. The Chamars are critical of the Brahmins
and have succeeded in splitting the village wide open, with
the Brahmins and other high-caste groups on one side, the
Chamars and others of low caste on the other. The intermediate castes are still oscillating between the two. A few
have allied themselves with the Chamars, while the great
majority of them are still with the Brahmins, though not willing to break their bonds of fellowship with the others. . . .

"The Brahmins stress that with the achievement of freedom the Chamars have literally become free. They were
emulating the Brahmins and other high caste people aspiring
to equality, claiming rights unheard of before. The Chamars,
under the influence of Gandhi's Harijan movement and national independence, told us that the impetus for their struggle came from other villages where the Chamars were in a
relatively happy position." The agitation received further
stimulus from the activities of the Pilot Development Project
workers who have regarded the removal of untouchability as
one of the main items in their program.

The acute phase of the trouble in the village of Sonwarsa
took the following form: The Brahmins being mostly the
landowners, the Chamars have mostly been landless laborers.

Until recently many of them cultivated land on a sharecropping basis. But due to the recent amendments in the tenancy legislation prohibiting the subletting of land for more than two consecutive years, the landlords withdrew their land, thus creating an acute land hunger among the Chamars. They have been compelled to seek employment in the village or outside on day wages; some drive carts, others work on the canals as casual laborers, while some are employed by the village people in such primary agricultural pursuits as plowing, weaving, manuring, harvesting. They receive less pay in the village than they can earn on the canal: a rupee a day in the village as compared with a rupee and a half in canal labor. (This and other grievances are regarded by Mukerjee as exaggerated; he quotes them as asserting rather irrationally that costs of living have been artificially inflated by the Brahmins.) Other brawls and personal animosities relating to the use of the wells and relating to the cutting down of trees feed into the general economic tension due to the essential loss of economic opportunity by the Chamars, and their determination not to yield but to rectify their situation.

The whole matter came to a head with the Panchayat elections. The Brahmins naturally wanted one of their own men to become the chief (*Sarpanch*). The Chamars nominated one of their own men. It was then suggested for the sake of compromise that someone from the intermediate castes should be chosen, and the Chamars nominated an individual whom they thought suitable. The Brahmins held that he was not qualified to hold the post. Then there ensued an argument about the electoral roll upon which were supposed to be the names of those qualified. The hostility became so acute that the Chamars decided to boycott the Panchayat election. They thus withdrew from the self-government pattern of the village, a fact which was expressed more articulately by their beginning to threaten the discontinuance of their traditional types of labor. They began to say: "Why should we remove the carcasses of cattle that die in the fields; let the Brahmins do it themselves." One can imagine what would actually happen were any large caste to withdraw completely from the execution of its traditional duties.

In the meantime, however, the Brahmins, being the moneylenders, were in the driver's seat, and the Chamars could do little more than threaten as long as they required cash in order to function. Feelings worked to a high pitch and the investigators came to the conclusion that minor episodes were being regularly inflated into items of considerable seriousness. The individual interviews with many of the Brahmins had to be compared with a sort of group interview with the Harijans, since they were unwilling to be interviewed except on this basis.

Following are typical materials unearthed: The Brahmins state that the Chamars no longer stand up or get down from their cot if they, the Brahmins, happen to pass by their door. Some of the Chamars complain that they could not remain sitting while a Brahmin was before them. The Brahmins say they have no objection to a Chamar's sitting on the same floor with them or even on the same cot provided they do not touch each other. They say the Chamars are in fact entering their rooms. The Chamars could if they liked draw water from the Brahmins' wells even though they had wells of their own. The Chamars state that they could never hope to sit side by side with the Brahmins, much less on the cot with them; that they were not allowed to enter their homes, could not draw water from their wells or could only do so under strict conditions. (Questioning revealed, however, that various lower castes maintain their own untouchability rules with respect to one another; thus the sweeper, for example, always sat apart from the others and grumbled that he could not mix with other people even at the time of the religious ceremonies.)

Professor Mukerjee came to the conclusion that a good

deal of this testimony seemed emotionally colored. The intermediate castes similarly misrepresented facts. Those among them who sided with the Brahmins denied the imposition of any serious disabilities upon them by the Brahmins, while on the other hand the group aligning itself with the Chamars emphatically denied any such leniency, and vehemently protested against the limitations imposed upon them.

Constructive steps

It does not follow that the solutions need take the form of violence or even of perpetual hostility. In addition to the recourse through legislation, and in addition to gradual conciliatory efforts based upon village discussion and the rectification of abuses and the universal process of compromise and adjustment, there are very concrete things which are being undertaken by local Indian leadership. Very practical indeed for example is the reorganization of village handicrafts such as tanning, leatherwork, woodwork, basket weaving, grass planting, and rope making. Such major steps as the abolition of debt bondage and the guarantee of freedom of contract and freedom of mobility are being taken care of. All sorts of minor easements can be made in accordance with the materials available, the skills and traditions of the local groups suffering the severest economic hardship.

In addition to economic matters, a few social matters are worth considering, e.g., the efforts by top and middle leadership to drop terms of greeting which do not convey a full sense of dignity and respect, and the effort to bring all castes into village affairs, with acceptance of their dignity and worth as individuals.

The degree of upper-caste liberalism in expressed willingness to forgo the special privileges of one's own group appears everywhere in our studies to be considerable. It occurred to Professor Mukerjee and his colleagues to inquire as to the acceptability of intermarriage from the point of view of various castes. One actually finds here, as we have been informed one finds everywhere in India, a certain number of members of every caste who are willing to accept the principle of intermarriage. In Mukerjee's sample, 16 per cent of the Brahmins were willing to favor intermarriage not only outside the caste but even outside the community (16 per cent would thus even favor marriage with Muslims). As one goes down the social scale one finds more and more individuals who express willingness to agree to marriage outside the caste. Of course this comes to mean more and more, as one goes down, the acceptance of marriage into a higher caste. Among the intermediate and lower castes a considerable number, sometimes as many as a third, are willing to contemplate marriage with Muslims; and the Muslims themselves show in this particular sample about the same acceptance of marriage into Hindu castes as Brahmins do of intermarriage with Muslims. It is of course *not* stated that these verbal expressions have any predictive value in relation to actual behavior. We are simply gathering data on attitudes which are plainly undergoing transition, and it will take observations of behavior to ascertain what relation between verbal expression and behavior may actually appear.

THE CITIES AS SOCIAL LEVELERS

As the scene of caste conflict shifts from village to city one finds that the essential relations of the castes remain the same. There is still nonintermarriage; noninterdining; homes are largely separate. The sense of status and ceremonial cleanness is still there. There are, however, many obvious changes related to the fact that workers of all castes may be found carrying out the same operation in the mill. Industrial jobs don't "fit" caste categories. We shall draw our data here primarily from the study of the industrial city of Kanpur, with some secondary data also from Ahmedabad. Mukerjee's associates interviewed all castes from Brahmins down to the sweepers, and included Muslims and Christians. Material in quotation marks is taken directly from Mukerjee.

"One must begin with the fact that a large proportion of the untouchables who seek employment in the cities are found in the lowest levels of work, having had no opportunity to acquire the requisite skills: one finds them in such low-paid jobs as those of doffers, reelers and sweepers. Such employment is not only the worst paid but is temporary and uncertain. Supervisory jobs are likely to be in the hands of upper castes. The social cleavage between the Chamars and the Muslim workers is a fertile cause of social tension. Not only in the factory but in the living quarters the familiar caste segregation lines are found, but with the beginnings of a marked reduction in the sharpness of separation as compared with the village. Castes such as the Pasis and Koris which are never permitted to live in proximity in the rural areas now dwell in common wards with the upper castes to the extent of about 30 per cent. In those workers' areas where the upper castes are concentrated, the old social distance is rigidly maintained, but where the lower castes predominate and have their own panchayats, temples and religious musical parties, they are able to maintain their morale in the alien environment.

"The upper-caste groups seem to have left their gods and religion behind in the villages, and hardly does an upper-caste area possess a temple of its own. Thus the slum temples and gods belong to the lowest caste groups and even the scavengers are permitted to enter a temple which serves the Chamars or the Pasis. While in the villages investigated 100 per cent of the Chamars and the Pasis suffer exclusion from wells in one form or another, we find here 45 per cent of the Chamars and only 32 per cent of the Pasis suffering from any such exclusion. Thus the water taps of the cities have become great social levelers. Both high and untouchable castes obtain water from the same taps. Indeed one may see a line forming, in which of course the upper castes have a better position, but the same sources are used."

All sorts of compromise arrangements are evident as indications of the breakdown of the tradition. One may thus smear the tap with clay for purification, "to appease one's conscience." Other very notable social levelers are the schools and dispensaries. Boys and girls sit on benches and mats without any discrimination based on caste. They play together on the school grounds. Mukerjee notes that unfortunately the school period is too short to have a permanent effect. Most working-class boys leave early to take jobs as coolies, shoeshiners, grasscutters, etc.

But as one begins to make about the same money as one's betters, there are all sorts of ways of asserting oneself. One may begin to obliterate distinctions in social status by means of display. "Our survey indicates that workers belonging to the inferior castes, especially their womenfolk, as well as the Muslim workers, dress themselves in finer apparel: colored shirts, muslin kurtas and pajamas testify to the insatiable desire for social recognition, especially in the evenings, when the drudgery of factory labor is over." (Note here that in the factory situation the *women* for the first time become prominent in the discussion.)

Equality in work and wages is largely responsible for bridging the gulf between upper and lower class groups, especially by conscious effort on the part of the lower class. "Contrast the shoddy, coarse apparel of the upper-caste workers. This improvement in clothing on the part of the lower caste is not viewed with forbearance by the upper castes. They show undisguised hostility. To a question as to what accounts for this difference in clothing, the man of the upper caste retorts that their women are inside the houses doing their household work while the women of the lower castes are engaged outside the home as ordinary workers or in more dubious pursuits."

Another form of change is in the loss of the traditional terms of respect to those of higher caste. In the bustle of market and cinema crowds, one uses a greeting such as *jaihind,* which may be used for persons belonging to any social stratum. In the political and labor demonstrations and in the observance of religious ceremonies, forms of social etiquette have developed which stress more and more an egalitarian attitude. Highly practical is the fact that trade unions cement high and low castes, notably in times of crisis, disputes, strikes. The trade union movement is, however, still weak in Kanpur and divided by ideological conflict, and men of the lowest castes do not as yet constitute more than 10 per cent of the total membership.

Among the factors which tend to *preserve* the caste system are the insecurities, responsibilities, and unknown dangers which might certainly be imposed upon men whose station is at present low if they should be forced to compete on terms which they cannot understand. A curious example is the following: the Koris and the Khatiks have protested against the recent decision of the government of the Uttar Pradesh to include them in the schedule of upper-caste Hindus. This is largely because of the feeling that an administrative decision cannot wipe out the social disabilities and educational drawbacks they suffer in the actual social situation, and might even aggravate these, as they would themselves be the underdogs in the upper social stratum, and consequently be discriminated against in respect to occupation of huts and the use of public wells. Within the schedule of the lower castes the educated among them would certainly have better opportunities for employment.

One is thus reminded that in a scarcity economy in a country with limited development of resources, ineffective utilization of natural resources, and a low level of technol-

ogy, those who are poor will inevitably constitute 90 per
cent or more of the total and will cling with the desperate
conservatism of the poor in many parts of the world to
such securities and adequacies as they already have. It is
only when they can see clearly where they are going that
they are likely to abandon such little refuge and certainty as
they already know. It is entirely characteristic of the world-
wide struggle for the improvement of one's lot that while
in India there is a constant demand that the government do
more for the status of the underprivileged, there is no intention of giving up anything that gives satisfaction in the
immediate life which one knows.

"The Brahmins, a large proportion of whom work in the
factories or as mechanics, though faring better than those of
lower caste, tend to feel that these jobs are below the standard demanded by their position, but under present economic
positions see no escape. They maintain their social superiority by avoiding water touched by lower castes and cooked
food prepared by the lower castes. A typical Brahmin who
was interviewed states himself to be quite sympathetic towards the aspiration of the lower-caste groups, and maintains very good relations with them; yet it turns out that he
never visits them at home and maintains his traditional caste
prerogatives. Issues may make continuous tension as when in
this instance men of a lower caste come about three feet
from the water tap or are drawing water, when higher caste
people are drawing water from the well. The men and
women of the lower castes resent this treatment but cannot
do anything about it." (One wonders whether in Western
society such a situation could long continue without blows.)
"In their turn there are occasional errors or lapses in which
a man of a lower caste happens to press the water tap when
the Brahmin is holding his bucket or pitcher for the water.
They tend to by-pass such irregularities lest they incur the
displeasure of the lower caste members.

"They are yielding somewhat in comparison with the rigid standards maintained in the villages. Even in the matter of intermarriage changes are appearing. A Brahmin is preparing to give his daughter in marriage to a Thakur, apparently because the latter is making good money as a clerk, while he, the Brahmin, would not be able to provide a large enough dowry if the girl were to be married to another Brahmin." [4]

As everywhere else in the world, small children are without prejudice. In our study in Kanpur it was noted that "children of the industrial workers belonging to the various castes were interviewed in the slums as well as in the schools to find out whether they maintain social distance between themselves. The children have unhampered personal ties. They are attached to their boon companions from the same school class and not according to their caste. In the classroom they sit on the same floor or benches without caste distinction. Discrimination, if any, in the seating arrangements in the class rests sometimes upon neatness and cleanliness of clothes which again depends upon the individual whim of the teacher concerned. In any scheme of social action research the school will have to be utilized as the fundamental unit in mass persuasion."

Yet in spite of this, and all the equalitarian pressures, it must be remembered that the children of different castes are brought up in very different ways, as would be true of children of high and low status in any country. Mukerjee specifically states: "The lower caste groups according to indoctrination received by Brahmin children are inferior in

. . . .

[4] Also to be emphasized everywhere is the fact that men of lower caste who win their way to economically desirable positions—when, for example, a laundryman passed the examination and became a postmaster—the status may move rather rapidly to that defined by the position of respect (especially in the case of a government position), and is therefore not anchored solely upon the fact of caste.

status and only meant for low and undignified occupations."
They are taught moreover that low-caste people are dirty
and crude even when the families are making the same income. When men of lower castes receive education and become their rivals in certain fields, the response is likely to
take the form of ridicule and sarcasm. Take the case of a Kori
employed as a clerk in a local factory. He does not consider
his present job dignified because he does not receive what
he regards as courteous treatment from his colleagues. The
Brahmin bearer or servant refuses to serve him tea or water
in the office.

CASTE TENSION IN SOUTH INDIA

In South India, which one can identify on the map in
terms of the states of Hyderabad, Madras, Mysore, and
Travancore-Cochin, caste lines are traditionally sharp. In
recent years Madras has been the center of a deep and cor-
rosive strife between Brahmins and non-Brahmins. The
Brahmin castes were looked upon as the exploiters. The
Brahmins had long been the educated people and it was
from them that the British government recruited its civil
servants, from the top to the bottom of the system. In the
state of Mysore all citizens who were not Brahmins were
looked upon as "backward classes" who needed special facilities to obtain education and ultimately to become eligible for government posts. "Backward scholarships" were in-
stituted to promote education among them. Government
posts were advertised in two categories, the "A" category
open to all citizens and the "B" category open only to members of backward communities, that is, all those irrespective
of religion who were not Brahmins. When the Justice Party
of South India organized itself, Hindus, Muslims, Christians,
and others joined it with the declared intention of secur-
ing equal opportunity and social justice to the downtrod-

den. As a result of mounting pressure by the non-Brahmins an order was promulgated defining quotas for civil service posts and for medical and engineering colleges and the like in terms of caste and religion. The effect of the whole Justice movement has been on the one hand to encourage the non-Brahmins to take the problem of their welfare into their own hands and carry on "anti-Brahmin restrictive activities," especially through legislation; on the other hand, to produce in the Brahmin a sense of victimization and ultimately a sense of hopelessness. Traditionally the Brahmin boys, for example, have always received an education and have always been eligible to receive desirable positions. Today, with definite quotas established, many of the Brahmin boys cannot expect to achieve the desired rewards, are essentially cast loose and flounder about; they cannot very well under Indian conditions find posts of a different character from those which Brahmins have held in the past. They are shoved out; they try to find positions to meet the dignity of their social status. Due in large measure to these conditions, South Indian Brahmins are found in all sorts of important positions in North India and in Bombay. We are credibly informed that many others become active elements in the dissident or communist ranks.

For these reasons the issue is not primarily the issue of caste Hindus versus Harijans, as it is in much of India, but the issue of Brahmins versus non-Brahmins. The law now gives the advantage to the latter to the point where a merit system is not strictly workable (many Brahmins being obviously better qualified from an educational point of view than many of the non-Brahmins who under the quota system replaced them). The question is whether the Brahmins can reasonably hope ever again to receive what they regard as their proper prerogatives. If we look forward to a period of universal education in India, it is hard to see how the traditional educational and occupational status of the Brahmins can be maintained. There is, in other words, a considerable rational basis for the pessimism and the hostility of the Brahmins. Moreover, until that remote date is reached when caste itself is forgotten, it is hard to see how the non-Brahmins can avoid tension based on two considerations: first, the sheer fact that they are non-Brahmins in a world in which Brahmin prestige means so much; and second, the fact that they have to keep forever pushing for their own rights as they see them in order to achieve ultimately an actual parity in education and opportunity, man for man, with those of the Brahmin caste. It must after all be remembered that though the Brahmins are on a quota system, still a higher proportion of Brahmins enter into desirable positions than is the case with members of other castes. We are dealing with a gradual relative displacement of Brahmins, not with a sudden equalization of all castes.

STUDENTS MOVE AGAINST THE CASTE SYSTEM

We report here in considerable detail the findings of Professor Kuppuswamy, of the Presidency College in Madras, dealing with the question of the attitudes of students in South India towards caste, because so far as we know it is the only empirical investigation in which quantitative data from large numbers of individuals have been gathered and analyzed.

The method used was the questionnaire, an excerpt of which appears in the Appendix. The respondents to this questionnaire are students from seven colleges in the city of Madras and from five nonmetropolitan ("mufusil") colleges. A total of 591 students took part in this investigation. Of these students, 468 were Hindus, 36 Muslims, 77 Christians, and 10 gave no response to the question concerning religion. Among the Hindus 118 were Brahmins, 279 belonged to non-Brahmin castes, and one was a Harijan. There were 397 boys and 194 girls.

To give first of all the over-all figures: When the students were asked to indicate whether they find the caste system satisfactory, tolerable, or intolerable, only about 11 per cent say satisfactory, about 32 per cent tolerable, and about 56 per cent intolerable. There is a very evident rejection of the caste system. This rejection is more marked among those students who responded in general that they do not conform to the customs of their families. The same problem may be phrased in another way by asking whether the caste system should remain, be modified, or be abolished. Only about 5 per cent want it to remain, about 37 per cent want it to be modified, and 58 per cent want it to be abolished.

Often it is said that the actual test of readiness to abolish the caste system is willingness to give up the prohibition against intercaste marriage. With regard to the question whether intermarriage should be restricted by caste, the extreme position is represented by approval of marriages between individuals of any caste or community whatever; 42.6 per cent of the group favor such universal permissiveness. In the matter of interdining, 81.2 per cent favor the removal of all restrictions (it will be noted later that the results from the Bogardus social distance tests differ slightly from these figures).

Professor Kuppuswamy also asked the "nonconformists" whether they would be willing to let their house, in case it fell vacant, to members of any group regardless of class or community, and found that 67 per cent of the "nonconformists" against 50 per cent of the remainder would set no restrictions whatever. From such data he proceeds to analyze the phenomenon of nonconformity in general. "There is a great consistency in the opinions expressed by the 94 respondents who assert that they do not conform to the social customs of the family. A large proportion of them assert that they look upon the caste system as intolerable and are prepared to abolish it. This opinion is reflected consistently with respect to the three important problems of marriage, dining, and the letting of houses. Most of them are also nonconformists in matters of religious practice."

We turn now to the question of attitude toward the caste system on the part of the Brahmins, the non-Brahmins, and the members of the Muslim and Christian groups. Only a small proportion of any group is to be found replying that the caste system is satisfactory. Among the Brahmins themselves, 11.7 regard it as satisfactory, 45.2 per cent as tolerable, and 42 per cent as intolerable. (No opinion, 1.1 per cent.) The non-Brahmin figures are 8.3, 26.6, and 64.8 per cent respectively. Though a larger proportion of non-Brahmins regard it as intolerable, one cannot say that either group strongly supports the caste system. The proportions for the Muslim and Christian groups show that over 50 per cent of both regard the caste system as intolerable, though it is of interest that a third of the Muslims regard the caste system as satisfactory, a higher proportion than is given by any other group.

In general, throughout these comparisons the women appear to be slightly more conservative than the men, that is, to be somewhat less resistant to the perpetuation of the caste system. This slight conservatism on the part of the women as compared with the men makes them actually comparable as a group with the Brahmins as a group, who are likewise slightly more conservative than the remaining group. The metropolitan group in Madras is definitely different from the mufusil group in two respects: (1) Among the mufusil women a considerably larger proportion are satisfied with the caste system and a considerably larger proportion find it intolerable—*both* groups gaining members at the expense of the intermediate position. Whereas the women in Madras tend strongly to accept the intermediate position, the men in the metropolitan and mufusil groups are practically indistinguishable. One can pursue the analysis further by comparing Brahmin and non-Brahmin men and women, in both Madras City and the mufusil areas. The result of course is to fractionate the groups down to numbers so small that statistical comparisons become hazardous.[5]

This fractionation has, however, certain value in that we may note the contribution made to total conservatism or total radicalism by various factors such as region, caste, and sex. Combining all three factors, we find the most conservative group to be the non-Brahmin women of the mufusil colleges. At the other extreme we find 73 per cent of the non-Brahmin men in the city and 69.6 per cent of the non-Brahmin men in the mufusil colleges regarding the caste system as intolerable.

Professor Kuppuswamy comments: "Probably quite a large amount of the antipathy between the Brahmins and the non-Brahmins may be due to this high degree of intolerance to the caste system in the non-Brahmin youth which may really be directed against the Brahmin community as much as against the abstract caste system itself." And it may be specifically directed to the competitive situation which exists and to the government order placing all upon a quota basis. Since the quota system operates relatively in favor of the non-Brahmins it is not likely that they are opposed at present to caste itself *as much* as they are opposed specifically to the Brahmin caste.

There is enough evidence, however, from the data from the women, the Muslims, the Christians, and above all the

. . . .

[5] In general we report here only those differences between groups which are significant according to accepted criteria of statistical practice; we admit only cases where the obtained differences might occur by chance less than once in a hundred similar studies.

Brahmins themselves to indicate clearly that the rejection of the caste system in its present form is overwhelming. It does not vary much from city to country, nor indeed does it differ from one to the other of the four language groups nor the five mufusil colleges; nor is there much difference between the students who live at home and those who live in hostels (dormitories).

One other factor of importance: family income. Whereas only about 10 per cent, more or less, of any of the economic groups studied here state that they are satisfied with the caste system, we find a very queer pattern when we turn to the responses in terms of "tolerable" and "intolerable." The poorer Brahmins and the poorer non-Brahmins alike observe caste rules more strictly than do those in more comfortable circumstances. We find therefore in both groups that as the family income goes up from a point below 900 rupees to a point of 6,000 rupees or more per month, the proportions finding the caste system tolerable go from 22.7 per cent steadily to 37.3 per cent with corresponding decline in the number who report it as intolerable. Incidentally those students who grew up in a joint family are even more hostile to the caste system than others.

As a check on the question regarding the satisfactory, the tolerable, or the intolerable status of the caste system, we have the question: should the caste system remain, be modified, or be abolished? The data are essentially similar, both men and women stating in about 5 per cent of the cases that it should remain. That it should be abolished outright is the view of 63 per cent of the men, 47 per cent of the women. But in this case the women from the mufusil colleges are as radical as are the men; for example, 62 per cent of them favor the abolition of the caste system (owing to the fact that there are only 42 women in the mufusil group, the difference between mufusil women and city women, while suggestive, is not statistically significant at the 1 per cent level).

To look more closely now at the question of attitudes towards intermarriage: We find about a quarter of the men favoring marriage within the same caste or subcaste (the traditional procedure); about a quarter favoring marriage between different castes; and nearly a half of the total favoring marriage with anyone at all. The women are a little more conservative on insisting on the same subcaste, and considerably more conservative on the matter of intermarriage with anyone. The non-Brahmins are considerably more radical than Brahmins all along the line; 81 per cent of the non-Brahmins approve of marriages outside the caste as against 50 per cent of the Brahmins.

Another way in which to approach the whole question of the mutual acceptance of groups is the Bogardus Scale of Social Distance (Appendix). Here we note that about 20 per cent of the students will admit to kinship by marriage any of the eight groups named in the scale, while nearly 60 per cent of them are willing to take food with any of the groups in their own dining rooms. The Bogardus Scale, being very specific, acts to screen out many tolerant responses which appear when the questions are asked in a somewhat vaguer form. There are a good many people willing to state specific rejections of other groups when the names of these groups are given who will ignore the fact of rejection when issues are framed in a more general fashion. The Bogardus Scale asks a highly personal question: Which groups would you admit to kinship by marriage?" This is a somewhat different matter from approving of intermarriage in general.

The Bogardus Scale also introduces a different terminology. The fourteenth question asks whether one is willing to dine with people of other castes, but the corresponding Bogardus item asks which groups the respondent would allow to take food with him *in his own dining room*. Interdining in a hotel or restaurant is a different issue from interdining at home.

The whole broad issue of equality of opportunity is defined as we have seen in especially poignant terms by the fact that there is a basic opposition in India between admitting individuals regardless of caste or creed and the principle of admitting them on the basis of manifest merit, as shown on the basis of examinations or any other objective test. The upper castes, notably the Brahmins, have everywhere in India and especially in Madras had advantages of many sorts (such as the advantage of education) for so long and in so thoroughgoing a fashion that to admit individuals to privileges on the basis of manifest merit alone would mean predominantly the admission of Brahmins. The Madras government, as we noted above, determined to protect the claims of the lower caste groups as a whole, established a specific quota system to permit non-Brahmins a large proportion of the educational openings that were available in the colleges. During the course of this investigation, namely, in 1951, the Supreme Court decided that this act was "repugnant to the constitution." There are, however, ways of effecting the same end and at the present time it appears that by means of amendments a way will be found to continue the present quota system and to further the claims of non-Brahmins.

In view of this difficult situation, it is of interest to see how students themselves feel about the issue. One of the questions asked in South India was this: "Should admission to colleges be on the basis of caste and creed?" About 20 per cent said yes, about 80 per cent no. The yes replies were in somewhat larger proportion among men than among women; this is true even in Madras City and true to an overwhelming degree in the mufusil colleges. As is to be expected, the number of affirmative responses from the Brahmins was negligible. At the other extreme, there is a fair amount of support among the Muslims for the acceptance of caste and creed as a criterion. Focusing more sharply the question of special facilities for the depressed classes—aimed specifically at the development of opportunities for Harijans—the reply is overwhelmingly affirmative from all groups. Since the offering of special opportunities to Harijans does, when taken literally, contradict the principle of admission without reference to caste or creed, Professor Kuppuswamy comments on this: "This shows the difference in attitude to a problem when it is general and when it is specific."

The same general issue of the quota system is next confronted in relation to government jobs. The question reads: "The principle of communal proportions in government employment is:" and here the student must choose between the two options "necessary" and "ruinous." About 30 per cent say necessary, about 60 per cent ruinous; and the remainder indicate that the principle is necessary for some time or decline to answer the question. Here again the number who regard communal proportions as ruinous is by far the highest among the Brahmins.

That caste and religious tolerance is on a high level among college students seems confirmed by the findings of Kali Prasad's Lucknow study[6] insofar as it deals with student groups. Here the pattern would compare closely with that of decidedly liberal groups of American college students. We find for example that the great majority of both Hindu and Muslim students indicate that they have close personal relationships with members of other communities, and in the majority of cases this applies not only to individual-to-individual relationships but also to family-to-family relationships. On the Bogardus Social Distance Scale the results are quite extraordinary: "Close kinship by marriage" with members of the various groups—Bengali, Christian, Harijan,

. . . .

[6] Kali Prasad was assisted by Mr. Saiyid Zafar Hasan, Mr. Ghanshyamdas Rastoji, Miss Irene Jacob, Miss Shafali Ghos, and others.

Hindu, Punjabi, Sikh, Sindhi, and the two Muslim groups, Shiah and Sunni—all give positive figures. Even in the case of the Harijans, 60 per cent of the Muslims and 90 per cent of the Hindus are favorable as regards this relationship; 70 per cent of Muslims and 90 per cent of Hindus accept Harijans as fellow diners; 70 per cent of Muslims and 80 per cent of Hindus accept them as intimate friends. The great majority of both the Hindu and the Muslim students moreover favor the encouragement of children of both communities to play freely with members of the other community, to take meals with them and to share close friendships with them.

In commenting upon these data on students' attitudes I would add that Indian intellectuals, notably the university staffs, are frequently involved in vigorous efforts to break down narrow-mindedness in their students. At Poona University, V. K. Kothurkar, Reader in Psychology and Director of the new Psychological Laboratory, recently made an experimental investigation of the possibility of modifying caste attitudes among college students. He made use of three methods: first, an orderly rational account of the backgrounds of the various castes and communities (including, of course, Muslims, Christians, Sikhs, and Parsees); second, an emotional appeal, urging his experimental groups to consider the desirable qualities of the various groups and their contribution to the life of India; third, a group discussion technique (in which he had had considerable experience). The hypothesis which he and I both entertained was that there would be more modification of intergroup attitudes as a result of group discussion than as a result of either of the other two methods. In this we were mistaken. The greatest changes arose as a result of the emotional appeals. This result is not statistically significant, but all the results from all the experimental groups are significantly greater than those from the control group. I admit some disquietude, owing to the possibility that the student groups may have been seeking to comply with the instructor's (the experimenter's) viewpoint; and consequently the greater the emotional force of his appeal the more they may have felt (consciously or unconsciously) the need to conform to his presentation.

It is a partial refutation of my point that Mr. Kothurkar found after the experiment that many of the students seemed deeply interested in personally discussing intergroup relationships; there seemed to be much more than an immediate and mechanical response to "classroom propaganda." On the basis of close personal contact he came to the conclusion that genuine interest and emotional involvement, not simply a desire to agree, was of importance. He also notes in a letter to me (October 28, 1951): "I am giving the results for what they are worth. I am however convinced about the validity of the main conclusion of my experiment that, so far as these boys were concerned, the emotional approach through an atmosphere of respect and reverence for other groups is a better method of modifying attitudes than either the factual or discussion method. Contrary to our original expectation and hypothesis, these young boys do not seem to be in a position to exploit fully the discussion technique, in bettering their social relationships. Does it indicate that our boys have got to be used to the democratic ways of discussion and at present prefer to be told what are the right attitudes rather than to be allowed to talk them out?"

Fortunately, further studies along this line are being continued at Poona University, and it is hoped that later a fuller report can be made available.

There is much other evidence both for India and for other countries that education tends in general to reduce intolerance, but to make such generalizations useful, we need much more specific information as to kinds of education, kinds of intolerance, and relation of verbal expression to behavior.

In over-all summary, we seem to find that one prominent form of social tension in India is the struggle of castes to improve their relative status; that urbanization and education are two of the factors tending to weaken the rigidity of the caste system; that changes in attitude occur more rapidly than changes in behavior; but that change in attitude has already gone so far as to set going new policies in both the central and the state governments which are already exerting their own pressures to undermine caste prerogatives.

7

The insecurity of the Muslims

In some parts of India there are villages with Muslim inhabitants only. For the most part, however, Muslims are specialists in certain economic activities; and this means that under the village system of economy they carry out certain specific functions just as the various Hindu caste groups do. They are, for example, weavers, or they may be workers in metals or in leather. They do not intermarry with the Hindus. Their services of worship are public and dramatic. But this again has not in itself constituted any special basis for isolation as far as day by day activities are concerned. One thinks immediately of European and American communities in which members of many European groups even with different languages are accepted by one another in a casual way. Lines of demarcation may be rather sharp without any hostility developing; indeed, there may be friendly greetings exchanged across such language or national barriers about as easily as between individuals not so separated. This may continue though in some other part of India there may be a riot going on, related perhaps to the economic conflicts between a Hindu landlord and his Muslim tenants or between a Muslim owner and his Hindu employees. Such a conflict in one region need not have any broad implications for another region. Village by village, people get along in their traditional way as neighbors.

When modern communalism developed in the late nineteenth and early twentieth centuries along the lines related in an earlier chapter, many Muslims felt themselves committed to a new effort to assert themselves politically and economically, while many others regarded their primary duty and interest to be cooperation with the Hindus and others in throwing off the British imperial system. In time the latter group came to work largely through the Congress Party, the former through the Muslim League. In some parts of India the Muslim League achieved considerable power and prestige. It could not, however, be asserted that in most of India any acute inflammation of intercommunity hostility immediately resulted. But as the tension between the Muslim League and the Congress Party gradually increased, the effects tended to spread downwards from the centers to the villages, and wherever the effect was to produce mutual suspicion one could find coming into use the term "communalism" and the conception that members of a given religious community constitute a functional unit which cannot accept the dominance of another community.

One aspect of this communalism was the "two-nation theory," the conception that wherever large blocs of Muslims could be identified within the same region they constituted a national group independent of the Indian nation. This was one of many factors tending towards the ultimate development of the atmosphere from which the Pakistan separation movement began. When finally the separation of India and Pakistan occurred, as described above, one finds villages varying all the way from one extreme to the other, i.e., from those in which every Hindu and every Muslim is in a state of extreme tension and fear with respect to the other group, to those at the other extreme (and far from the borders) where little change in Hindu-Muslim relations occurred.

Important in the latter situation were two facts: (1) the Muslims were personally known and offered no threat; and (2) their economic services were needed. The economic life of the village depended upon the fact that the Muslims, like the rest, had fixed and necessary duties to perform. Still others had so great a stake in land or job that it would have been economic suicide to leave. "We can't go; we're married to the land," said a taxi driver in Patna who would have liked, as so many other millions of Muslims would have liked, to try his hand in the new country. Millions who made the attempt in Pakistan found it very difficult; in fact many of them were like the "Okies" of *The Grapes of Wrath*, starting for the new country on the assumption that land and opportunity would be theirs, but finding on arrival that there was actually no place for them, no economic future in which they could have confidence. A great many of them existed at a less-than-subsistence level, and a great many of them came back to India. Those who came back might, if fortunate, find that their land or their shops had been held vacant; if they had stayed too long, they might find that these had been lost and that they must start over again.

Those Muslims who were in undivided India prior to the time of partition probably numbered nearly a hundred million. The partition lines were in a general way drawn so as to include most of the Muslims in the new nation. About two thirds of the Muslims are now in Pakistan (East Pakistan has a larger population than West Pakistan). About a third of the original number, perhaps thirty-five million Muslims, remain today in India—largely, I suspect, because of the economic uncertainties involved in pulling up stakes and migrating to the new country.

How many of the Muslims of India today would prefer to live under Pakistan rule it is of course impossible to ascertain. It is our impression, however, that two statements could be made which are reasonably close to the truth, which may on the surface appear contradictory. The first would be that most Muslims, like most other human beings, are interested in making the best of life as they know it, providing for themselves and their families with such comfort and decency as they can, and that they consequently have no great desire to embark upon a strange new life for which they are unprepared. They would, in other words, like to stay in India if conditions do not become too catastrophically difficult for them. On the other hand, I am of the impression that many Muslims, belonging to a strongly organized social group with a great deal of fellow feeling and loyalty to their own people and tradition, would like to function under a regime which is definitely Islamic in its orientation. This does not necessarily mean that they wish a religious rather than a secular state. It does not necessarily mean that if they had a flying carpet they would prefer to live in Pakistan. It does mean, however, that they look upon Pakistan as a land of real promise and that they stay in India largely because of the economic and other physical difficulties involved in making a move. It is possible that these two statements are really in contradiction; but neither of them is offered as a literal and verbal summary of attitudes. For reasons which will be very obvious to the reader, we did not ask point-blank questions of the sort involved. But the material given below will perhaps serve to suggest that there was a rather large measure of truth in our assigning both of these attitudes to very large numbers of Muslims and in believing that in fact many Muslims entertain both of these attitudes at the same time.

As far as the reality of further migration is concerned, there is not very much use in pursuing this matter further since it is improbable that much more migration across the India-Pakistan border will occur or is likely to be economically valuable if it does occur. Most of the thirty-five million Muslims are in India to stay. The enormous majority of them accept Indian institutions, talk the same or essentially the same language as the people about them, have their own economic, social, and political functions well defined, operate as we noted like a caste within the Hindu system, are law-abiding and economically self-reliant members of the body politic. They contribute notably not only to the economic, but also to the literary, scientific, professional, and educational life of India. It is therefore of the utmost importance to them and to the Hindus to understand one another as well as they possibly can. Partly because their number is so very much larger than that of any other minority group in India (they greatly outnumber the Sikhs) and partly because the relations between India and Pakistan are economically and politically so closely tied to the attitudes of the people of both states, it was the wish of the Indian government that special attention be paid to the relations of Hindus and Muslims within India.

Now just how are these relations to be conceived? The first background factor is the original invasion of India by the Muslims, the voluntary or involuntary conversion of many Hindus to the Islamic faith, and the long military domination of large parts of India by Muslim rulers. At no time, however, did the Muslims live as aliens in the land, as the British did, separating themselves in language and culture from the Hindus. In fact, Muslim rulers learned a great deal and borrowed a great deal from the Hindus. Nevertheless, Islamic art, Islamic literature, Islamic philosophy, the Islamic faith in God and His relation to His prophet Mohammed, together with the God-ordained system of religious tradition, makes the Islamic community separate in fundamental respects from the Hindu. A good Muslim believes that all religions are *intrinsically* equally good; but he also believes that all religions other than Islam have suffered corruption, while a unique contribution of the Prophet was that he preached a faith that cannot be corrupted. A good Muslim cannot therefore believe that the Hindu pantheon or indeed even the Hindu caste system is morally and spiritually a rightful competitor with the Koran and the prophet's life and message. Muslims as conquerors were more than men of arms who by force could establish themselves in parts of India. They were definitely persons who regarded themselves as having a superior tradition. From the Hindu point of view, the Muslims were aggressive—aggressive both in the sense of the use of naked force and also in the sense that their tightly knit, compact, and effective culture and social organization had an erosive effect upon those aspects of culture which directly contradicted them.

There is, however, this enormous difference between the conquest of India and let us say the conquest of the Americas by the white man: there was relatively little in the culture of most of the New World which could stand up effectively against the competing culture of Europe. One thinks perhaps of Aztec art as an illustration of something which might have withstood it, but civilization in Mexico today is essentially a Spanish civilization rather than Aztec. In India, on the other hand, the resistance of Indian culture to Islamic culture was rather successful except under the immediate shadow of the sovereign and the power which he wielded; that is to say, Hindu temples, Hindu dances, Hindu traditions might be pushed back a few yards or a few miles from the person of the Muslim sovereign. Indian architecture might actually be pushed aside or in a few dramatic cases mosques might be built upon the foundations or even upon the ground structure of a Hindu temple. But this did not mean that Hindu civilization was washed out. It was merely pushed back by force in a few areas. All these factors, then, related to the mutual acceptance of Muslim conquerors and Hindu conquered. At the same time the mass of the Muslims increased as time went on through the voluntary or forced conversion of Hindus. Intermixture was moreover the rule. The physical types of Hindus and Muslims are today identical despite the fact that the Muslim conquerors were mostly of lighter skin, being of Middle Eastern or Central Asian origin.

Despite 200 years of British rule, the fact that the

Muslims had been conquerors and the fact that they stood
for a dynamic and expansive civilization were never completely forgotten. Even though for many decades the British
favored Hindus as against Muslims in the development of
their civil service and came relatively late to the development of a Muslim civil service and constabulary to serve
them, the Muslims had nevertheless much reason to think
of themselves as a dynamic, powerful, conquering people; as
subordinate along with the Hindus to British rule, they could
nevertheless think of themselves as more active and in some
ways superior to the Hindu population with which they
lived.

These factors are, I think, not altogether unrelated to the
arousal of Muslim aspirations and Muslim nationalism in the
late nineteenth and early twentieth centuries. Of course
these aspirations for a return to Muslim supremacy were fed
from many sources, of which one was the obvious desire of
educated young men to be civil servants or functionaries not
merely in a regime to which they were subordinate but in
their own regime, their own Islamic land to which they began to give more and more explicit thought. Even aside,
however, from the elite who received the education and
training requisite to their becoming civil servants, there was
in the rank and file of the Muslims the feeling of their great
tradition, the insecurity associated with minority group position whenever a challenge of power broke out. When, for example, a distant riot or even altercation came to one's attention, the question was: what is our status as a minority
group? The same behavior could be regarded by a Muslim
as necessary to self-protection and the definition of one's
special privileges, and from the Hindu point of view as arrogant, or insistence on a domineering role. Whatever value
judgments we may pass, there is not the slightest doubt that
the Muslim community wielded more power and influence
in many parts of India than its numbers would by them-

selves have guaranteed; even where Muslims did not constitute 50 per cent of the population they frequently were a
strong, well-organized, and effective group.

MINORITY GROUP PSYCHOLOGY

All of this is background for the understanding of the situation in which the Muslims after the creation of Pakistan
found themselves a minority in India. Not only were they a
minority; they were a minority acutely blamed by Hindus
for the partition of the country, a minority regarded as representative of an anti-Indian hostile, divisive, and subversive
influence which had shattered the aspirations for national
unity; which from the Indian point of view had been responsible for the internecine struggle, the slaughter of the innocent, the sufferings of the refugee migrants from West and
East Pakistan, and most of the ills to which modern India is
subject. From the Muslim point of view the Muslims are a normal, hard-working, reasonable element in the body politic
with a great tradition and capable of effective work, but subject today to all sorts of discrimination and exclusion from
employment, ostracism and blame, and even countless petty
personal indignities.

One can imagine, by reference to our own situation, why
such an incident as a Hindu band's playing in front of a
mosque takes on two entirely different meanings. From the
Hindu point of view there may be a few rowdies or troublemakers who are so stupid or so boorish as to enjoy annoying
a few Muslims by playing music while the services in the
mosque are in progress. From the Muslim point of view one
has here a gross and violent manifestation of sacrilegious
and vindictive hostility not only to individual Muslims but to
the sacred tradition of Islam; and not only are there a few
uncouth and brutal rowdies who have no feeling for the elementary decencies of life, but the Hindu community as a

whole is standing behind them, refraining from punishing them, refraining even from any sort of curb or moral control concerned with basic decencies. I am reminded of some incidents of attacks by hoodlums on American synagogues and even of a meeting of the Fellowship of Reconciliation attacked and subjected to violent and indecent language by a hoodlum crowd whose members had another religious outlook. Hindu-Muslim relations then are in one respect the relations of a minority to a majority under conditions where the minority cannot and will not accept second-class status, cannot and will not regard itself as subservient or merely a minor contributor to the national life as a whole. The Muslim minority is sure of its ground, proud of its tradition, and eager for full acceptance as a powerful and effective group within India. It feels that such status is not being accorded it.

So far we have been speaking largely in terms of status and dignity. We must move now to a deeper level, the level of sheer economic opportunity and even physical safety. In the Aligarh study, it is clear that the Muslims predominantly regarded themselves as discriminated against in the matter of jobs, and their tone is one of resentment. The sense of persecution has run through the Muslim publications of recent years, and those publications coming from Pakistan which insist on the injustice to Indian Muslims are widely read by the Muslims in India who more and more come to regard themselves as a dispossessed and persecuted minority group.

The basic statistics are not available to indicate whether in fact there is any discrimination against Muslims in the matter of jobs. If one stops to consider the nature of jobs in India, one would realize why the claim is difficult to support. For one thing, jobs go according to caste. Muslims work, let us say, as locksmiths, as weavers, as leatherworkers, at many other tasks, many of which hold high respect. If the Muslim community is able to accommodate a newly arrived Muslim, he will typically find employment along the lines of the accredited Muslim occupations. He may assert that people are not willing to lend him money and probably to some degree this is the case. For one thing, the Muslim population has in the last few years been rather unstable and a great many individuals have gone suddenly to Pakistan with no certainty that they would ever return. This makes the Muslim group as a group poor "risks" from the point of view of loans, without impugning anybody, whether Muslim or Hindu, with regard to personal morals. The important thing, however, is not the statistical assemblage of facts regarding the actual economic hazards, but the fact that the Muslims are so insecure as to believe themselves subject to continuous economic discrimination. As long as they believe this, the fact of their belief is of fundamental importance in social adjustment. If they believe this they cannot but act in accordance with this belief. If, moreover, they are constantly acting on the assumption of discrimination against them, annoyance on the part of the Hindus is sure likewise to result.

The Muslim problem is naturally regarded by the Muslim population as very urgent indeed, both in its immediate historical background and in its present status. From the point of view of most of the Hindus encountered in our studies, things are settled: Pakistan is Pakistan, the Muslims have settled down to be citizens of India; let's all work together and what's all the shouting about?

Again, from the Muslim point of view: we are being discriminated against; life is difficult; we can't get jobs; our children can't get an education; the future for ourselves and especially for them is dark; relations with Pakistan are difficult; Kashmir hasn't been settled; we don't know where we stand; we want action; we want the end of promises; we want guarantees; we want to be sure that our status as Muslims separates us in no way from the general body politic, the privileges and opportunities which are available for all other citizens of the community. From the Hindu point of view this is all a rather quaint, special, unnecessary kind of talk: We all are in the same boat; every Hindu caste is a minority; the situation is hard for us all; Muslims have their own Pakistan; now that you've decided to stay in India you're just like any other group; why do you ask for more? Life is difficult as it is; we'll do the best we can; take your share and stop protesting.

One Muslim professor who had heard the essence of these two points of view so many times that he was sick of it all told me in secrecy just exactly what he and his family had been through. "You know at the time of partition and several times since then, they have been out to get us and actually it is a lucky thing that I had a rifle. I didn't have to use it, you know. The Hindu mob gathered around the house; they were going to lynch me. They had things quite well organized until they found I had the rifle. They would certainly have done the same to me that they did to others. They stayed around most of the night. Nobody had quite the courage to force the house. Finally they went home. That last of these episodes left us all rather in a pulp. Then as things blew over they decided everything was all right. 'We want to be friends.' That's fine! We want to be friends, too. I wonder if people realize the rather different way it looks to you after you've been on the defending end from your house, with a black angry mob out there in front of you that would like to lynch you, and knowing that it wasn't their desire to be friends but only your rifle that carried you through. Even today of course they won't try to dislodge me from my job, but how about my boy's future? You're never treated just as a human being; you're treated as a Muslim. Your position as a professor, your past achievements, your research, your teaching are never just taken for what they are; it's always a question of 'this is the work of one of our Muslim professors.' "

The Western scholar will recognize the universal problem

of the disturbed relations of minority to majority groups. In the same way the Negro scholar or doctor would like for a minute to forget that he is a Negro scholar or doctor and just be a scholar or doctor, doing what any other scholar or doctor is doing. The Jewish social scientist or novelist would like for a moment not to be the Jewish social scientist or the Jewish novelist but just the social scientist or the novelist. One remembers perhaps Albert Einstein's comment on the book about "Jewish scientists." Why not the red-headed scientists? Why not pick out human beings on the basis of external criteria and deal with them as a category instead of accepting them simply as individuals? The feeling of the Muslim today is that he is marked, that he stands out in the sense in which the members of other caste groups do not stand out. He thinks that the very fact that he stands out makes discrimination possible and he wants the end of discrimination. To the Hindu, regarding society as a composite of many elements, and religion, notably Islamic religion, as an important and striking element which stands out against the landscape, the idea that religion be forgotten or that the Islamic tradition be given no special attention is meaningless.

There are many forces working toward a better understanding. All over India there are as usual the movements led from the top and the movements led from the bottom. The Prime Minister has over and over again used his political sagacity and his hard-driving energy and courage to create his secular state, a nondiscriminating state in which religion is to play no role in the political and economic cleavages, in which all religious groups are to have the same economic and political opportunities. The jockeying for power, caste by caste, community by community, can be replaced by functional groupings in which people choose representatives standing for real economic-political positions. For the Prime Minister and much of the Indian leadership of today the problem of communalism is a problem in which overemphasis has been given to religious or social diversities. The primary task consists of resolutely insisting on mutual respect and freedom of opportunity, and developing joint projects in which men of different caste and communities can work together. The positive program of education, industrialization, agricultural rehabilitation, sanitation and public health, and every other measure for the improvement of the lot of the people is to be developed jointly by men and women of all castes and communities. This is the positive program of India and the program to which enormous energy has been devoted in these five years of independence and with reference to which huge progress is being made.

PARS RAM'S ALIGARH STUDY

Much of the following study on Muslim insecurity will deal more concretely with one aspect of Hindu-Muslim relations as they were intensively studied by Pars Ram in Aligarh, a city which has a large and politically alert Muslim group (and through its university earlier played an important part in the establishment of the State of Pakistan). A random sample of fifty adult Hindu males and fifty adult Muslim males was so drawn as to give comparable representation of the two groups with respect to region in the city and with respect to economic class. After a qualitative picture of the Aligarh studies has been given by describing the way in which rumors spread in the city, the interview data for these two groups will be considered.

Pars Ram writes:

"An analysis of the rumors, gossip and fantastic evaluation of persons current in a particular community can be a fascinating study in its own right. More than that, such an analysis reveals the hierarchy of relations in the given community and of the roles which the various sections of the community take upon themselves at a time of stress. Every rumor, according to Gordon Allport and Leo Postman, has its *public*, and consequently every rumor reveals the social structure of its public. Since rumors serve as clues to the problems and perplexities of the rumor-affected sections of the community, a careful note was kept of the various rumors having a bearing on group tension in the town of Aligarh. Though the lack of adequate facilities has stood in the way of an exhaustive analysis, the following account throws light on the needs and attitudes of groups and the functional value that rumor, gossip and fantastic evaluation of persons can represent."

A suggested approach to the analysis of rumors

A rumor is essentially a group phenomenon. It is not one individual's effort at understanding a perplexing situation, and his personal exercises in arriving at a stage of belief which can be given the name of rumor. Many persons feel baffled in understanding a situation which has vital concern for them. One of them has a "new idea," a "brain wave," which gives a meaning to the situation. This "brain wave" has a social reference, too. Many others readily accept his meaning. But they do not stop at that. They are keen to tell it to others. There are also silent spectators who submissively accept the meaning given to the situation, and dull their curiosity about any possible alternative meaning. The whole activity of manufacturing and spreading the rumor produces certain results for the community or for a section of it. As a social force, the rumor has to be understood in terms of its effect and results for the group. These comments suggest the following questions as an approach to the analysis of rumors:

1. What was ultimately achieved by way of group action, or of modification of group or individual attitudes, through the propagated rumor? The answer to this question will reveal the social functions of the rumor.

2. Through what channels was the rumor transmitted?

(Informal group, organized groups, persons of a particular class, age, profession, etc.).

3. What were the essential features of the original statement, and how had these been modified, elaborated, and sharpened?

4. What determined the contents of the rumor?

With this approach in mind, we shall now analyze some of the rumors on which data are available.

Rumors about Hindu-Muslim riots

The rumors. There were widespread rumors in the month of February, 1951, about the Hindu-Muslim riots which, according to the rumor, were to be started in Aligarh —according to one account on February 28, 1951; according to another on March 2; and according to a third, on the occasion of the Holi festival (from March 22 to March 24).

Effect of the rumors. These rumors resulted in the following: Muslim traders were afraid of buying fresh stock for their stores. Some Muslims reported that they were not undertaking any repair or improvement of their houses. A few decided to stay away from Aligarh for the period.

Group action prompted by the rumors. As a result of these rumors, prominent Muslims waited in a deputation upon the District Magistrate and urged the Government to take the necessary precautions. A number of Hindus were consequently taken into police custody as a precautionary measure, and an additional police reserve was kept on hand to meet any emergency that might arise. The Nawab of Chhattari invited Hindus and Muslims to celebrate the Holi festival at his residence on the eve of the Holi. There is reason to believe that the police would not have taken special precautions and drastic measures to detain Hindus on the Holi occasion in the absence of these persistent rumors about the preparation for riots. Nor perhaps would the Muslim elite have cared to celebrate jointly the Holi festival at the Muslim Nawab's house. We may assume therefore that the rumor alerted Muslims and that they in turn alerted the police, and also took steps to meet the leading members of the Hindu community by way of a gesture of good will.

There was peace in Aligarh before and during the Holi occasion in 1951.

Sections affected by the rumors.   While the rumors about the fear of riots were being widely circulated, the Tension Research Team interviewed a number of Hindus to find out if they had heard the rumor about riots. Here are the typical reactions:

A Hindu schoolteacher expressed surprise at the alleged Hindu preparation for riots. He said he would have known about the preparation if there were to be any and added: "These Muslims will always manufacture some device to blackmail us."

A Hindu stationery storekeeper said, "All Hindu-Muslim conflicts take place in the heads of the UNESCO Research Team. None around here." He, too, had not heard about the riots.

A Hindu lawyer said about the rumor: "A clever way for the Muslims to contact the higher governmental authorities. I don't know of any preparation by the Hindus."

Two leaders of Hindu students' organizations were approached. They stated that they had no plan to create or take part in any riot. Two Hindu college teachers and the principal of a college answered questions about riot rumors after the manner of the Hindus quoted above.

Hindus were on the whole ignorant of the rumors, with the exception of higher government officers who are concerned with the administration of the city and leaders of certain political parties and the few who lived in the predominantly Muslim localities.

In contrast with this, the Muslims were quite excited by

the rumors. A number of Muslim storekeepers did not place orders for a fresh supply of goods for the general period of the Holi festival lest their stores be broken into and the stock removed. Muslim women in a Muslim locality seriously believed that the All-India Radio had announced the date on which a general massacre of Muslims would take place in Aligarh.

Not all Muslims had been equally affected by the rumor. The Muslim University teachers did not show signs of taking the rumor seriously, though some of them had heard about it. The lower staff of the Muslim University was quite affected. The Muslim gentry outside the University living away from the crowded areas had not been affected very much. But they all had heard about these rumors.

Origin of the rumors. Every effort was made to trace the man who had allegedly first heard the "radio announcement" of the riots in Aligarh. Whenever a call was made at his house he was announced as out. "Will return tomorrow." "Returns home very late in the night and goes to his work very early in the morning." In another case it was alleged that a Hindu vendor had told the following to his Muslim customer, a small girl: "Enjoy the pleasure of buying eatables now and for the next few days. You will not be here after the Holi."

Our persistent efforts at getting at the source from which the rumors had emanated met obstructions. The very presence of P. B., a member of the Tension Research Team, made Muslims noncommunicative and apprehensive. She was taken to be an agent of the police. Instead of a straight answer to our inquiries, questions were put back to us: "Who are you, by the way?" "Let my uncle come back from work. He knows all about the rumor. I shall consult him and then you can call here again."

Very scanty information is available regarding the Hindu sources from which the communications about riots had been passed on to Muslims. Only two sources have so far been located:

1. A Muslim owned a house in a locality where the majority of the inhabitants were Hindus. He left his own house and settled in a Muslim locality in the town in March, 1950, on the occasion of the Hindu-Muslim riots. His house had, in the meanwhile, been occupied by a Harijan having a bad police record. It was reported that he was keeping a kidnapped woman in the house and was also wanted by the police. Now this Muslim was keen on returning to his own house and often visited the locality with that end in view. The Harijan occupant of his house was in no mood to vacate the house. This Muslim had given evidence in a court of law which went against another Harijan and he therefore always expected trouble from Harijans. When the Muslim owner of the house and the Harijan occupant of the house met at a ration shop, the Harijan warned the Muslim against any plans to get his house back and added the following: "Our weapons are sharper and deadlier than we had on the occasion of the last Holi" (1950). When the President of the City Congress Committee was requested to visit the locality he was told that the Hindus in that locality did not approve of the Harijan's ways. They also confessed complete ignorance of the threat that the Harijan had been making to the Muslim.

2. About January 20, 1951, a number of Hindu boys waylaid a couple of Muslim boys who, the former believed, had insulted the sister of one of the boys while she was in the Exhibition. While assaulting the Muslim boys the Hindu boys are reported to have made the following remark: "You have forgotten all about the last year's Holi bloodshed; you have to be taught the lesson afresh."

Roles in the rumor. The utterances that the Hindu aggressors in the above instances made while assaulting their Muslim victims had a tremendous social significance. The

Hindu aggressors took the role of the saviors of the Hindu faith, who had licked the *Mlechhas* (Muslims) and achieved thereby an agreeable opinion of their criminal acts. The verbal communication implied roles for the Muslims which they accepted after the manner of robots, and started fulfilling them. It was open to the Muslim boys who had been assaulted to tell their assailants that they were not the ones who had teased the girl in question. They could have contacted the parents of the Hindu boys and told them about the criminal activities of their sons. They could have approached their warden and could have asked him to contact the principal of the college to which the Hindu boys belonged. They could have gathered their friends and reciprocated with complement the treatment meted out to them by their Hindu assailants. However, all these possibilities apparently did not occur to them; if they did, they were ruled out as unpracticable. Anyway, they started behaving like victimized Muslims, hiding their scars from every Hindu, talking about the impending danger to the Muslims (and not giving the whole story of their conflict with Hindu boys) to their distant relatives in the town. There have been many instances in which Muslims have given their Hindu neighbors "as good as they got" without taking the role of the persecuted Muslim; they often hold their own amidst the Hindu majority.

It is significant that the rumor of riots spread amongst sections of the Muslim population which could play the role of the helpless and which could not have taken any other role: women and unskilled laborers, for example.

But to play the role of the helpless is by no means necessarily to play a passive role. While the infant is helpless in many ways, and many beggars in India play the same role, the role makes others active. Moreover, the passive role played by one and the active role by others tend to be integrated. The social climate established by this relation does enduring injury to the ego development of the dependent section. Sections of the community made active in the rumor situation were the active political workers and others in a prestige position. Their role in elaborating the rumor is interesting. They have to convince the governmental authorities of the reality of the preparation for riots. In their account of the rumor all the minor incidents were knit into a coherent whole, which suggested the presence of an organized Hindu gang in the city which promoted assaults on Muslims after the manner of guerrilla tactics. Whether such an organized agency for promoting assault on Muslims was present in the city or not is not known. It was therefore not possible to gauge the relation of the contents of the rumor to the facts of the case.

Reactions of the Hindus of Aligarh to the Muslims approaching the government were not friendly. "Muslims have not given up the old habit of poisoning the ears of the Government against their Hindu neighbors even when the British rule is no more operating in India." "Muslims have managed to put good Hindus behind the bars and they will pay for it." "Muslims know the art of agitation and camouflage."

The data on which the above analysis has been based were meager. The analysis of roles hinted at here is applicable to the kind of rumor discussed here and not to all kinds of rumor. But the conclusion suggested is important and should be put to a rigid experimental test. The rumor conserves the prestige and dependence relations operating in a community. It inhibits people's taking new roles.

Distortion of the situation in the rumor

Extracts from our diaries given below are revealing in this connection:

January 29, 1951. X, a Muslim who keeps himself well informed about Muslims in the town, was seen this afternoon. Talking about the Hindu-Muslim relations in the town, he said there was nothing to report except that the Muslim rickshaw-pullers are engaged by Hindu students, and are not paid for the services rendered by them and are often mis-handled. "Both Hindu and Muslim rickshaw-pullers complain of the behavior of the students."

February 6, 1951. X was seen at his office. Three other Muslims were also present. One of them said that his family could not get much out of the Exhibition because most stores advertised their wares in Hindi, and his family were familiar with Urdu only. Another in the audience said it would be impossible for Muslims to visit the Exhibition because his younger brother had been assaulted for no reason. "Hindu bad characters have been let loose in the city." After a while the assembly broke up with a very despondent note about the future of the Muslims. "We shall accept whatever is in store for us."

February 12, 1951. Met X at his office at 8 P.M. I discovered that his office is the meeting place for Muslims from all over the town and even from the countryside, who may bring their grievances and perplexities. In one corner sits a man whose brother is not giving him a due share out of the joint family property. A returnee from Pakistan seeks X's aid to have his business premises, which are now used by a refugee, restored to him. A third narrates his grievances about the neighbors who take liberties with Waqf property (property dedicated exclusively to a Muslim religious organization). X's place serves as a clearinghouse for information on all kinds of tortures experienced by Muslims. Yesterday's skirmishes near Subzi Mandi made up the topic engaging the attention of the audience at the time. A Hindu while driving his cattle damaged some wares belonging to a Hindu store owner. The cattle owner gathered his supporters and attacked the shopkeeper, and one or two Muslim neighbors. The incident was the occasion for comments. Some of the comments are noted here:

"If a refugee fights the local Hindus, Muslims become the victims. If the *Jan* Congress*(a political organization) has a row with the Congress, Muslims suffer. If Hindu Mahasabha rattles swords with the Congress, Muslims are the victims."

"If there is an occasion for a Hindu festival, Muslims pass restless nights. I do not know what is in store for us on the Holi day. One hears of Muslims being tortured everywhere."

"Riots on a small scale are already on." (Here the various members of the audience brought reports they had heard of the victimization of the Muslims.)

February 20, 1951. Women's gathering in a Muslim Mohalla† (eight individuals). Time 2 P.M. Here are a few extracts from their conversation which give an idea of the group atmosphere usually created in gossip meetings of Muslim women:

"We have seen no peace in the new setup. The administration is never just to us."

"Even a small Hindu child goes about with the air of the prime Minister about him. These children will create trouble."

"Who told you that?"

"I heard this at the hospital a month ago. Even communists and socialists have turned anti-Muslim. Hindu students shout at our boys, 'Go to Pakistan.' Muslims are as good as dead here, yet Hindus think Muslims are very strong."

"No one takes Muslims seriously when they say they had fought for the freedom of the country. No one regards Muslims as generous and capable of being virtuous. All faults are attributed to Muslims—even when Muslims are the sufferers. Their houses are searched; they are arrested."

"The baker around the corner said that the Muslims will have a tough time on the occasion of the Holi festival. We do not see any good in repairing our house. We may have to leave."

* *jan sangh* , *sangh* = association
jan = people

† *mohalla* = locality

"That is what a nephew of mine, a student in the University, said."

"It will be worst in June when Hindus gather from villages to bathe in the Ganges."

Comments. It has not been possible to trace the modification and distortion of such remarks as have just been noted. But we know of a number of informal groups which serve to spread gossip, such as Muslim women waiting at an outdoor hospital, Muslim shopkeepers meeting after prayers in a mosque (particularly so after the Friday prayers and office of religio-social organization). Usually cut off from the rest of the population, they meet amongst themselves, and in most places (there may be a few exceptions) an atmosphere of defeatism is created through exchange of notes about the treatment of the Muslims. This atmosphere implies a frame of reference for judging all incidents. And the burden of the frame of reference is this: Muslims are not receiving fair treatment at the hands of the non-Muslims and the government officials. If some evidence comes forth to the contrary, it is treated as an exception and its validity questioned. "There will be no more exceptions in the future. These are vestiges from the past prestige of the Muslims."

The development of a rumor

We were, moreover, able to trace the development of one rumor, stage by stage. The series of statements quoted below constituted contents of the rumor at various stages of its intensity:

Facts of the situation. Thousands of Muslims participate every evening at the annual Exhibition Fair at Aligarh. Muslim shopkeepers from different parts of Uttar Pradesh have their commercial stalls there, and there is brisk trade. One evening, in an out-of-the-way corner near the exhibition ground, a few Hindu boys assaulted a few Muslim boys for the latters' alleged misbehavior. This did not disturb the peace. The assault was deliberately planned in a way to attract no attention.

The first modification. "Muslim boys were assaulted by the Hindu boys." (The context and the grounds for the incident were omitted.)

Second modification. "Muslims were assaulted by the Hindus with a view to demoralize the Muslims."

Third modification. "Muslims were assaulted at the exhibition ground. A Muslim's house was forcibly occupied in Serai Qutub. There may be trouble in the future."

Fourth modification. "There are many cases of the Muslims being harassed. These are preliminaries to the massacre of the Muslims on the Holi day."

Fifth modification. "There is an organized agency to uproot the Muslims."

These statements are given in chronological order, taken from the record kept of interviews with individuals and of the meetings of informal groups. It will not be far-fetched to suggest that the distortion of the facts in the rumor is the typical expression of the Muslim tendency to interpret all events happening around them as deliberately planned to annihilate them.

There is plenty of evidence to support this. Recently the Socialist Party organized a people's march in the Capital of India to present the people's demands to the President of the Indian Republic. Muslims, Sikhs and other minorities were represented in this demonstration out of proportion to their numbers. When illiterate Muslims in Aligarh were asked about this particular event, they replied in such words as these: "We have heard there will be riots in Delhi; Muslims will be massacred in large numbers on June 3."

A few words about the way these ideas come to acquire stability: *We are not examining at all the basis of these norms in the actual treatment meted out to Muslims.* To inquire into the actual handicaps of the Muslims compared to the rest of the population requires the active cooperation of many agencies and above all of the various departments of the Government. We were not equipped to conduct this kind of inquiry. Our primary concern is with the *attitudes, and the way the symbols of reality acquire significance for the development of attitudes*. For purposes of research it is important to isolate the *frame of reference* of the Muslims, and to inquire systematically into the factors which enter into its determination.

The one factor which is most potent in giving stability to the frame of reference amongst the Muslims is the Muslim Indian-language press, particularly the Urdu press. The influence of newspapers works somewhat in the following manner: An illiterate Muslim is discriminated against. He keeps his grievances to himself and offers a smiling face to his Hindu friend and even Hindu aggressor. He unburdens himself of his torture to a Muslim who has read in a newspaper about similar discriminations against Muslims elsewhere and the editorial comments thereon. The tone of the Muslim press tends on the whole to delight in dilating upon grievances. The literate Muslim accepts with faith and confidence the attitude toward the problems recommended by his newspaper and he transmits the same interpretation to his illiterate client. He reads about what happens to Muslims in Hyderabad, Bihar, etc., and he is eager to arrive at a generalized picture of the plight of Muslims.

HOW TWO SUSPICIOUS GROUPS SEE THEMSELVES AND ONE ANOTHER

How Muslims perceive themselves

Any study of social tensions must take into account the way the members of a group perceive themselves as a group. This perception has an important bearing on the social relations obtaining between the various facets of the ego operating in the individual. One's perception of his group carries at least the following meanings.

The way others regard his group. When a Hindu says that Hindus are not united, he is partly reflecting the opinion of alien observers of the Hindu social system. In a similar manner when a Muslim says that Muslims are carried away more by ideological than by realistic considerations, he is reflecting the opinion of non-Muslims whom he holds in esteem.

The way he wishes his group to be regarded by others. This is reflected in such statements as the following: "Hindus are a reflective people." "For Muslims, religion is not so much a personal experience as a highly institutionalized way of living one's day-to-day life, to discipline oneself for a particular spiritual reality."

An effect of the way in which he reacts to other groups. Reaction to others helps him to build a notion of his own group. "Muslims as rulers acted with vigor in promoting justice." "Hindus take a long time in arriving at a decision and appear to be passive." These opinions are the aftermath of social relations of a particular kind. Many other forces operating in determining one's notion of his group could be mentioned. It is evident from the above that one's notion of his group reflects certain well-established ways of thinking and behaving toward other groups. The way one perceives one's group carries the meaning of the *roles* one's group plays towards others. Our first task then in studying Hindu-Muslim relations is to find out the notion which Muslims and Hindus have of themselves.

Muslim's notions of themselves. Analysis of the data revealed the following different kinds of notions that Muslims entertained about themselves:

1. There were those who felt hurt at being called Muslims instead of Indians. In their civic and economic life they

wanted to be accepted as Indians, like the rest of the population in India.

For example, a Muslim worker in a mill said, "Muslims are as happy or unhappy in India as the rest of the population. We swim or sink with the prosperity of the mill. If there is a profit we get a bonus, as anyone else does. If the mill runs at a loss, we also suffer. There are no special difficulties of the Muslims which are not difficulties of everyone else."

2. Then there were those who felt that Muslims were poor, or at a disadvantage, or less educated, compared to non-Muslims. But these interviews showed no tendency to blame either the non-Muslims or the government for their backwardness. These interviewees showed a healthy criticism of Muslims without indulging in mud-slinging. Nevertheless they retained Muslim consciousness.

A Muslim general merchant said: "Much of the unemployment amongst Muslims is due to the following facts: there was a goodly export of locks manufactured in Aligarh to the part of India now called Pakistan. With the partition of the country, Aligarh was deprived of the trade and this had an adverse effect on Muslims more than the Hindus because more than 60 per cent of the money realized through sale of locks in Aligarh goes to Aligarh Muslims. Thanks to the trade policy of our neighboring Muslim State of Pakistan, our income has been drastically reduced."

There is also the unpalatable fact of many Muslims leaving India without paying the bills they owed to the Hindus. This has made for a mild distrust of the Muslims. People hesitate to advance loans or goods on loan to Muslims. This again is a difficulty created by Muslims themselves.

3. Another opinion prevailing amongst Muslims was that although they were receiving pinpricks at the hands of the non-Muslims and the petty government officers, they were nevertheless in no danger of being exterminated or expelled from India. Some of them had faith that this phase would

pass away. They wanted specific complaints to be dealt with in a specific way, and did not build fantasies of being persecuted.

A Muslim hotelkeeper told the following incident: "A Hindu ordered tea from my restaurant. After a minute or two he discovered that I was a Muslim. He angrily walked out without paying for the tea and blaming me for deceiving him. This left a bitter taste in the mouth." This interviewee kept cool and was not very much excited about the incidents.

4. A fourth trend in Muslims' opinion about themselves was that they were being rejected by the non-Muslims. In contrast with (3), these Muslims tended to blame the Hindus for this rejection.

A Muslim schoolteacher felt that the Hindus did not trust even the most respectable Muslims. "We are regarded as Pakistani spies: we are not given responsible positions in the police and army lest we betray India's secrets to Pakistan. I know Hindus have sufficient justification for behaving the way they do towards us. That does not mitigate our sufferings."

5. A fifth trend in the Muslims' notions of themselves is that they are in a hostile territory. They regard Hindus (and they identify the present government with Hindus) as plotting to uproot Muslims.

"Muslim houses are looted and Muslims are murdered and no action is taken against the culprits."

"Muslims are threatened with dire consequences if they do not leave India."

Now about the number of Muslim interviewees in each of the above categories:

Convinced that Muslims are not discriminated against 5

Critical of the Muslim political outlook and conscious of Muslim backwardness without holding Hindus or the government responsible 3

Conscious of pinpricks Muslims receive and regard these as sporadic and temporary...................................... 13

Feel Muslims rejected by Hindus and characterize this as a pervasive trend.. 4

Feel that Muslims are persecuted by Hindus and believe this to be a pervasive trend... 12

Regard Muslims as both rejected and persecuted................ 13

Total Muslim sample....................................... 50

MUSLIMS' PERCEPTION OF THEMSELVES IN RELATION TO SOCIAL CLASS

	Working Class (15)	Lower Middle Class (20)	Upper Class (15)
Convinced that Muslims are not discriminated against.......	4	1	0
Critical of the Muslim political outlook and conscious of Muslim backwardness without holding Hindus or the Government responsible.........	1	0	2
Conscious of pinpricks Muslims receive and regard these as sporadic and temporary......	6	3	4
Feel Muslims rejected by Hindus and characterize this as a pervasive trend..........	0	2	2
Feel that Muslims are persecuted by Hindus and the Government and believe this to be a pervasive trend...........	1	4	7
Regard Muslims as both rejected and persecuted.......	3	10	0

Why do Muslims feel rejected and persecuted?

Over half of the Muslims feel rejected or persecuted by the
Hindus. This high incidence of a suspicious attitude amongst
the lower middle class and the upper strata of the Muslim
population is a fact partially independent of the question
whether such suspicion is actually warranted by the situation.

Spontaneous references to the Hindus were listed from the
recorded statement of each Muslim interviewee. These listed
references were then classified (classification was suggested
by the list itself). The most common references were those
of *insecurity.* The following are typical:

"It is dangerous to live in a Hindu locality because they
may abduct and rape our women."

"Hindus may attack Muslims at night."

"A part of the Hindu society called the R.S.S. are harm-
ing Muslims and are trying to uproot us."

"Hindus don't offer work to Muslim artisans."

"Hindus charge heavy black market prices for goods they
sell to Muslims, but not to their Hindu customers."

"Hindus oust Muslims from Government offices. Capable
Muslims are unable to find scope for their work."

"Petty officers show favors to Hindus and give pinpricks to
Muslims. Hindu officers discriminate against Muslim con-
tractors, lawyers, clerks, etc. They shout at Muslims: 'Why
don't you go to Pakistan?' "

"Hindus are superficially good to Muslims but inwardly
nurse a grudge towards them."

Of the spontaneous references classified above, the first,
second, and third indicate an acute kind of insecurity—an
insecurity which touches upon the very right to live and move
about. The fourth, fifth, and sixth references indicate insecurity caused by handicaps in earning a livelihood, while the
seventh and eighth refer to comparatively minor pinpricks.

* The same is true of Hindus
in Pakistan — the same pattern of
insecurity, prejudice, rumors and
ingroup feeling.

Hostility shown by Muslims to Hindus in spontaneous references takes the following forms:

"I cannot have close personal relations with Hindus because they are outside the circle of Islam."

"I cannot eat with Hindus because they don't say grace in the Muslim way before eating." ?

"I don't like Hindus because they are growing uppish."

"Hindus and Muslims are made different, and the best thing for them is to stay apart."

Many Muslim interviewees, while mentioning their grievances and insecurities, preferred to use a generalization in the passive voice: "Muslims are *being charged* higher prices." "Muslims *are not selected* for commissions in the army." The systematic way in which the passive voice was used attracted our notice. The passive voice made it necessary for the interviewer to throw out a probe to discover the reference to the agent producing insecurity. Though such phrasing is by itself no sure sign of ego weakness or of delusions of reference, yet it deserves further study.

Some working-class Muslims refer to the Hindus as offering work to Harijans in preference to the Muslims. Jealousy dominates their mental horizon in this situation, and their impoverished ego on that score perceives Harijans as competitors for comfortable and prosperous positions. "Harijans are having their day. They have started occupations which were formerly the monopoly of Muslims." Here is a statement from a rickshaw puller: "Hindus, who are the main customers, prefer Harijans to us." Jealousy comes out clearly in remarks of the following kind: "Let the city people fraternize with Harijans; the village peasant will always show the Harijan where he belongs."

Remarks of the following kind have been taken as an indication of jealousy of Harijans:

"Even the government of the day favors them."

"Hindus give them work."

---

* Hostility shown by Hindus to muslims ought to have been recorded. Violence, lack of sophistication and limited liberalism in marital relationship are the three most important things a common hindu would associate with muslims. Both the common

"The untouchables of yesterday are showing their teeth (becoming aggressive to the Muslims)."

References of insecurity in relation to Harijans are not direct, as with Hindus, but the presence of jealousy *implies* insecurity.

The following are the stereotypes about Harijans collected from interview data:

1. They eat pork—a prohibited article of diet for Muslims.
2. Harijans are dirty.
3. Muslims are forbidden to eat with Harijans.
4. Harijans are untouchables.
5. The very idea of Harijans is repulsive and sends creepy sensations through the whole body.   ✳

HINDUS' REFERENCES TO MUSLIMS

	Frequency
1. Hindus are appeased by the present government at the cost of the Muslims...............................	1
2. Muslims are dirty....................................	4
3. The past of the Muslims has been aggression upon Hindus	1
4. I can run errands for Muslims but I cannot eat with them	1
5. Muslims regard Pakistan as their homeland and are disloyal to India....................................	2
6. Muslim metalworkers are absolutely necessary for lock manufacturing in Aligarh.........................	1
7. No Muslims or Christians will be left in India in the twentieth century, says a proverb of Muslim origin..	2
(There is a saying amongst Muslims regarding their having a bad time 1,400 years after the birth of Mohammed)	
8. Muslims cooperate with Hindus these days............	1
9. Muslims are no longer in power......................	2

*nities accuse each other of uncleanliness
cf. A Passage to India : E.M. Forster. See page 158.*

✳ Compare the situation of the Harijans in Pakistan.

10. Muslims are bigots and cannot be fair to minorities under
their rule... 4

11. In my personal relations I find Muslims bigots........ 2

12. Muslims are clever people and defy evacuee property
rules before leaving for Pakistan.................... 1

13. Muslims have nothing to complain about in India...... 3

14. If Muslims behave and do not become aggressive or disloyal they have a good future...................... 4

15. Muslims prefer to remain aloof from Hindus.......... 1

These references can be classified under the following
categories:

   1. Favorable to Muslims (Nos. 1, 6, 8)...... 3

   2. Neutral or statement of facts (9, 13)........ 5

   3. Unfavorable:

      Dirt reference (2)...................... 4

      Political behavior (3, 5, 14) 10

      Religious bigotry and aloofness (4, 10, 11, 15) 5

      Through popular saying (7) 2

      Muslims crafty (12).................... 1

The helpful concept of "time perspective"

We thought the way in which one community perceives the
other might be revealed to some degree through what Kurt
Lewin has called "time perspective."

In March, 1950, there were widespread Hindu-Muslim
riots in the Uttar Pradesh, including Aligarh. The first question in the interview asked of both Hindus and Muslims
was, therefore: "Have you heard or seen anything of the
conflict between different groups or communities (a) during

the past year; (b) during the past six months; (c) during the past three months; (d) during the past week?" There were differences in the approach of the Hindus and Muslims in answering this question.

The typical Hindu approach: temporal reference to tension. An appropriate answer to the question as asked should not have any reference to the historical background of Hindu-Muslim relations. But twenty-five Hindu respondents who belonged to the upper classes began with reference to the conflict in terms of events some time in the past. Hindu teachers and students answered this question in terms of the events that took place in 1946, when the Muslim agitation against the Hindus had been intensified by Pakistan slogans. One Congress adherent started with 1857, and with the founding of the Muslim College by Sir Syed Ahmed Khan, and commented on the behavior of Muslims in the heyday of the Muslim League. Logically viewed, all these replies dodged the real implications of the question.

Later on, while the Hindus made copious references to the past, they referred as well to the March, 1950, events, but treated them as minor disturbances. They were positive that there had been perfect peace in the city since April, 1950.

The Muslim approach. The Muslim description of the Hindu-Muslim conflict started with August, 1947, or more specifically with March, 1950. (There was the solitary exception of a Muslim professor who referred to the conflict situation in exactly the same way the Hindu Congress adherent had done.) They referred to the pre-1947 period as of peaceful relations between the two groups. *

Whereas the Hindu stopped his version of conflict at April, 1950, the Muslims referred to little incidents—beatings, thefts, etc., rather than riots—that took place *after May, 1950,* and even to *October, 1950,* when interviews were held.

There is every evidence that the interviewees from both the communities were genuine in their statements. To a stu-

* Situation in Bengal was different: Dacca disturbances.

dent of human affairs, the temporal references to the conflict are of profound significance. The Hindu approach implies a roundabout detour before coming to the point. The
Muslim approach is loaded with emotion, which is soon replaced by another emotion of equal intensity.

In the same kind of time perspective the characteristic
Hindu response to the question: "If you had the power, what
would you do about communal strife?" is like this: "We've
had these problems a long time, and it will be a long time before we are through with them." The characteristic Muslim
response is: "The police can stop it tomorrow if they want
to."

Two hypotheses occur to the observer: (1) The difference
in time perspective may be due to the vast span of time
conceived by Hindu cosmology, the agelessness of all reality
as contrasted with the dynamic or explosive nature of
Muslim history, with event crowding upon event; and (2)
the difference may be due simply to the high anxiety level of
the Muslims, the fact that the shoe pinches *now*, and that
one is aware of what happened yesterday and may happen
tomorrow. There is more to be said for hypothesis No. 2, but
perhaps hypothesis No. 1 also has relevance.

The temporal reference to the perception of riots invites
comments on the channels of communication prevailing in
the two groups. The Hindus are blind to the little incidents of
discrimination to which the Muslims refer. Even when these
incidents are brought to their notice, they are vigorously
denied. On the other hand, a Muslim appears fully informed
and up-to-date regarding the minor incidents of ill treatment, although sometimes these incidents relate to a Muslim
living in a faroff locality of the city or relate to acts of innocent frivolity. It is presumed that a city is a civic unit, so that
what happens in one locality or to some individuals or
groups should be reflected in the observation of members of
all groups. What happens is that one kind of communication

Compare situation in Pakistan.

is completely shut off from one set of people and has tremendous emotional significance for the other.

Reference to participants.   Muslims invariably referred to the students of local Hindu colleges as the villains of the piece, acting as tools in the hands of the people who plan a Hindu Raj in India. These students, according to the Muslim version, have as their camp followers men from low occupations and castes, who loot Muslim shops and bag the looted articles. Eighty per cent of the Hindus believe that the riots were started by the Muslims' striking Hindu boys and shooting Hindu men. About 25 per cent of the Hindus seriously believe that Muslims have committed horrible atrocities on the Hindus even though the latter are in the majority in India. Only 20 per cent of the Hindus admitted that riots had been started by the unruly element in the Hindu population.

Reference to the instigation of riots.   Forty-eight per cent of the Hindus seriously believed that the riots had been engineered by the Muslims in the following ways:

1. The Pakistani agents were interested in the migration of Muslim artisans to Pakistan to ruin the lock industry in Aligarh and then to rebuild the same in Pakistan. They deliberately brought Hindus in conflict with the Muslims.

2. Many Muslims awaiting their trial in Aligarh courts, or heavily in debt to Hindus, wanted riots and staged them as an easy escape out of an embarrassing situation.

3. The riots were created by Muslims to blackmail the Indian government through demonstrating that Muslims had been compelled to migrate.

Forty per cent of the Hindus regarded the riots as comparable to any street quarrel which arises spontaneously. Twelve per cent of the Hindus said that riots had been engineered by Hindus under a definite plan to turn the Muslims out.

Of the Muslims, 72 per cent were of the opinion that the

* Educational qualification of these twelve per cent is ~~important~~ significant.

riots had been a part of the government policy to drive the Muslims out. Forty-eight per cent definitely stated that the Uttar Pradesh riots aimed at uprooting the Muslims from their zones of influence in the field of trade, property, culture, etc., such as Agra, Philibit, Shahjahanpur, and Aligarh. They believed that riots would be engineered until every Muslim was either killed or compelled to migrate. Twenty-eight per cent of the Muslims thought that the Government was all right, but thought that many in the Congress and the administration did not follow the governmental instructions in relation to minorities. "All of the Muslims" thought that powerful Hindus staged occasional riots to threaten the Muslims, as a part of their plans to exterminate the Muslim minorities. Many Muslims reported the story of the Hindu man in the street who openly told the Muslims: "Your days are numbered. This year Holi will be celebrated with the Muslim blood."

The majority of the Hindus do not know that Hindus have played any part in planning riots. They continue in the comfortable beliefs that the Muslim hooligans around the corner are the troublemakers. They view their own group as non-violent. The Muslims on the other hand feel that they have been "sitting on a volcano."

What did the Government do? The Muslims had been prohibited from leaving their homes during the Holi holidays (promulgation of "Section 144"). This gave an opportunity to the Holi crowds to loot Muslim shops and attack Muslim houses. Though the Collector of the District had issued this order in consultation with his Muslim and Hindu advisers in the interest of the safety of the Muslims, it was interpreted as a deliberate act of the Government to inflict injury upon the Muslim interest. Forty per cent of the Muslims believed that the government is weak, but still managed to check the riots in time; 60 per cent, however, blamed the government.

Sixty per cent of the Hindu group thought that the government had done all it could to ensure safety to the Muslims; 40 per cent blamed the Government for being hard on the Hindus and arresting the innocent amongst them for alleged crimes.

CAUSES OF "LOW TENSION"

Primary emphasis in Kali Prasad's Lucknow study was placed upon the fact that Lucknow has traditionally been a low-tension center as far as Hindu-Muslim relations are concerned. The first point to make is, therefore, his demonstration that to a considerable degree the Hindu-Muslim social distance or hostility is at a lower level than elsewhere in our Indian samples. This is related largely to the fact that the history of the city under Muslim rulers over a long period involved cordial relations and much utilization of the Hindu community for many responsible posts, and that it was contrary to the thought of the Muslim regime to cultivate hostility with the subject Hindu population. As we shall see a little later, the respondents in Lucknow themselves named some of the factors which had been responsible for low tension in Lucknow.

From the point of view of method, the first thing to note was that most of the Lucknow investigation was based upon a written questionnaire administered in Hindi, in Urdu, or in English to respondents thoroughly capable of written responses. This means that the samples are comparable not to the total samples from elsewhere but only to the samples which we have called "educated" and "literate" (the former comprising those able to read English; the latter comprising those able to read only a vernacular).

A second major difference in method lies in the fact that two large populations were used: one based upon sampling certain regions of the city, so that individuals could be handled one after the other rapidly without necessitating traveling about the city looking for the individual who had been selected; the other consisting of student groups.[1]

In the former study, the nonstudent group, we have four Hindu groups totaling 165 individuals, four Muslim groups totaling 132 individuals, and two refugee groups totaling 35 individuals. As noted below, stratification within the Hindu and Muslim groups is made in terms of sex, education, and income.

The primary evidence that Lucknow has in fact been in some sense a low-tension city appears in two matters: first, the fact that the great majority of the respondents in both Hindu and Muslim groups state that as children they played with members of the opposite community; second, the fact that the great bulk of subjects both Hindu and Muslim are ready to accept members of the opposite community in interdining and as intimate friends. The figures for intercommunity acceptance, group by group, typically run from 50 to over 90 per cent, with the central tendency about 75 per cent; very strikingly and consistently, special tolerance is shown by the educated Muslim group at a relatively high income level, where the figures have a central tendency at nearly 90 per cent for the acceptance as intimate friends of members of all the various groups mentioned in the questionnaire, such as Bengali, Christian, Harijan, Hindu, Punjabi, Sikh, etc. It is remarkable, for example, to note that intimate friendships with the Sikhs are affirmed by 70 per cent of this Muslim group and by 77 per cent with reference to the Sindhi group who, as will be recalled, are in the forefront of the refugee problem. It appears to us that whatever

. . . .

[1] In addition, a short *interview* method was used consisting of only a few questions, administered to a population selected by means of the ration cards of the city, but not much was done with this method and our attention will be given to the two studies just cited which make use of the written questionnaire.

complications attend the conception of a low-tension center, Kali Prasad has established the point that at the level of verbal expression, at least, the educated Muslims in relatively favorable circumstances are very extraordinarily tolerant of other groups.

Various possible reasons for the low-tension status of Lucknow were offered for consideration to the interviewees. These factors which were to be affirmed or denied were as follows: (1) common culture of Hindus and Muslims; (2) greater social contacts between Hindus and Muslims; (3) common language; (4) common dress; (5) common observances of certain festivals; (6) greater tolerance and better understanding in the people of Lucknow; (7) traditions of commonness and pride in peaceful living; (8) better administration; (9) existence of acute differences between Shiahs and Sunnis (Muslim subgroups) in Lucknow; (10) efficiency of police. Substantial majorities affirming the reality of these factors in regard to the first eight reasons are obtained from both Hindus and Muslims and even higher from Muslims than from Hindus.

The ninth factor relating to the Shiah-Sunni difference is regarded by about half the Hindus as important but is rejected by almost all the Muslims. The last factor, the efficiency of the police, is affirmed by a little less than 40 per cent of the Hindus and a little more than 50 per cent of the Muslims.

It is of some interest that among the refugees, who could hardly be expected to know very intimately what the factors responsible for low tension in Lucknow have been, the number of affirmative responses right down the line is smaller than it is in the other two groups with a central tendency at about 50 per cent. Professor Kali Prasad writes: "More than half of the Hindu subjects are of the opinion that the communal relations in Lucknow have been adversely affected by the influx of refugees in the city. The majority of the refugees, about 60 per cent, do not of course agree with this.

Both Hindus and Muslims frequently give as reasons for the deterioration of Hindu-Muslim relations the advent of the refugees. Some of the Muslims refer to the propagandist efforts of the RSS and Mahasabha (strongly Hindu and consequently at times anti-Muslim organizations), and a considerable number in response to this and other questions indicate that they regard refugees as less cultured, more unmannerly, likely to be uncouth, brusque, unable to make courteous contact. An interesting question arises as to whether we are dealing here simply with mutual misunderstandings between people of different cultures or whether the stereotype of uncouthness and discourtesy is one which arises as a result of these conditions of deprivation and suffering.

Despite the general agreement that Lucknow is a low-tension center, it is of interest that the great majority of Muslims believe themselves to be discriminated against, especially from an economic point of view; for example, with regard to "services, permits, licenses, etc." About 80 per cent of the Hindus think that the Muslims have an economic future in India and refugees are not far from the other Hindus in their beliefs on this point. Among the Muslims a little over 50 per cent share this optimistic outlook. Somewhat over half of Hindu, Muslim, and refugee groups believe that the central government is taking satisfactory steps to solve the communal problem.

The great majority of the Muslims, despite the general level of tolerance, state that they will not pass through a Hindu locality,[2] and an even greater majority will not pass through a refugee colony. An equally great majority of local Hindus and of refugees will not pass through a Muslim locality. Fear and suspicion are still to be reckoned with.

. . . .

[2] Note that this refers to a time of stress, and no attempt should be made to generalize to all periods.

* Rashtriya Sevak Sangha, involved in the trial about the assassination of Gandhi.

This means of course that segregation is a fact accepted and acted upon by practically all; it does not imply that the majority of any community are hostile to members of other communities. One simply plays safe.

Some attention was given to the characteristics attributed by each community to the members of other communities and the like or dislike of such characteristics. The attributes of Muslims which are favorably responded to by most Hindus and refugees are: belief in one God; simple marriage ceremony; brotherliness; group prayers; widow marriages; and loyalty. The attributes of Muslims which are disliked by Hindus and refugees are beef-eating; prayers five times a day; unsatisfactory personal hygiene; wearing of the beard; fanaticism, opposition to other religions; purdah (the seclusion of women); and burqa (the veil); conversion; divorce; and marriage with near relatives.

Specific grievances mentioned by Muslims refer to a local unpleasantness on the occasion of a recent Muslim festival; to the case of an indignity suffered by a mosque; to the prohibition of cow-slaughter on a day of special Muslim significance (Bakrid); to being told by Hindus that they should go to Pakistan; to the use of pure Hindi separated as far as possible from Urdu; and the governmental and personal acts suggesting to Muslims that they are second-class citizens, for example, being given no effective voice in the administration. A substantial majority of all the Muslim groups believe that the attitude of the Hindus in India has stiffened against the Muslims since the time of the partition. A considerable number of Muslims, however, state that this is not characteristic of all Hindus. They tend to be especially afraid of the advent to power of the RSS or Mahasabha and in general are insecure regarding the future of their children.

We should like to offer a few words regarding the bearing of our data upon the much discussed issue whether the

* Bakr' Eid = Annual religious festival of the muslims.

Hindu-Muslim strife is primarily a function of the *actual hostilities*, the competitive relationships, the damage and threats through which the two groups have passed; or whether, on the other hand, it is primarily a function of the basic differences in *cultural outlook*, the basic incompatibilities which make it impossible for members of one group to feel at home in or to understand the outlook of the other group. On such a point as this, the reasons commonly given for dislike of the other community group are of some importance, even though these may be to some extent rationalizations and actually unrelated to the causal dynamics of the situation. It is worth noting that the things which are resented most by Hindus among the alleged Muslim character traits are dirtiness, fanaticism, and cruelty. "Cruelty," at least, is not merely a function of cultural diversity but apparently a direct expression of hostility, a direct reference to damage which the groups have inflicted upon one another. This would tend to suggest that the factor of cultural diversity is perhaps to be given somewhat less weight than specific damage.

Even more clear is the fact that the Muslims give as their primary objections to the behavior of the Hindus such factors as the tendency of Hindu bands to play music in front of mosques, and the interference of the Hindus in the cow-killing and beef-eating habits of the Muslims. At least the playing before the mosque is not considered by Muslims to be just cultural diversity but is felt as direct aggression. They feel that Hindus are baiting the Muslims, trying to raise the hostility of the Muslims to the boiling point. Behind these two and many other objections which Muslims voice to the behavior of Hindus is the dramatic statement which was made to us by several members of the group of Muslim leaders whom we met in Bombay: "They try to dominate our lives; they won't let us alone. They want us to live according to their plan, not ours." When this feeling was voiced, there seemed to be a general feeling around the table that this had hit the nail on the head. There is also a good deal in the interview material suggesting that the primary complaint of Muslims from the point of view of intercultural contact is not *diversity* of culture but *interference* by the majority group in the ways of the minority.

Finally, we should like to note the caste differences among the Hindus in their attitudes toward Muslims—the higher castes appearing in general to place the Muslims at a greater social distance—and the evident feeling of the Muslims that they would rather associate with high-caste than with low-caste Hindus. Actually, of course, it is not the Muslim at all who constitutes "the low man on the totem pole." Everywhere in India where we were able to collect any data on the matter, it was the untouchables or Harijans rather than the Muslims who got the brunt of the most severe discrimination. Untouchables, in contrast to the upper and intermediate castes, are considered unclean and permanently separated from the main body of the Hindu community, which makes even more dramatic the Gandhian movement against untouchability as voiced and vigorously followed in recent years.

At the conclusion of his Aligarh report, Pars Ram notes that Hindus and Muslims have been isolated from one another for about two decades. Many Hindus grow up without ever meeting a Muslim on a friendly or personal basis.

Pars Ram adds that people are unaware of the purposes of the governmental policies on control of prices, etc. This leads to all kinds of rumors unfavorable to the prestige of the government. When the prestige is lowered, it results in intergroup tension. People can suffer restrictions cheerfully, deny themselves certain luxuries and face hardships once they know that the governmental regulations are in the interest of the whole nation. There is no agency in operation to build a better understanding at the *grass roots*, where people and the government officers of humbler status come together. A few experiments on bringing rapport between the masses and the government are called for.

THE PROBLEM IN BOMBAY

The lack of intercommunication between Hindus and Muslims is also emphasized in the Bombay study. Indeed, the Bombay study shows how, despite much close childhood association, the Hindus and Muslims draw apart, enter different ideological and cultural worlds, read different newspapers, think different thoughts. This is phrased by Professor Vakil in terms of a pervasive "provincialism" which is likewise expressed in caste distance and language-group distance; and he stresses the huge importance of a broad educational program based on the replacement of provincialism by a sense of a common destiny shared with all other citizens.

The partition of India had sent enormous numbers from the far western portion of the old India, people from Sind, flocking eastward into the Bombay region. A great many of them had been landlords, money-lenders, businessmen, people of substance who by selling what they had were able to finance their trip but who felt the shock of impoverishment with special severity. Many of them had gone nearly a thousand miles on their way to their new homes. An enormous number, in fact, had established themselves in the Bombay area without homes. They had been established by the government in such places as the huge refugee camp at Kalyan, a group of inter-communicating cities with a total of 95,000 persons. Many of the refugees had however scattered in small or large groups in the City of Bombay or its environs. It is estimated that there were about 150,000 Muslims in the city. We had a morning conference with the twenty leaders of the Muslim community in Bombay, who were very frank and direct about the situation. They had some skepticism until they were shown the completely objective nature of the investigation and were informed that they would see the report.

With the aid of statisticians who worked closely with the economists, sociologists and psychologists, it was possible to devise a suitable method of random sampling by using the ration cards of the city. Time and money allowed for the study of only seventy-five individuals in each of the three groups. The ration cards are in large blocs in file cases. After taking care that the geography of the city was adequately represented by the various blocs with which we were to work, it was only necessary to take one family-head out of each hundred cases (or whatever number was appropriate in relation to the total). Emphasis was laid upon interviewing the actual person designated by this method, so planned as to give us the requisite quota of educated, of literate, and of illiterate persons. Time and trouble were taken to locate the person selected and to overcome reluctance or resistance to participation. It was necessary to have some ice-breakers in effecting such working conditions.[3] Despite all efforts, the *uneducated* Muslims could not be adequately reached, so that the inquiry was limited to *literate* or *educated* ones (the term "literate" means able to read one's own vernacular; the term "educated" means capable of reading English, simply because English is required at the intermediate or high school level and those therefore unfamiliar with English cannot be considered educated).

. . . .

[3] Thanks are especially due to Mr. M.M.A. Baiji and Mr. Mustafa Shiakh, who helped in making contacts and assisting volunteers to do the interviewing. The interviewing was done by graduate students of the School of Economics and Sociology of Bombay University, and of the Tata Institute.

An attempt was made to have the interviewer[4] always a member of the same sex and community group as the interviewee, but this did not prove feasible in all cases.

The Bombay study thus represents a well integrated social-science approach, utilizing the facilities of an exceptionally strong staff, and the cooperation of many qualified students. While the Aligarh study emphasizes individual viewpoints, the Bombay study gives expansive economic and sociological analysis of the interview data from the three communities studied. The pervasive influence of this Bombay study appears throughout this book, so that space need be given here only to the summarizing of a few main trends.

Now to generalize the main results.

The resident Hindus

To begin with the resident Hindu group, the most striking thing is its relative unawareness of the problems of the other two groups. It does not share in the channel of communication which carries news and complaints from one to another of those whose lives are marked by fear and trouble.

One notes that while they place the Muslims relatively low in terms of general social desirability, and, at great social distance, there is not much evidence of actual hatred of them. The refugees, almost all of whom are Sindhis, do not as a matter of fact fare very much better in the eyes of the Hindu resident group. Many relatively direct evidences of rejection of them are clear; for example, when the language groups of Bombay are to be compared, the Sindhi-speaking groups are near the bottom of the list in acceptability. From the point

.   .   .   .

[4] In connection with the training of the interviewers, special mention should be made of Dr. Lakdawala of the Bombay School of Economics and Sociology, Dr. P. H. Prahbu of the Tata Institute of Social Sciences, and Miss P. A. Dordi, a social worker in the city. As noted earlier, the overall deputy director of the study was Dr. A. R. Desai.

of view of the provincialism of India, the Sindhis are after all foreigners in many major respects, their language and caste system being strikingly different from those of the Bombay population. It would be ridiculous to expect a Pan-Indian sense of brotherhood to dominate the scene at the present time. There is not much evidence that income, caste or education of Hindu residents influences very greatly their attitude toward either the Muslims or the refugees. This is not to deny in any way the role of economic factors in the tension pattern.

As far as attitudes toward the activity of the government are concerned (no differentiation was made here between central government and state government), there are a few who think the government is doing almost everything pretty well; a few that think it is doing almost everything very poorly; a few who emphasize rationing and food control as things well done; a few who emphasize these as things poorly done. There is no general indictment of the government, but neither is there any blanket approval.

It may be worth while here to cross-reference with the material of Pars Ram, gathered in Aligarh, which strongly suggests that there is a tendency to be more lenient towards the central government than towards the local administration. It is assumed that the Bombay respondents were thinking primarily of their state and municipal administrations. There is no evidence that the majority of the Hindu residents regard the government as blameworthy either for too lenient or too hostile an attitude toward the Muslims. The majority seem to expect ordinary equality for Muslim citizens and seem to feel that such equality is being provided.

The Muslims

Now as to the attitudes of the Bombay Muslims. The first point to stress is that the illiterate members of this group declined altogether to participate in spite of the prodding from the Muslim leaders of the city. This is important not only in indicating their probable fear of revealing their attitudes, but as bearing indirectly on the question of the validity of the interview method, since it was impossible within the time and budget limits to carry out the check interviews which had been planned. Our primary evidence of validity lies in two things: first, the fact that the majority of our Hindu residents and refugees at all levels cooperated without difficulty and that practically all literate and educated Muslims cooperated, giving expressions of attitude along the general lines which had been expected; second, the fact that very outspoken and extreme bitterness came from most of the refugees along the lines of our expectation, tending to confirm the feeling that cooperation at least at the conscious level was good. There is of course not the slightest doubt that some evasion and a considerable amount of seeking to please the interview staff must have occurred. This is one of the natural hazards of the method and nothing is gained by attempting to minimize it.

One might perhaps adequately summarize the typical Muslim attitude in Bombay by saying that it is not so much hostile and not so much frightened as it is tentative, cautious, uncertain and groping. Here and there marked hostility to Hindus and to the government is evident but the general position seems to be to ask simply for equality in citizenship status. Moreover, not very much hostility to the refugees was noted here. The Muslims as a group evidently expect the government to keep its promises regarding nondiscrimination, to give all groups including the Muslims themselves and the refugees equality under the law.

A number of other constructive steps regarding Hindu-Muslim relations will be surveyed when we have established a broader perspective.

8

The frustration of the refugees

It is hard for the American to get any idea of the scope of the problem of the refugees in India. In the United States we have known miserable people in the dust-bowl areas and in some of the mountain "hollows" and half-abandoned mining towns, living in squalor and ill health, dejected and hopeless. In American cities during the depression there were vacant lots where men without families or resources lived in box-huts in freezing winter weather with nothing but a kerosene wick to warm their hands over; in Harlem today there are "apartments" where several families live, five or six to a room, where plaster falls from the ceiling and rats scurry from the basement to the garbage in the courtyard. But with all of these one does not see anything quite like the large masses of suffering, angrily bitter and hostile people in some of the refugee camps in India. Their problem is not difficult to understand; few people have gone through an experience such as theirs.

In India families rarely leave their land unless they are forced from it. During the period of the partition, there were in some cases a few months of staggering uncertainty, working gradually toward the obvious climax. One knew of disaster that had happened to others who had waited too long; one reluctantly sold what was saleable; the women's jewelry provided some of the wherewithal for the journey. There might be a bullock cart or two available to help on the way. The government might provide transportation by train and ship. One said good-by not just to a plot of land but to one's entire tradition, one's home life, and one's language group, the shrines of one's fathers. The departure was not, from their point of view, like a departure from one state to another. Indeed, it was like the forced departure of Longfellow's Acadians, or the long journey of Russian or Polish Jews to the western shores of the Atlantic. Yet in the case of these latter groups there was a chance to create a future. In the case of the Indian refugees there was a loss of homeland, a process catapulting one into a world of increasing miseries and no clear future whatever.

Even if one's goods could be sold, the journey was not necessarily safely undertaken. There was always a risk; hundreds of thousands were caught as they tried to make their escape and butchered on the way. The ultimate destination of those who survived was by no means clear. One knew that there were some types of help offered by the Indian government, but not what this would entail. The sufferings of the huge hopeless mass whom we visited at Kalyan near Bombay were more than matched by the sufferings of the pathetic disintegrating group from East Bengal whom we encountered north of Patna. The former had been merchants and landlords; the latter a group of villagers, accustomed to effective and competent farming in their own land, now thrown onto a type of soil which they did not know how to cultivate, with practically no equipment, with no guarantees from the government, with not even a fairly bearable day-by-day existence. The first thing to keep in mind then about refugees is that they are not like the refugees from Europe to our American shores—people endowed with a great hope for new life—nor like the people escaping from Europe as refugees to Israel—people who are fulfilling a sort of ancestral destiny of their cultural and religious community— but rather a group of straggling sufferers trying to pull together the fragments of a life lost, and unable to do so.

PATTERNS OF BITTERNESS

Let us make the acquaintance of a few Sindhi refugees, who in consequence of the partition had to escape from West Pakistan. They were interviewed in the Ahmedabad neighborhood by Mr. N. L. Dosajh, a psychologist with considerable experience in interviewing and in the use of projective tests, who received a small UNESCO stipend and made the Ahmedabad refugee problem his specialty during the time when we were in India. His method was to select two or three individuals per block in the large refugee camps on the fringes of Ahmedabad, a total of fifty individuals. In developing his method, he at first used a free conversational approach. After establishing his initial rapport with the individual, he allowed him to talk as freely as possible. On the basis of these preliminary tests it was found that the areas of tension could be broadly divided into *tensions against* (1) the government, (2) the Muslims, (3) the local people, (4) living conditions, (5) rations and food, (6) the various political organizations, (7) the mukhis (camp supervisors), and (8) a miscellany of remaining items, including neighbors, other castes, and employers. On the basis of this experience, the talk was more definitely structured in the main investigation. The refugee was allowed to talk as freely as he liked, but information was definitely secured under the eight heads indicated. The interview was recorded verbatim, but in a few cases, when this could not be done, it was recalled from memory after the interview.

The following records and interviews are typical:

A former merchant from Sind, 63 years of age, interviewed in his shop, tells how he used to handle sugar and made an average monthly income of 300 rupees. To the question: "How did you get out of Haripurahazari in the time of the riots?" he replied, "I was helped by the military and came to Kakul which I left by steamship after escaping from the mass slaughter. I thus came to India with my family and I was saved by the grace of God."

To the question, "How are the people of Ahmedabad?" he replies: "They are very rich; and also half of the world is very poor and unhappy. The Gujaratis of Ahmedabad are very good. There was a man who spent almost 400,000 rupees in giving away food and clothes. If such persons do not make their appearance, then it is only God who takes care of us." "How many members are there in your family?" "Five. I have two daughters, a wife, and a son twelve years of age. The son is studying."

"How are the Muslims behaving towards you?" "They shall prove a traitor, for they have taken cow's meat. But the people of this city have confidence in them."

"What about living conditions?" "Most of them are broken down; the difficulties are many, but what to do and where to go? In the cities the rents are very high, the income is not enough to maintain us. So I talk of a residence."

"What is the Congress government doing?" "Why are you taking down notes?" ("I have been assigned to report on the condition of the refugees.") "We are having difficulties for three years for the want of rations of wheat. There are also difficulties with water."

"How is the water supply?" "Eight taps are shared by 120 residents. For the remaining eight huts there is no provision at all. When we sent deputations to the collector at Ahmedabad it had no result.

"I have two brothers. We lived together, but now live in different quarters. One of the brothers is in Delhi. We maintain good relations. We were very happy in our native land. What can be done? It is only God who can redress our grievances. Most of the people from my native place are now in Delhi. The five or seven of us who are here from Haripurahazari are not helping one another in our need."

Here Ramchand, the younger brother of the interviewee, comes and begins to speak. The interviewer asks him "Where do you come from?" He replies: "I come from Haripurahazari. I have opened a shop because the mill in which I was working was closed."

"What was your business in your native land?" "I was a grocer and general merchant."

"Are there any difficulties?" "Yes, there are, but by the grace of God we are successful in evading them as much as possible."

"What was your income?" "My income in my country was 6,000 to 7,000 rupees. I left many bills uncollected and all my goods locked in my house and thought that I might return to the shop. But now it is impossible. I have four members in my family: a son, a mother, a wife, and myself. We were to have had better quarters, but I think someone pocketed some money."

Another man, Teramal, after telling how he had tried to establish himself in Gara and lost money in the venture, points out that he cannot establish himself without capital and that the rations are insufficient. "I have got nothing from the Congress. It only gave food in the beginning and sent us in a ship. Then to Gara. We are living in one room; it is very small; the ration is not enough. I get some from the black market. I borrowed in order to buy a buffalo, but I cannot make out on that. The animal does not get grass. In the beginning the Congress did well, but afterwards nothing."

Another man says: "Now I am living like a ghost in a jungle. I have consumed all the gold I had. There are many insects crawling about, and their bite is dangerous."

The records are monotonous. The complaints of crowded, filthy quarters, inadequate water, insufficient rations, and above all, insufficient support from the government, are almost universal. Feeling against the government extends to the point where the interviewer himself was suspected of being a government spy. Some of the interviewees begged him not to make known that they had given information.

They are suspicious also of the camp supervisors (Mukhis). Some of the refugees suggest to the interviewer that he talk directly with the Mukhi. When he replies that he is taking a few people in each block and that they want all points of view, one of them says, "Yes, that is right, because these Mukhis don't give true facts to the officers and other people who come here. They say everything is going on well. They manage things for themselves, get loans, quarters, and keep the people in the dark. The government also listens to them, listens only to those who are already rich but not to the poor who are simply dying. The commandant and other officers and the Mukhis all work hand in hand. To whom shall we complain?"

The interviewer asks: "How about Gujaratis?" "They don't even want to see us, they hate us, they do not let us do any business in this city."

"And the Muslims?" "Well, they are enjoying life; the government backs them up. The government hates the refugees but it helps the Muslims."

"How are living conditions?" "Yes, we have rooms, but no arrangement for washing clothes. My wife has to go a long distance to the well and there is a crowd there."

"What about your food?" "We are eating stuff which we used to throw away in Pakistan for the birds to eat."

"And the Congress Party and other organizations?" "They don't help us. For the sake of one's stomach, and in order to feed one's family, one has to do everything, even the meanest job. Each one looks to his own personal interest. The cleanliness problem is terrific. I have never seen a sweeper and the latrines are terrible."

In this latter instance, the interview seemed to have some relief value for the interviewee. He started out in a restless

and boisterous tone, but as he relieved himself of his hostilities he relaxed and at the end was positively smiling as he
sat on a bench and thoughtfully smoked.

The following is an example of a free narrative rolling on
and on without requiring questions:

"We have suffered a good deal by coming over to this side.
It would have been better had we remained there and
changed our religion. But my wife compelled me to come on
this side, otherwise I was ready to become a Muslim. Our
government won't be able to do anything. Those who are just
living a very ordinary life are now big ministers. They have
got a number of cars, one for each family member, and
three English teachers are employed in their home to edu-
cate their children. There is a lot of bribery and corruption;
no one is there to check it. If anyone points it out, he is at
once crushed."

To the question, "How about the Gujaratis here?" "We
have no dealings with the Gujaratis, but they help their own
class."

"And the Muslims?" "Muslims are all right, here as well
as there. Our government is protecting them. I think the
reign of such Muslim rulers as Akbar was better. At least
they heard the poor people, but now no one listens. The officers when we approach them turn us out and deal harshly
with us.

"In Sind, though my pay was not great, I was leading a
very good life. We were getting very good things to eat, but
now everything is of the worst. This milk that we are getting
is so poor it will affect our eyes. The Sindhis here are quarreling among themselves. There is a lot of rivalry. We do
have a Panchayat. The president is a good man but other
people around him are wicked and do not let him do good.
They put obstacles in his way."

"What about these various organizations?" "Well, the Congress is dead; it was only in existence as long as Gandhi

was living. But now the Congress leaders put on suits and ties and live in palatial bungalows like Westerners. They accept bribes and indulge in all sorts of foul ways to make money. The black market is rampant. Now it is only the name of the Congress which is being exploited to harass the poor."

It should be noted that there seems to be general feeling that political pressure is useless. The government cannot "count on votes from the refugees." There is no way to exert pressure as aliens upon the local regime or upon the New Delhi government.

The problem of the relation of the refugee to the local people everywhere can be phrased in terms of one of these Sindhi refugees in Ahmedabad. When asked, "How about the local people?" he says: "They say we have spoiled their business. Now where should we go? We have also to earn our livelihood so we have got to do business, but the Gujaratis hate us for that very reason."

The following statement is a highly concentrated expression of the major aspects of tension against the Muslims and against the government together, fused by one refugee into a single narrative: "In some of the principles enunciated in the Koran, like the killing of enemies, Islam has been propagated as a principle of bloodshed. The followers of Islam, the Muslims throughout their history, follow these principles in practice, so the civilization that has crept up in Islam is not a human but an animal type. Muslims, particularly in India, were and are economically downtrodden, politically subjugated, educationally illiterate, having no sense of ideal living. Since the separate electorates of Hindus and Muslims, the British government has been separating them and of course the hatred has helped Mr. Jinnah to carry out the Pakistan plan for the Indian Muslims. Being poor in economic matters and blind in faith has made all this trouble, starting with Direct Action Day in Calcutta, up to the mass murders; and they have totally looted what has been left by the Indians in Pakistan. Their economic gain has been built on the looting and the massacre of Hindus."

The following is from a Punjabi: "Our native place was very dear to us; there was good water, everything. Here time is passing. We can't help it. In the first place, I am not getting a job. I was a permanent hand there, twenty years of service as a building overseer and a bicycle merchant. The government has not done anything. Our clothes have gone to pieces; everything has been used up. I remained honest there as well as here. The government is not helping, at least it is not helping the refugees. The Gujaratis are not helping either. They, at least the business men, don't like Sindhi business men. I am not in touch with the Muslims. In Nasik the Muslims give bribes to the police. Though we have got free quarters from the government, they are just like a tent. After a month or two they will charge 700 rupees, though the actual cost is not more than 350. The rations are very bad; the rice and other food are very inferior. We are not accustomed to it and the quantity is very small. It is not even enough to live on; we have to purchase in the black market. It is the government which is encouraging the black market. One of my friends has a ration shop. He told me how he had to bribe the officer of the department; otherwise he cannot carry on. They expect things in the black market. The officers take sugar. They can't help it. Everybody is saying sweet words but doing nothing. The government is interested in maintaining its own power and the Hindu Mahasabha and other parties cannot do anything because they are not in power."

In contrast, another refugee, a man of twenty-six years, appears rather contented. He lost much property at the time of partition, but his general response to the question about his economic condition is: "I am all right. The government has done what it could, but the refugees are blaming the government. Whatever loan the government makes to them, the refugees waste the money in enjoyment and drinking and then blame the government for not helping them. In fact, the government made a mistake in helping the refugees with free rations and food. This made them idle and easy-going. Their rooms allotted are quite all right but they keep quarreling. They have formed parties; there is no union. This is because of lack of education. The Gujaratis at first helped them, but then the refugees deceived them so they turned against them. The Gujaratis are such that once they are deceived they will turn against the person. The Muslims are very strong in Gujarat and they don't like the policy of the government regarding the Muslims. They are trying to re-habilitate their own people. Our rations and food are just like those of other people; it is the same for all."

The interviewer notes that this whole picture depends upon the man's getting a good job immediately upon arrival in the Ahmedabad area.

Almost everywhere one finds that Pandit Nehru is exempted from the general blast against the government. "Our government is useless. All are thieves collected together. Only Pandit is all right; the rest are all worthless and self-ish people. The Pandit himself says what can he do; the rest of the machinery does not work."

Everywhere, of course, the question arose how the interviewee felt toward the process of being interviewed. It had been determined that the studies would be described as university studies. The following throws some light on the problem:

"Who is there in whose house there are no quarrels? Wheresoever there are two pots they are bound to strike against each other. Husband and wife do quarrel. I don't mean my family in particular but this happens everywhere. You should not enter into our private affairs." ("I am sorry; I only wanted to see if this partition has affected your family life in any way, but if you take it ill I shall not ask.") "No, it's all right; I am ill. I have been working from early morning; I am very tired and I want to go now and take rest. Excuse me if I have uttered any harsh words."

In these Ahmedabad studies a projective test known as the Sentence Completion Test was also used. One filled-out example will be given here:

1. I feel angry when *somebody goes astray.*
2. I feel happy when *I am in my home.*
3. Something I hope for is *that what I am getting may continue.*
4. The kind of people I like is *Sindhis.*
5. The best thing for India would be *that she should become prosperous.*
6. Independence has brought *nothing for me.*
7. The present government is *lazy.*
8. Before partition India was *going on very well.*
9. The migration from Pakistan to India has caused me *a lot of misery and pain.*
10. Muslims as a whole are *dishonest and insincere.*
11. The Gujaratis in general are *ordinary people.*
12. I spend my leisure *in rest.*
13. The other communities in this country are *not close to me.*
14. The Congress Party in India is *selfish. It does not care for the poor.*

Upon completion of the interview, each individual was rated on his degree of tension, a score of two indicating very high tension, one, average tension, and zero, no tension. The rating was done by two individuals quite independently. The correlation of the two raters (for 50 cases) was .91.

The sample consists of fifty individuals as follows:

    6 middle class, illiterate, employed
20 middle class, literate, employed
    6 middle class, illiterate, unemployed
    9 middle class, literate, unemployed
    3 poor, illiterate, employed
    3 poor, illiterate, unemployed
    3 rich, literate, employed

"Rich" means owning property of 100,000 rupees or more and one's original home in the land of origin; "middle class" means owning from 5,000 rupees up to 100,000; and "poor" means owning less than 5,000 rupees. It will be seen from the table that the tensions are more or less evenly distributed among the various categories.

In the sample of fifty, the high tensions recorded, as estimated by the two raters, X and Y, appear as follows:

	X	Y
Against the government	33	30
Against the Muslims	31	25
Against local people	24	26
Against living conditions	34	31
Against rations and food	29	29
Against political organizations	30	26
Against Mukhi	23	22
Against other things	11	15

Mr. Dosajh offers the following general findings: (1) The middle class show greater tension than the poor in all areas except living conditions; (2) the descending order of tensions in the middle class is government, living conditions, political organizations, rations and food, Muslims, local people, Mukhis, and other things; (3) the descending order of tensions among the poor people is living conditions, rations and food, various political organizations, the government, local people, Muslims, other things, and Mukhis. In every area of the eight covered, the middle-class unemployed showed greater tension than the middle-class employed. As a whole, the middle-class, literate, unemployed are those showing the highest over-all tension level.

In the Bombay study of the interrelations between refugees, Muslims, and Hindu residents, there is abundant evidence of similar distress and tension. It is, however, made clear that economic frustrations are of major importance and that economic rehabilitation is now the primary problem.

PROBLEMS OF DEPENDENCE AND OF SELF-HELP

So far, our attention has been given to refugees from West Pakistan, comprising mainly Sindhis and Punjabis. We have, in addition, an extensive study of refugees from East Pakistan, by Dr. B. S. Guha and his collaborators[1] of the Department of Anthropology of the government of India. At the planning conference in New Delhi in August, 1950, Dr. Guha decided to utilize in the present project some of the research methods of anthropology and psychology which had already been used in his international industrialization study. The study of refugee camps, however, was made long after the industrialization study had begun, and different kinds of social tension appear in a village disturbed by industrial change and in a village comprised of frightened and impoverished refugees. Moreover, while the use of projective tests had been emphasized in the industrialization study, it seemed more appropriate in the present investigation to use methods directly related to the misery of the refugees and their attitude toward what the government was doing for them; and at the same time to utilize methods which would permit a comparison between the refugees of Bengal and those of the West.

Dr. Guha decided to compare two refugee settlements, one of which was under government supervision and the other of which represented autonomous activity of the refugees, a "self-help" settlement. The former was the Jirat colony, comprised of about two thousand persons who had left their homes in East Bengal after the huge upheaval, terror, and carnage of 1950. Since a formerly prosperous village lying about 40 miles west of Calcutta had deteriorated over
. . . .

[1] Dr. B. K. Chatterjee, Dr. Parimal Das, Mrs. Uma Guha, Miss K. Gnanambal, Mr. P. C. Ray, Mr. R. K. De, and Mr. S. Kundu.

many decades, considerable land was available for a new settlement, the labor being supplied by the able-bodied men among the refugees, and the capital being provided by the government. Each able-bodied male worked five or more hours per day, largely at tasks of excavation for the development of new tanks (artificial pools) or the rehabilitation of old tanks, or road building. A modest cash wage was paid. Other individuals, that is females and very young and very old males, were given standard cash doles. The government appointed an overseer who was responsible for the maintenance of the group, including its schools and its health facilities. The attitude of the refugee group was therefore one of dependence upon the government. A good many of the men were able to eke out their earnings by continuing with traditional trades, such as those of shopkeeper, hawker, and fisherman, but in general the group felt that the government did not take much trouble about this matter; for example, land assigned the fishermen was often far from the streams.

In reading the full report transmitted by Dr. Guha, one gains the vivid impression that these people were in a wretched state, inadequately housed and nourished, with inadequate health facilities and insufficient attention given to schools; but the most important aspect of the whole situation was their uncertainty about the future. There was no clear goal, no clear plan of ultimate rehabilitation toward which they could aim. On the other hand, it must be remembered that those who had escaped at the time of the upheaval in 1950 were grateful to have preserved life and limb, and to be able to hold the family together; and they looked towards the government, however inadequate its aid, as the protector upon which they must lean. When it comes to group and individual differences among the refugees, we must remember that in general the prosperous (mostly upper-caste) people had lost more than the poorer (mostly lower-caste) people, simply because all were now reduced to a level not much above that of sheer subsistence.

The procedure used involved first the selection of a random sample by the technique of assigning numbers to families and choosing families on the basis of the random numbers alone, so far as a proper balance between sexes, age groups (those over 35 and under 35), and caste groups (simply upper and lower) could be maintained in this way. Individuals within families were also randomly chosen, insofar as this is compatible with what has just been said. A hundred individuals were thus chosen. This will give us, in general, about a dozen individuals in each category "homogeneous" as to caste, age, and sex. We may, if we like, compare the fifty upper-caste with the fifty lower-caste individuals, or the fifty older with the fifty younger, or the fifty men with the fifty women, or we may make subgroup comparisons of any desired type, subject to the statistical difficulties involved in working with small samples.

The anthropological survey of the situation having been made, the primary method employed was the interview, in which the life history was supplemented by the administration of a rather long series of questions. The questions dealt mainly with attitudes toward the Muslims, other castes, the government, other members of the family, and the future. The questions were so randomized that the same topic was not pursued and finished before raising another general class of issues. Rather, one question might deal with the Muslims, another with the government, and another with the family, and then we might find another dealing with the Muslims. The questions were all of the five-point scale type, the interviewee being told that he could indicate his position anywhere from full agreement to full disagreement with each statement that was made.

The questions were as follows:

ATTITUDE SCALE
>No.
>Name
>Age
>Sex
>Caste
>Education
>Date

DIRECTIONS

Mark each of the following statements in the left margin according to how much you agree or disagree with it. Write +5, +4, +3, +2, +1, depending on your intensity of favorable or unfavorable attitude.

> +5 : Strongly favorable
> +4 : Favorable
> +3 : Undecided
> +2 : Unfavorable
> +1 : Strongly unfavorable

A. ATTITUDE TOWARD MUSLIMS

1. Muslims are to blame for my troubles.
2. Some Muslims are good people.
3. All Muslims should leave the Indian Union.
4. Hindus should treat Muslims as Indian citizens without any discrimination.

B. ATTITUDE TOWARD OTHER CASTES

1. There is good reason for tension in this locality between upper and lower caste Hindus.
2. I do not like to enter into marital relationship with other castes even when they are at par with my caste educationally and economically.
3. In comparison with other castes my caste is getting much less opportunities and advantages.
4. We should help the people of other castes when they are in trouble even when they do not help us when we are in trouble.

C. ATTITUDE TOWARD GOVERNMENT

1. The present Government is responsible for our miseries.
2. The Government is doing all it can for us.

3. The present Government is too weak in its dealing with Pakistan.
4. Government officials in the refugee camps are generally sympathetic.

D. ATTITUDE TOWARD OWN FUTURE
1. It will never be possible for me to be what I was.
2. I believe that my family can re-establish itself.
3. If I am very active, I can improve my lot.
4. I have no hopes for the future.

E. ATTITUDE TOWARD LOCAL PEOPLE
1. The people of West Bengal are not sympathetic toward the refugees.
2. There can never be intimate social relationships between the people of East and West Bengal.
3. We should integrate ourselves with the people of West Bengal.
4. People of West Bengal are generally doing a great deal to help us.

F. GENERAL ATTITUDE (INTERPERSONAL, INCLUDING FAMILY)
1. The members of my family are more difficult to get on with than before.
2. The happiness of family life makes up for all our hardships.
3. The relations of husband and wife are better than they used to be.
4. The relations between parents and children are getting worse.

All of these questions are relevant to our problem of tensions, being expressions of feeling for or against certain groups or activities. It is not denied that some of them have definite factual reference. These people have suffered intensely. Many members of their groups had been tortured or killed; much rape and robbery had occurred within the area of their immediate experience. No attempt will be made here to disentangle the rational from the irrational, the "justified" from the "unjustified" attitudes.

Before saying anything about the subgroups, we may generalize that there is one major response (and there are two secondary responses) which are generally characteristic of the whole population studied. First, their suffering at the hands of the Muslims was intense. Even where no physical damage of any sort was done them, they lived in a world of insecurity or terror for a matter of months. The partition had occurred in 1947. But these were people who had waited a long time, and who had not actually torn loose from their ancestral lands until the situation became altogether intolerable. The great majority, being somewhat negative toward Muslims before the period of partition, became, thereafter, intensely hostile and bitter. The two secondary responses to be noted are a tendency to feel that the government is not doing all it could for them, and a tendency to feel that the local people surrounding them lack sympathy and friendliness. The attitude toward the government is exemplified by the fact that they cannot understand why they have no adequate schools. The government started three primary schools, but these are housed in thatched sheds, with no protection from the sun and rain, no chairs or benches, no blackboard or chalk. There is not even paper, and the children must write on palm leaves. The refugees cannot understand why, in this as in many other matters, they did not get the privileges they think belong to them simply as citizens of India. Of course they need to make the most of opportunities for work as artisans or shopkeepers, and find themselves in competitive relations with the local people. They feel that they get not only no help but no sympathy in addition. This latter situation is much harder on the women than on the men, the women being shut up in the household, bewildered, lacking normal gratifications of the need for neighborliness and support.

Now as to the findings by groups and subgroups. The men are, in general, in a more advantageous position to make an adjustment. The able-bodied men within the age range considered are mostly at work, and while the physical labor involved in digging and building is regarded by the formerly prosperous members of the group as a form of degradation, still the use of one's muscles, and the observation of something accomplished from day to day, help in the process of adjustment. Partly, also, because in general they have much more education, the men as a whole are able to understand a little bit more clearly what is happening to them. The women are, in general, much more conservative, notably in matters of religion. They have less adequate resources, by way of contact with the outer world and by way of education, to deal aggressively with the fate which has befallen them. Part, indeed, of their conservatism may be related to the need for some sort of definite emotional anchorage in a life which has tended to become impoverished. The fact that the women actually suffered grave and continuous anxiety during the last years in Pakistan with reference to the likelihood of attack may be psychologically related to the greater hostility at present toward the local people; for since the Muslims are no longer immediately there to be feared and hated, some of what was directed to them may be displaced to other persons who are not friendly. Indeed, Dr. Guha suggests that there is, likewise, a tendency toward a "scapegoating" response to the government, the government's activities being self-evident day by day and the Muslims being for the most part in a world of the past.

Moreover, in view of their lower degree of education, Dr. Guha suggests that the behavior of the women in seeking comfort or desiring to lean upon the government may perhaps be related to the regression or "primitivation" of behavior arising from the frustration experienced; under catastrophe people often become childish. While this is an interesting suggestion, it is subject to some reservations. For one thing, there are more pessimists among the women than among the men, only 2 per cent of the men giving responses which average at point one or point two on the five-point scales for hopelessness regarding the future, while 20 per cent of the women belong in these pessimist categories. It can safely be said that all the factors taken together which serve to support the morale of the women are insufficient to give them the kind of support which the men, in their relatively active situation, receive.

These figures on optimism and pessimism, especially among the males, constitute one of the reasons for my own personal belief that these verbal attitude responses are essentially authentic. Granted that there may be a strong tendency to please the interviewer and some lurking suspicion that a favorable attitude toward the government may, in the long run, help one's own status, it seems likely that a group of people in distress will emphasize, rather than minimize, their misery and will tend to admit the pessimistic features in their whole situation. Consequently, the prevailing optimism here is striking. Incidentally, the data from this study tend to support a generalization made by Pars Ram (page 164) regarding a general tendency to respect the distant government but to blame petty local officials for all that goes wrong.

Regarding caste attitudes, the similarities between upper-caste and lower-caste attitudes seem in general more striking than the differences. The upper castes have suffered a greater relative decline in their fortunes, but they have intellectual and other resources which are more adequate to meet the situation. The pervasive hostility towards the Muslims is shared to about the same degree by the two groups. The attitude of upper-caste groups and lower-caste groups toward one another seems to be undergoing liberalization as a result of their experiences, even the Harijans benefiting from a very considerable relaxation of the traditional rejection aimed at them.

Regarding the differences between older and younger adults (age 35 being the cutting point), about all that is worth saying here is that younger persons seem to be somewhat more aggressive toward Muslims and toward the government, perhaps because of greater physiological intensity or because of lack of background of more fortunate relations in earlier years.

The sentence completion test

Dr. Guha gives special emphasis to the sentence completion test (cf. page 176) which appears here in a new form. It is reproduced in full in a footnote.[2] Here, instead of requesting that responses take a yes-no form, or that one indicate one's position on a five-point scale, one allows the interviewee to finish the sentence in any fashion he likes. The question, "One thing which sets me against Muslims is. . . ." appears to serve a function which is not served by the five-point questions. One digs momentarily beneath the surface, getting a spontaneous form of expression, and discovers the relative importance of factors contributing to an attitude, not merely an indication of the intensity of the attitude. The commonest answers to this question are: (1) manners and conduct; (2) cow-slaughter (and beef-eating); (3) use of torture. The concepts "dirty" and "fanatical," quoted earlier in connection with the Bombay study, appear relatively infrequently, and appear to be of small weight. Taken in connection with the life history, it is clear that specific experiences during the period of conflict lie behind the general phrase "manners and conduct"; and indeed a good many respondents go ahead to give examples of what they mean. Their emphasis upon cow-slaughter and beef-eating may seem extreme to the Western reader; he must remember

• • • •

[2] Questions:
1. One thing that puts me against Muslims is . . . .
2. The thing that makes me distrust the Muslims is . . . .
3. Muslims are people who . . . .
4. I dislike Muslims whenever they . . . .
5. I like Muslims whenever they . . . .

that the cow is a mother symbol or that the cow's sacredness is deeply fused with feelings of the sacredness of giving birth and nourishment. The large number in all groups here and in the other camp who emphasize torture suggest that we are confronting not vague stereotypes, but specific horrors which live in the memory.

The over-all intensity of feeling can perhaps be fairly well summarized in the single fact that the unfinished sentence, "I like Muslims whenever they. . . ." (giving the interviewee a chance to say something favorable) results in a reply of "I do not like them at all," or its equivalent, in over half the total number, though some praised them as good agriculturists, some liked their religious attitude, some noted their unity, and some their honesty.

A modified form of the Bogardus Social Distance Scale was used, ascertaining the number of persons in each group and subgroup who are willing to accept members of other defined social groups in relations of various sorts: marriage, friendship, interdining, and social mixing. Here we find considerable relaxation of rigid attitudes about intermarriage; a relaxation greater, of course, among males than females and greater among the lower castes than among the upper castes. Acceptance of members of other castes as friends is taken for granted by almost everyone, and social mixing by just about 100 per cent. In this particular sample, the attitude favoring interdining is relatively conservative among the upper-caste groups; the lower-caste groups are eager for such acceptance. A pervasive pattern of greater conservatism and greater clinging to one's own world appears in the case of the women.

My own general interpretation of this material would be that these people can definitely be rehabilitated at any time. They have not deteriorated psychologically, so far as the data indicate, to any great extent. Their grievances are real, their difficulties huge, their pessimism remarkably little;

there is no direct evidence of disintegration. All they need is good, strong, substantial help in defining a new goal and working toward it. It is not a question of receiving a larger dole; it is a question of a new objective toward which they can confidently work.

A self-help group

In contrast to the Jirat study, which reflects in so many ways the dependence upon the government, stands the Azadgarh study, selected by Dr. Guha to bring out some of the problems of self-help prevailing among refugees.

A group of people from East Bengal, living in Calcutta before the partition, made up their minds to help the refugees by making available to them a large tract of neglected land adjoining the home of one of the initiators of the plan. The offer of a sum in payment to the owner brought a refusal, and after due consideration they took the "calculated risk" of encouraging the refugees to seize the land. Though the plots of land amounted only to a twentieth of an acre per family, the refugee group set to work with great energy, leveling the land, clearing out jungles, building homes, arranging for roads and a water supply, elected their own central committee, and made themselves responsible for their own group life. The owner of the land opposed them with goondas (hired strong-arm men) as well as with the police; the latter, while not succeeding in evicting them, stood in their eyes as symbols of government disapproval. Their hostility became still more acute when the Eviction Bill, later called the Rehabilitation Bill, was passed, specifically providing for the ejection of settlers from land illegally seized. The entire subsequent course of their life is colored by continuous acute anxiety regarding the role of the government. They have maintained a rather tight morale, not only fighting off these outside threats but organizing clubs and festivals, schools and medical facilities, which are of course far from adequate; the point is that these services arise wholly from the group and not from outside support.

The method followed by Dr. Guha is essentially the same as the method used at Jirat. We have, then, a hundred individuals randomly selected, with breakdowns by sex, age, and caste. The initial contact with the subjects was much more difficult, since the whole atmosphere in the camp was one of suspicion toward outsiders—and with very good reason, since they feared that the research workers were spies. It took a long time to thaw them out. This was, however, ultimately achieved, and warm friendships sprang up between the research team and the refugees.

Despite the uniformity of the method, one great difference between the groups prohibits our interpreting the main differences between them solely in terms of the fact that one is assisted by the government, the other a self-help group. The Jirat group escaped under difficulties after the violent upheaval and conflict of 1950 had occurred. The Azadgarh group had, however, left Pakistan before the most acute phase was reached. One might expect from such considerations (as in fact one finds) a lesser degree of anti-Muslim feeling in Azadgarh, along with the expected greater hostility toward the Indian government. Somewhat offsetting this difference is the fact that the local population apparently found equal difficulty in accepting the strangers. Both groups suffer from loneliness, and show hostility toward the local population from whom, originally, kindness and support had been expected.

Dr. Guha and his collaborators also offer some interesting suggestions regarding psychodynamic factors which may complicate all these relationships. They think that the government may stand as a father symbol, in such fashion that the hostility and sense of injustice experienced by the Azadgarh group may unconsciously bring on grave guilt feelings, as being essentially responses against the father. Identification of government care with paternal care is by no means an unreasonable suggestion. We are not, however, able in this report to give the considerable space which would be required for a fair evaluation of this hypothesis.

To state the most general impression gained by Dr. Guha himself and, I think, by almost any reader who carefully studies the report, the chief sufferings of the group appear due to uncertainty about the future. We had occasion to note in the Kalyan camp evidence of the deterioration of personality related to the fact that the plans of the government are not known to the refugees. The same was the case in the interviews of the Ahmedabad project. In the present study it would appear that acute anxiety derives from not knowing from week to week where the future will lead. Almost any definite plan could give some sort of adaptive response, but an uncertainty related to so many grave difficulties for themselves and their families produces anguish and may in time produce deterioration.

The attitude scale was used just as it was at Jirat. Questions were asked regarding hostility to the Muslims. It is striking to note, despite what the refugees have been through, that about 20 per cent of the males manifest no hostility (tension). This reminds one of the situation in Aligarh, page 144ff. The percentage of females here showing tension is 60 per cent (it will be remembered that in Aligarh only males were interviewed). The lower-caste group in Azadgarh shows more hostility than the upper-caste group, the difference appearing clearly in both sexes.

The attitude toward the Government, when tested by the same conventional measures, is about equally hostile, when all categories of responses are considered. Actually only 4 per cent show a definitely favorable attitude toward the Government. The situation is the same among men and among women.

As in Jirat, hostility toward the local people is considerable in the case of the women; but among the men it does not appear in quantity. Not very much intercaste tension is evident in this study. There is some evidence that recent movements toward liberalism of the higher towards the lower castes is having an effect here; the common experiences that all have shared are apparently producing some degree of unity of feeling. One interesting difference between Jirat and Azadgarh is pointed out by the investigators, namely the fact that the Jirat refugees prior to their permanent settlement in the village were constrained by circumstances to dine together in the government camps in relief centers without caste distinction. This appears to have influenced their attitudes and to have modified their caste conservatism. No such experience was shared by the Azadgarh refugees.

In the attitude scales we find, as we found before, a general conservatism of the women as compared with the men; a smaller number who are willing to consider marriage outside the caste group, but nevertheless will accept the social mixing with all castes as a matter of course.

Despite the differences in experience between the two refugee groups, and despite the differences to be expected between refugees and others, one finds in the present refugee groups the same general relaxation of caste rigidities and the same tendency to seek new human relations which are found elsewhere in modern India.[3]

. . . .

[3] Dr. Guha's recent follow-up observations indicate that since completion of the present studies a considerable change in the situation of the two refugee colonies has taken place. In the Jirat group the number of persons who support themselves by gainful labor has significantly increased, and their physical, social and psychological condition has improved. A more active and productive orientation appears to have replaced the "regressive" tendencies frequently observed during the

PSYCHOLOGY OF THE REFUGEES

Now let us see if we can throw any light upon the deeper psychology of the refugees of India. Our first psychological hypothesis here is that which goes by the name of "frustration and aggression." We are told by this hypothesis that people who insistently demand something which they deeply need, and cannot obtain it, express their frustration in *aggression*, usually directed toward the person conceived to be the source of the frustration; one may seek a victim at times who may be unrelated to one's frustration; or one may turn the attack upon oneself ("kicking oneself"), the attribution to oneself of the unpardonable sin or the cause of all human suffering, a form of inward turning of aggression to which sometimes the term masochism is applied. If the hypothesis is relevant, refugees will be furious not only against the Muslims but against other Hindus, and even against themselves.

In contrast to this frustration-aggression idea, there is the conception that under some circumstances people fall back to a less mature, more infantile condition. In psychoanalytic language they *regress* to a period of more primitive organization. A classical experiment at the State University of Iowa found that most children under conditions of frustration became quite suddenly and very clearly much less ma-

---

earlier investigation. Recently, the Jirat refugees have formed their own welfare and social activities society. The government has contributed to the new trend by construction of a high school.

On the other hand, conditions in the self-help colony at Azadgarh are deteriorating. While only a few of these settlers are gainfully employed, most of them have exhausted their cash funds or lost their small business investments. In addition, the constant threat of eviction and the feeling of being abandoned by the government have drained their moral strength.

ture than they had been before. From this viewpoint, the refugees would tend to become childish.

A third hypothesis is offered us in the study of an Austrian "unemployed village" which was deprived of its industry completely by the post-World War I treaties and in which everyone lived on an inadequate dole—likewise in a study of the unemployed in the city of Warsaw during the same period. In the Austrian study one common response to frustration was absolute *apathy*. People who had struggled fruitlessly to find some sort of work had discovered that there simply was nothing to do and had become essentially like vegetables in their daily existence, not having even the stamina left to read, to seek amusement, or to think. In the Warsaw study this period of apathy was again found, but typically only after a long period of vigorous and even frantic struggle to find employment.

In the light of these three hypotheses, what can be said of the refugees in response to their terrible frustration?

In attempting a reply to this question, we have several sources of information. First, we have the fact that in some parts of India refugees have been given vigorous and effective work to do in rehabilitating their lives and that of their families. An outstanding example is Nilokheri, eighty miles from Delhi. Another example is Faridabad, a few miles from Delhi. Here, through a plan developed by Kamla Devi and others and with government support, over 20,000 refugees were given the task of building a city with homes and shops and factories. This adventure attracted the attention of Senator Brewster and through him some other members of the United States Senate, and the possibility of multiplying similar experiments has been discussed in the press.

One relatively comforting fact about the huge government enterprise of caring for refugees has been the relative adequacy of the preparation of the boys for dignified and rewarding work. Certainly the crafts instruction at the Kalyan

Camp prepares boys of fifteen or so to undertake woodwork, linoleum block printing, leatherwork, simple metalwork and many other activities. One might go on marking the map with examples of good things done on behalf of refugees. It must be remembered, however, that these are tiny drops sprinkled on a vast area. The refugees cannot be given employment under present conditions without the expenditure of considerable capital nor without pushing others out of employment. One sees a typical illustration in the spread of shops through Lucknow where the refugees by the very fact of their success in running little stores have become competitors to the traditional owners and have become the butt of considerable hostility. In our Ahmedabad inquiries we found that the refugees were trying, in order to establish themselves, to undersell the local Gujarati merchants, with results which can easily be imagined. The genuine assimilation of the refugees is an economic problem for which the government has altogether inadequate resources.

Now as to a decision between these different hypotheses: First, we would certainly say that the word "apathetic" would be the *worst* possible description of the refugee faces and the refugee words with which we have made our contact. In the Kalyan Camp I was asked to meet some sixty representative men who would talk to us about their problems. The meeting got out of order in a couple of minutes with dozens of men trying to talk at once, so full of suffering, bitterness, resentment, and hate that they could not listen to one another; shouting, screaming at us their demands that the government stop talking and help them. The picture left upon us was one of steaming bitterness, not of "resignation" in any form.

In the camp in Bihar where the refugees had arrived somewhat more recently, as a result of the East Bengal troubles of 1949 and 1950, we saw just as much suffering but of a somewhat different sort. People gathered together in small groups talking to the members of our troop who had gone to visit the village; there was no organized public meeting, there was no speechmaking. There was, however, a continuous stream of misery involving hopelessness towards the future and a great deal of self-pity, the self-pity of people who have no real positive hope to which they can give their attention; blank and wretched faces alternated with contorted and suffering faces. An old man down whose cheeks the tears poured put it very simply: "We escaped the Muslims but now it would be better to have been torn apart by the bullocks."

There is of course a great deal of suspicion among the refugees regarding the authorities who have control of the refugee situation; notably one hears many expressions of distrust, and charges of graft and corruption. The hostility, however, is also directed toward the Hindu community at large. "We are the people who made the sacrifice. We are the people who were driven from our homes. Why do they do so little for us? How can it be that these Hindus, our brothers, stay on the other side of the road, who hardly even turn to look at us?"

In connection with this journey to the refugee village in Bihar, an extreme illustration of this came to light. The camp had been placed side by side with an aboriginal village. Here a few hundred aboriginals were engaged in adequate and normal subsistence farming. They had tried during the first few weeks to offer little things for the comfort of the refugees. The refugees could not understand why it was so little. They had thought of themselves as Indians who had come to the land of India from the new and much dreaded Pakistan; they thought that both the government and all those surrounding them would welcome them with open arms, lend them things, and not expect immediate return.

One sees the same sort of thing everywhere in the world. The refugees expect what cannot reasonably be given from the point of view of the traditional settlers. The things they lend they expect to be returned and they do not expect to make large gifts, only enough to carry the refugee over. But for how long a time must he be carried along? The refugee is established; he does no work. The government does not even provide work for him. There are not the tools, there is not the land. The refugee goes on idling there, consuming goods which the villagers nearby offer through their hard work. From their point of view the refugees are an idle and complaining lot. From the refugee point of view one is dealing with men whose hearts are of flint. The situation cannot be handled at the grass-roots level of the two contending parties; it can only be handled by administrators wise enough to provide in the very beginning for a joint cooperative economic enterprise involving the various component parts. This in turn cannot possibly be done except with a type of capital outlay which will make possible the effective labor of the newly planted refugees.

But what of the attitude of the refugees toward the Muslims from whom they escaped? Is it an attitude of unlimited bitterness? One is surprised to find two general principles that seem to cut through any characterization of the Hindu-Muslim hostility. The first is the fact that in Hindu samples which we took we found about 20 per cent practically free of any special bias in favor of their own group; about 20 per cent, that is, who say that there are always misunderstandings, that all human beings are essentially alike, that there are good people and bad people in every group, and specifically that the Muslims are no worse than Hindus or the Hindus no worse than Muslims. One finds likewise among Muslims this small but substantial and clear-eyed minority group, who refuse to take sides in the current animosities and name-calling hostilities. Even civil war does not by any means uniformly produce an unbridgeable gulf of noncommunication between two groups.

Second, however, there is the curious fact that the experience of suffering operates in terms of *group membership* rather than in terms of the purely personal frustrations which each individual has encountered. In each group of refugees we appear to find a good deal of evidence that it is not one's personal loss of property, or even loss of members of the family, which determines one's degree of hostility to the Muslims. In a small but very carefully planned study, Miss Malhotra of the Institute of Applied Psychology at Patna demonstrated that the hostility toward Pakistan and the specific hostility toward Muslims among the group of refugees which she studied were independent of the severity of one's personal misfortune. The same sorts of data have come to us from several parts of India. It is as if one went through a collective experience with others sharing the same sufferings; and it is the collective experience, the shared suffering of the group as a whole, which appears to determine the general level of anti-Muslim hostility. Now of course it is true, as we already noted, that some individuals are free of such animosity, but these are not by any means necessarily the same individuals who suffer the least. In fact, the individual tolerances for Muslims appears to be related not to the large or small amount of one's own suffering but to entirely different variables related to temperament and early upbringing. There seems to be some evidence that the children of all these groups played with Muslim children when they were little, and there seems to be in the Calcutta material some evidence that those who played the most with the Muslim children are those who incline toward the least hostility as adults. At any rate, some foundation for mutual understanding between Hindus and Muslims was established in childhood and though interpreted differently in different ways by different people, serves as one of the important factors in making possible such mutual acceptance as now exists.

Of course the sufferings of the refugees are related to the problem of intergroup hostility not only in a direct and obvious way but in a very indirect and circuitous way. The refugees naturally spread the word regarding their sufferings; and through the press as well as through oral communication the Hindu community is reminded more and more of the sufferings of Hindus at the hand of Muslims. This does not necessarily help the immediate status of the refugees, but it can hurt Hindu-Muslim relations in general.

An example of this became strikingly evident in the city of Lucknow. It will be remembered that Professor Kali Prasad made a study of Lucknow as a low-tension center. His extensive data on the hostilities obtaining between Hindus and Muslims do clearly support his view that Lucknow has been a low-tension center. In view of the centuries of effective government of the city by Muslim rulers and the two centuries of effective collaboration of the Hindu and Muslim communities in the life of the city during the period of British rule, his case is certainly well supported in suggesting that Lucknow is a city in which communal strife has played a rather small part. Nevertheless, even in Lucknow it has been quite evident that the advent of the refugees has served to stir up a degree of anti-Muslim feeling which did not characterize the city before. We encountered in Lucknow what we had encountered likewise in Bombay and Aligarh, namely, the feeling: "We Muslims are insecure. Look at what we've gone through. Eyes are on us now. We are suspected of being disloyal, hostile, unfair, tricky, arrogant. Our future is difficult indeed."

Of course one might argue that the refugee camp was in itself a great mistake, that the only thing that could be done with refugees was to get them established as normal members of the community. One finds exactly this being attempted in Lucknow and elsewhere through allowing the refugees to establish their own shops. And one sees difficulties in that, too. The fact appears to be that it costs a great deal of money to establish refugees in business and that in India where capital is so hard to get hold of, and so many projects for the industrial and agricultural development of the country are afoot, one can hardly expect a good standard of living or even the general problem of refugee rehabilitation to be given a "top priority" in government plans.

Indeed one may wonder whether much can be accomplished by research on the tensions problem as it relates to refugees unless rehabilitation becomes a more urgent item in government planning. This of course is just one aspect of capital expenditure. I am no economist but it seems to me essential that the labor, the personal economic value of the refugees, several million strong, be turned to account. It seems to me also to be of the utmost possible importance that the refugees themselves contribute to the rehabilitation of their country and become identified with it. At the same time it is of the utmost importance that Indians think of the refugees not as competitors for the few jobs and the few economic opportunities that exist, but as men and women who share with them in the upbuilding of India. Turning thousands of them into retail trade is no solution. This means that almost complete support of the refugees until they have useful work to do, and then a diminishing schedule of support, is imperative. Nothing can be more demoralizing than the year-by-year rotting to pieces of tens of thousands of people that one sees at places like the refugee camps already described.

A single illustration will be spelled out in more detail. At the Kalyan Camp hopes were frequently expressed in our hearing that electrical power might be made available to the camp. There had been vague suggestions by the government over and over again that such power might be supplied. Look at all the shops and small industries which could be supplied; look at all the goods that could be turned out;

look at all the artisans that could be trained! Nothing would be more important. Worse, however, than a flat "no" was the endless dallying, toying with the idea, and the failure of the government to take any action. Finally, after all this talk, visualize the effect of a tremendous cutback in electrical power effective in Bombay in 1951. This put the hundred thousand people in the Kalyan Camp even more darkly in the shade.

It seems clear that as soon as the refugees can be given the equipment and the training, the land or the shops or the goods necessary to give them a new life, they should be steadily pushed into a position of complete self-support. They expect to pay back and they should pay back; not charity but a lift to one's feet is what is involved. Everywhere in India, so far as I know, such a lift to the feet has proved well worth while. We mentioned the refugee city of Nilokheri, where thousands of refugees, with government aid, built their own homes, shops, factories. Refugee rebuilding is an aspect of capital outlay comparable to the sinking of wells or the establishment of industries. If the economic contribution of the millions of refugees be taken as seriously as the economic contribution of unreclaimed land, India can enormously reduce her problem of social tensions.

9

Hostilities and hopes of textile workers

The movement from farm to city has been going on for centuries in the West. It shows itself in the dramatic fact of about 94 per cent urbanization in Britain, the first country to undergo industrialization. In the United States within the last few decades the rural population has dwindled from over 50 per cent to about 20 per cent, and in spite of "back-to-the-farm" movements it continues. The industrialization of India is a relatively recent matter. Following upon the establishment of the railway network, British capital was here and there used for the construction of mills, factories, and mines, and Indian capital was first represented on a large scale in the investments of the huge Parsi industrial empire of the Tatas.

Several misconceptions nevertheless remain regarding the rate and form of industrialization of India. To a very large degree the raw materials extracted or cultivated in India have been and still are shipped to British ports for processing. One of the greatest of all industrial developments, that in the textile industry, became a great bone of contention between British and Indian claims during the twenties and thirties. The huge phalanx of textile mills all across Yorkshire and Lancashire bore testimony to the possible threat which might be felt if Indian demands for self-sufficiency in textiles should be granted. Nevertheless, to some degree before the time of independence, notably in

Bombay, Ahmedabad, and Kanpur, Indian as well as British capital was used for the establishment of Indian mills. Some of these mills, as in the case of the Sarabhai family in Ahmedabad, are now in the hands of the third generation.

The impression might be given in the West that "India is undergoing a rapid industrialization." It is true that such industrial empires as already exist, such as those of Tata, Birla, and Dalmia, are still expanding. It is *not* true, however, that the rate of industrial expansion is rapid by Western standards. There are probably not over three million industrial workers in all India, about 1 per cent of the population. The arrival of industrial workers in the urban regions is largely a result of the extreme pressures upon the land already noted, and there is no strong desire to remain beyond the time required. Inquiry for example among the Ahmedabad workers indicated that those who had come from the country districts preferred to go back. Many had fantasies of what they would do when they could quit work, and in most cases this involved establishing a bit of land and carrying on their own farming outside of the city of Ahmedabad.

Moreover, a back-to-the-land movement is actually occurring in a form which expresses another very different aspect of industrialism. Machine-made products do to some degree displace handmade products, and the development of the factory system may thus lead to the collapse of the market for many handicraftsmen who thereupon are forced to return as best they can to the family land. A. R. Desai[1] has presented some evidence to suggest that this return movement of the handicraftsman to the land is even greater than the movement of the dispossessed into the industrial positions in the city. The government, however, has made it a primary point since independence to put a large proportion of the

. . . .

[1] *Social Background of Indian Nationalism*. Oxford, 1946.

available capital into industrialization. This will certainly add materially to the urban population within a few years. The fact, however, that the government is also doing all it can to rehabilitate the farms may well result in a decrease of pressure upon the land. Rapid industrialization in the sense in which the Western world would use the term is not confidently to be predicted. Nevertheless, for reasons already given, industrialization and urbanization are of huge importance with regard to the social evolution of India, partly because an industrial population with all its levels and types of workers represents a major force in the modernization or, if you like, the westernization of Indian thought, and also because, as we have seen, the urban mentality is bound to have an increasingly marked effect upon the rural mentality which has characterized the conservatism or backwardness of the Indian masses.

In the light of the foregoing it may be understood why so much importance is attached here to factors of industrial morale. From a purely managerial point of view, one naturally wants one's employees to be contented. When contented, they work steadily and well; the turnover is relatively small; the breaking in of new employees, eager to learn, does not take so long; and the demand for shorter hours, higher wages, and more expensive comforts and facilities reaches a relatively stable level. Motives vary among managers in India as they do anywhere else, but one thing upon which managers in general can agree is that high morale in the sense of eagerness to work well and steadily is a factor worth rupees just as in the West it is worth pounds sterling or dollars. Actually very few owners or managers anywhere seem to have done even this kind of elementary thinking about the psychology of their workers; but to these few belongs any future which the present factory system may have, and we shall feel justified in highlighting one of the progressive Indian managerial movements.

In describing the mill situation, I should like first to give a few personal impressions, and then draw upon data gathered in the Ahmedabad study with some cross references to fragmentary material drawn from Kanpur and Bombay.

THE LIFE OF A TEXTILE WORKER

The reader may or may not know what the noise, dirt, crowding and confusion of a textile mill is like. He may or may not know, or guess, on the basis of what he has read, that mill life, like most life in India, is very hard. Without entering into detail, I will merely remind him that men put in their lives at a grinding, deafening, sweltering job at a wage which just supports life, without any retirement allowance or health insurance. There are some women, too, in the reeling, doubling, and winding sections, and in activities such as mending of broken cloth. Boys of fifteen are often brought by their fathers to begin their lives in the mills. Few individuals choose it spontaneously. It must be remembered that the population pressure and the fragmentation of the land have year by year driven people off of their land. Sometimes completely unforeseeable events like the government's seizure of a region to make an airport or a factory may in a most literal sense drive people off (we saw just such a ruined landless village). A fairly large proportion of the mill workers in Ahmedabad, according to our questionnaire data, look forward to a time of retirement and having their own village life again. Most of them, however, are not saving; indeed most of them are in debt; and these hopes do not appear to be very realistic. A general acceptance of the situation rather than open protest is characteristic. It would be a great mistake, however, to assume that the population is completely supine or apathetic. During the time of the huge Bombay textile strike which occurred in September, 1950, the Ahmedabad workers were constantly talking about the Bombay strike and about the general situation in the textile industry. We had been told that the workers were concerned only with immediate here-and-now issues. This did not prove at all to be the case when samples of their conversation were quietly collected in various parts of the mills.

This does not in any sense imply that the textile industry is the worst industry in India. Indian industry is mostly a hard, hot, heavy, disagreeable proposition for the worker, with poor organization, low wages, and no retirement or health allowances.

In some ways the mill situation in Ahmedabad is exceptional because Gandhi had lent his assistance in the early days of the founding of the union in the late twenties. It is not a strong union from a Western point of view, but it is a strong union from an Indian point of view. It has a well-organized system for processing grievances, so that the union can actually make its voice felt whenever injustice has been specified by any of those who experience it. It has not carried out what we would call collective bargaining, and the disastrous effects of the huge textile strike in Bombay are not likely to encourage local leadership to attempt anything very vigorous. Nevertheless, as a factor creating a sense of unity among the workers and as making available a responsible body with whom employers may deal, it is important and doubly important because it has the great sanction of the Gandhi name. Quite characteristic also of the state of westernization and the conflict between humanitarian and profit-making impulses is the fact that one of the most powerful organizers and supporters of the textile union is a sister of one of the larger mill-owners.

The actual situation of the industrial worker should perhaps be spelled out in a little more detail. A single dramatic item will make clear perhaps to the West what degree of physical impoverishment the typical Indian faces. Undernourishment is the rule. The average weight of the adult male textile worker in Ahmedabad, we are informed, is 105 pounds. They do indeed look skinny and spindly, lacking in physique and in energy. Later a similar item came to our attention in Bombay, where the average weight has been reported to be 98 pounds. We cannot vouch for the exact figures, but appearances and photographs suggest that these are not far off. To the question whether these men are constitutionally small, the only reply that we can give is that the difference between very poor and very good nutrition typically makes a difference of some three inches in height (as exemplified by Japanese reared in Japan contrasted with Japanese reared on the West Coast of America) and of 20 or 30 pounds. We cannot be certain of the possible effects of better nutrition in India because the basic physical anthropology of India has never been done, and we do not know what these conditions of malnutrition and of health hazards may mean in terms of stature. We do know, however, that in some parts of India, such as the Punjab, the men are notably taller and more rugged. The suspicion forced upon us is that the Indians are men of a stature which is constitutionally or natively about like that of Americans, but that they are somewhat shorter and very much lighter simply by virtue of inadequate nourishment.

SOCIAL TENSIONS IN A TEXTILE CITY

How much social tension as such does one actually find in textile cities? In Ahmedabad we find a considerable amount of hostility to the supervisors or jobbers who are responsible for the general flow of production. Up until recently these supervisors had the power of hiring and firing in their own hands, and a fraction of a man's wages upon employment were turned over to the supervisor. This system has now been abolished, but the supervisor still has the indirect power of firing insofar as he gives warnings for what he regards as serious failures of production, and in most instances three warnings mean loss of job. The loss of a job is terribly serious in India. One does not easily pick up another. It was therefore felt reasonable that the UNESCO study in Ahmedabad should emphasize data on attitudes toward supervisors. At the same time a good deal of material was also gathered on general attitudes toward the industrial situation as a whole. The data appearing in detail below suggest that relatively few are really contented and that relatively few are really in a violently hostile or revolutionary mood. Contrary to the widespread opinion that it is the better-paid elements who are the most articulate in their protest, there appears on the contrary to be a direct positive relation between earnings and morale. It is not those who are near the top of the job hierarchy and who take over some middle-class ideas who are actually most restless. It is rather those who are at the very bottom of the wage ladder.

Hostility towards the Muslims, who appear in the textile industry mainly in the role of weavers, is not marked. There have been some riots in Ahmedabad, but few and far between, and in general of rather limited social importance. It must be remembered at the same time that when a riot occurs it has a "sobering" effect, or a "threatening" effect, if one likes, upon the minority group; in the same way, one finds that the Muslim group, although in general not living in acute fear, keeps out of certain regions at certain times, particularly regions where riots have occurred, and one feels that a certain potential animosity, always just around the corner, would greet any attempt of the Muslims to reassert themselves. It cannot be maintained that there is any active discrimination against the Muslims, that is, discrimination in a western sense. In India castes typically live by themselves and find quarters more or less in accordance with their general income and standards of life; and the Muslim group, as we already noted, is treated as a caste and its situation is in general comparable to that of other castes in the lower-middle region of the caste hierarchy, but is definitely better than that of the lowest Hindu groups (Harijans or "untouchables"). When one of the mill-owners introduced "bubble fountains" in place of tumblers for drinking water, he was waited upon at once by a solemn delegation. "What's wrong?" "It isn't human to lap up water that way; that's the way animals drink." After two hours of similar rationalizations the delegates finally said that the trouble was that the Harijans would be *drinking from the same fountain;* and the mill had to go back to tumblers; which at least permitted discrimination!

And just as we find that the better paid are the most satisfied, so we note that the best of the mills in Ahmedabad, instead of nurturing attitudes of belligerency in the workers, nurture attitudes of appreciation. One is fortunate indeed if he gets work in the "Calico Mill," where working conditions are good.

The primary source of information regarding worker morale is the series of complaints which are constantly processed by the union at its headquarters. A secondary source of information lies in interviews with something over 300 workers and with a group of labor union officers and of managers. The interview work was done in a high-tension mill and a medium-tension mill, as determined by the number of complaints received by the labor union. In both instances the spinning department and the loom shed were the primary centers of inquiry. In the high-tension mill, moreover, all jobbers in the loom shed were interviewed with regard to their attitudes toward workers, management, wages, hours of work, conditions regarding leave, and other jobbers in the department to see if their attitudes had any relation to the efficiency or morale of the working group. Other data on mill efficiency were offered by the records of absenteeism,

mill breakage of cloth, and actual productivity of the machines.

Almost all the spinners are Harijans, whereas the weavers
comprise both Hindus and Muslims. Comparison was
made between older and younger workers, forty years being
the division point. Total number of persons interviewed was
137. The questions asked deal with two broad groups of
issues: first, the physical conditions in the mills, such as tem-
perature, ventilation, illumination, cleanliness, canteen, lunch
shed, washroom facilities, and drinking water; while another
group of items was concerned with the process of supervision and with management policies. Information was obtained
from each worker regarding the size of his family and education and income and living conditions. Personality data were
secured through the life history, the inquiry regarding interpersonal relations of the family and in the community, the
future aspirations regarding the family and oneself, and the
Social Distance Scale, i.e., distance felt to exist between the
individual and various other castes and social groups. Four
graduate students of sociology acted as interviewers, having
been given a ten-day training by Mr. Dayal; three of them
had already had experience with the workers. The attempt
to use a nondirective or open-ended method of interviewing
was not, however, successful, for though the workers were
willing to talk freely, they had to be probed with numerous
questions. There was for the most part no difficulty in establishing good rapport.

Differences between the level of dissatisfaction in the high-
tension and medium-tension mill prove to be in the expected direction and to be large and statistically significant.
In both groups the dissatisfaction level is greater in spinning
than in weaving. That this is not due to a general attitude of
complaint on the part of spinners as such is suggested by the
fact that for conditions which are common to both, namely,

conditions outside of the department in which they work, the dissatisfaction level is approximately the same.

It must be remembered that the spinners are all Harijans and are a class suffering from social discrimination on many issues. They are today, however, becoming more conscious of their rights and this fact may well be of major importance in the high general level of dissatisfaction expressed by them.

The workers in both mills feel moreover that management will not show true profit figures, and consequently desire a fixed bonus rather than one which is supposed to vary with profit.

In connection with our concern all through this volume with the problem of Hindu-Muslim relations, it is gratifying to be able to give this specific information as to how a Hindu group and a Muslim group working under identical conditions respond. Such responses almost certainly reflect the different social background and in particular the changed situation of the Muslims since the time of the partition of India. The ATIRA material shows that in general the dissatisfaction level is higher among Muslims than among Hindus, both in respect to physical conditions of the job and with respect to the matters relating to the other conditions of work. In terms of the unrest of today, it is not surprising to find that workers below forty years of age are in general slightly more dissatisfied than are the older workers in matters related to the physical conditions, while in other matters the differences are small and uncertain.[2]

. . . .

[2] In all these matters the question of the presence of a general attitude which runs through all the items was pursued by a method known as split-half reliability, which proved to be in the first part of the study .74 and in the second part .55. This means that workers who are dissatisfied with one area tend in general to be dissatisfied with other areas and the more satisfied in one area are the more satisfied in another area. This may well arise from the fact that dissatisfaction generated by

As to the validity of these data, in the sense that the expressions of attitude are correlated with actual facts of human behavior, the most definite evidence lies in the fact of absenteeism and labor turnover. Secondarily in the matter of productive efficiency, since the housing and living conditions of the workers in Mill A and Mill B are quite comparable, there seems to be reasonably direct evidence that the attitudes of the workers while at work are directly related to the other signs of behavior interfering with efficiency.

THE PSYCHOLOGY OF EFFICIENCY

It was possible also to seek information as to the effect of supervision upon the efficiency of work done. The physical conditions of work in eight sections of Mill A which were compared were all similar, yet their efficiencies varied greatly. For example, damage was 16 per cent higher in one of the sections than in the one with the least damage.

Immediately it became evident that differences between the ;obbers and their attitudes toward workers were quite marked. The jobber whose section has the highest efficiency level proves to be highly understanding. He is the only one in the course of the interviews who makes remarks such as these: "I get work done by persuasion"; "A worker understands when addressed in a sweet tongue." He believes that the workers do not complain without reason and that if responsibility is given them they discharge it very well. He is also satisfied with his relations with the management.

On the other hand, the jobber in the section which shows the lowest efficiency level remarks: "I have to give suspension notices in order to warn workers to be careful." He be-

---

certain unfavorable aspects of the job tend to spread and contaminate the rest, or may be due to other general factors in personality or environment.

lieves that fear is the motivation for work. His health is bad; he appears also to be partially deaf.

In over-all comment upon the Ahmedabad findings, it should be noted that although the view that workers are dissatisfied with wages is certainly correct, a large number of other factors appear likewise to be important. What may appear to the outsider to be relatively minor physical conditions affecting the job appear under these conditions to be of considerable weight. Even the matter of the attitude of the immediate supervisor is important.

A primary factor in perspective on this whole situation is the fact that current wages are just about enough to make both ends meet. Under these conditions, the great majority are in debt. The low earning power is related on the one hand, of course, to the low level of labor organization and bargaining power, but on the other hand to the rather low standards of productivity. A great deal of the machinery is antiquated and enormously less productive than is modern machinery. The experiment being carried on in the Calico Mill in Ahmedabad is of interest, showing what may happen as greater levels of productivity are sought. An enormous amount of new machinery has been installed which makes it possible for a man to tend many times the number of machines which could earlier be tended. The result, of course, is to produce much more per man; and incidentally there is a great reduction in noise, dirt, and crowding. The Calico Mill is regarded generally in Ahmedabad as one of the best mills in which to work.

The first question which one raises is whether the improvement in productivity will not displace a great many workers. It will, of course, do so if application of the method is mechanical and arbitrary. There are, however, several other steps which can and are being taken. The first is to train workers for other types of employment for which there is known to be a demand, so that it is possible, before relinquishing one's job in a mill, to fit oneself to take over some other type of needed occupation. Second is the possibility of making the reduction in the working force in such a way that only those who die or are retired from mill work are actually cut from the roll of workers. When a man dies or retires he simply is not replaced. In this way the firing of a qualified worker becomes unnecessary.

About two fifths of those now working in the mills would choose this kind of work if they had their own decision to make. About a fifth would go into trade or business, about a tenth into farming, and the rest into miscellaneous jobs representing 1 or 2 per cent each. Yet only 12 per cent of the workers are willing that their children should take up mill work. Many hope that their children can enter business or farming, and a considerable number say "Any other job than mill work." [3]

    • • • •

[3] In the course of his physical examination of workers in a motor engineering company, a printing press, and a paint manufacturing concern in Madras in 1948, Dr. A. Devasagayam gathered extensive interview material on four major issues which confront workers: first, indebtedness; second, work grievances; third, worries and troubles aside from work; and fourth, education. He found that nearly 80 per cent of the workers there were in debt; interest rates were high; and for the great majority the debt was increasing so that no escape was very likely. Imprisonment for debt still being enforced by law, there was no recourse. The itemization of the cost of living indicates that the great bulk of the income goes for food (a fact which appears to be authenticated elsewhere in our Indian observations) and that items like "black market rice" are essential for meeting food requisites at the same time that they add to the enormous burden. Only about 40 per cent complain of their wages. Of course the same issue could be phrased in terms of the high cost of living. Again low income is in some cases due not to low wages but to irregularity of work. There seemed to be a general feeling that it was not easy to raise oneself to a better job. There was no way to demonstrate ability or to earn promotion. There appears in general to be a suspicious attitude towards employers. Large individual differences in supervisory staff are re-

Two basic questions arise: first, how fast India will be able to improve working conditions, and second, how this improvement will keep pace with the rising westernization of the workers' minds, their sense of the fact that it is a world in which workers are more and more articulate and demanding, and in the long run likely to get most of what they ask. I speak not at all as an expert. I would offer with some caution only the following point: In the first place, there are huge individual differences among the mill owners in their readiness to modernize, rationalize, reduce noise, dirt, poor illumination, and confusion; their willingness to reduce somewhat the magnitude of their earnings for the sake of the workers' welfare; their general sensitivity to the social science approach and their awareness of the terrible payoff which will come if a modern viewpoint toward labor is not rather early developed. There are in Ahmedabad a few mill owners who understand that the tide is rising.

---

ported here, as they are in Ahmedabad, some winning loyalty and others only deep bitterness. Among the workers' worries are to be mentioned extreme crowding despite high rents; the absence of health precautions and medical care and insurance are of major importance. One can get medical aid only by going into still further debt. All this despite the fact that the literacy rate in the sample is 60 per cent.

IO

Prejudice — Indian and American

In India I was asked a great many times to discuss in small
groups or on the lecture platform the problem of prejudice in
the United States and its similarity to the problem of prejudice in India, and found myself developing more and more a
sense of the basic oneness of this world-wide problem. As I
worked out my lecture outlines I became more and more
aware of the detailed similarities between prejudice, as described in the foregoing chapters, and its manifestations in
the Western world. It is of course easy enough to think of
differences; take, for example, the fact that skin color is not
in India an important factor in social cleavage. Nevertheless,
the onenesses completely overwhelm the disparities.

Before I attempt some broader generalizations as to the
basic dynamics of social prejudice, I shall try to define a few
obvious similarities and dissimilarities in the group attitude
toward the Harijans in India and the Negroes in the United
States.

HARIJANS AND NEGROES—A COMPARISON OF STATUS

In the first place, we are concerned in both cases with a
relatively sharp status problem in relation to which there is
exclusion. The untouchable or scheduled castes in India,
though they vary in their own degrees of status and although
the higher castes among them are not technically very far
below the lowest of the "intermediate" castes, are in many
regions rather sharply defined. One might perhaps point out

215

that although in the United States Caucasians carry out a certain amount of discrimination against Orientals, against American Indians, and others of skin color other than their own, nevertheless they carry out a rather special, well-defined, intense, and not easily escaped type of discrimination against the Negro. This exclusion is based to a considerable extent upon conceptions of status, that kind of relationship which in the vernacular is expressed by "being as good as" some one else. It is always easy to reply that within the majority group there are many variations; that in the white community the Scandinavians may sometimes be regarded as "not as good as" the British; the French-Canadians regarded as not as good as the "France French." Still, no one even in the most prejudiced northern city could escape the fact that the relation of the Negro to the white towers above any special problem of subdivisions of prestige within the majority group itself. A second fundamental point of similarity relates to the fact that economic, educational, and other advantages are regarded as "too good" for the members of the rejected group, and that therefore, whatever the origins of the situation, a circular relation is established between primitiveness of outlook (lack of education) and on the other hand social status. Many in India have regarded the Harijan as not needing any special access to a higher walk of life. It would be too good for him; it was something which was beyond his potential anyway.

The pressure of modern Indian humanitarian and progressive thought has of course all been in favor of the elevation of the lower castes. One cannot say that the same degree of unanimity exists in the United States, although in general it could be said that thoughtful people in both countries have come to agree that discrimination is an injury both to the rejected and to the majority group involved, that the nature of the democratic process is interfered with, and that the economic and other cultural contributions of the minority

group cannot be effectively used for the benefit of all unless
the more rigid forms of seclusion are abrogated.

Here, however, a very large difference in feeling can be
defined. Untouchability has no exact equivalent in the Western world. One thinks not only of handshaking, which may
take place between whites and Negroes even though equality
by no means exists, but also of routine and casual processes,
such as, for example, giving a tip, which involve the touching
of hands. We may be dealing with status differences but not
with an aversion to physical contact in quite the same sense.
The Negro may enter the white man's home, he may care
for him, make him comfortable; he may, as servant, be physically close to him. This is not permitted to the Harijan.

The attitude from which the concept of untouchability has
sprung appears to be related on the one hand to physical
filth and on the other hand to ceremonial uncleanness. Those
who handle the bodies and excreta of animals, those who
deal directly with dirt, as in the case of the laundryman and
the sweeper, are subjected to a sharp exclusion even though
in some cases a certain degree of technical skill is permitted
in these operations. On the other hand, many of the exclu-
sions are clearly related not to physical dirt but to ceremonial ideas. We may illustrate here from the role of the hog in
the eating habits of the Jews and the Muslims. It would be
difficult to demonstrate that ham need physically be filthy in
any sense which would not be true of fish, chicken, or other
meat. Nevertheless, the hog is unclean and the food rituals of
the Jews and the Muslims have standardized the conception
of an uncleanness which is here ceremonial rather than literally physical.

One might go on to an uncleanness of a still higher order
in the sense that a sin is held to leave a sort of ceremonial
uncleanness on him who commits it, or in the sense that
even the thinking of certain thoughts may make the soul or

even the body of the individual unclean. At a rather primitive level of social organization, all these different types of uncleanness are poorly disentangled. They are almost equivalent. That which is unclean physically conveys its uncleanness to the word which describes it and even by the utterance of the word may contaminate the body or soul of the speaker. One thinks of the washing out of the mouth of the child who has been guilty of profanity, and one thinks of the ceremonial use of water, as in baptism, as an expression, an "outward and visible sign" of the process by which inward sin or guilt is washed away. Certainly at the level of the Indian peasant there is nothing surprising about the fact that uncleanness is not a very well analyzed quality.

Now I think it might probably be argued without undue stressing of the point that the untouchable in India is not only low in status and "by right" excluded from certain educational, occupational, and other privileges, but is *unclean* in the eyes of the intermediate and higher castes in a sense which would not be true of the patterns of prejudice which are familiar to us in the Western world. Whether this makes the problem more difficult to deal with is of course another story. It certainly adds to the emotional loading. Mukerjee notes: "The upper-caste persons expressed their view during the course of our discussion that the Chamars, Pasis, and Dusadhs are considered low because their food habits and mode of life were not liked. It was said that low-caste men eat the undigested grain which cattle excrete in the dung and the meat of animals which had died in the fields. Low-caste persons have sunk to such degradation through poverty; poverty also leads to vice and prostitution." The question whether the emotional loading of the rejection makes an approach to its resolution more difficult could only be answered by knowing whether the factors which lead to the emotion can be swept away by a sort of shock effect at the same time that the poverty itself is removed.

THE BASIC DYNAMICS OF SOCIAL PREJUDICE

However, all modern studies of prejudice—Indian, American, or otherwise, reveal certain underlying dynamics which I shall try to outline briefly in the following pages.

The "conditioned" prejudice

The term "prejudice" does not as a rule carry the same meaning in reference to *group* attitudes as to *individual* attitudes. When we say, "I dislike Jones and I really don't know why; I suppose I am just prejudiced," this represents a kind of response which may well be due to one disagreeable incident in the past or even to an incident which did not concern Jones himself at all, but someone who looked like him. It may be that in early childhood we were caught redhanded and given a good shaking by someone who shared some superficial physical attribute with the Jones of today, something like a mustache or stooped shoulders or a long nose. It must be granted that this simple type of carry-over from an earlier sharp experience does occasionally play *some* part in the phenomenon of prejudice. In general it is easily discussed under the heading of the "conditioned response" (just as the dogs in the old St. Petersburg laboratory began to water at the mouth when the sound of the master's footsteps came across the floor, simply because in the past these footsteps had always preceded the presentation of their regular ration of meat).

A certain amount of human prejudice may be due to single dramatic experiences or to recurrent experiences of a very simple sort, involving either gratification or frustration. In these cases we become prejudiced *for* or *against* an individual.

As a matter of fact, this type of very simple acquisition of prejudice has been recently studied by Gregory Razran, with an accurate method for measuring the human salivary response. During the course of a long laboratory session, students read the names of various ethnic groups, such as Italians, Hungarians, Finns, Japanese, Germans, etc. Also, from time to time they were given sandwiches. To them there was no connection between any particular name and the distribution of sandwiches. Actually, however, when a record was made later of the amount of hostility which they expressed toward each of the ethnic groups, it became very evident that those groups which had been mentioned at the same time that sandwiches were administered went up in the social scale as compared with those who were not accompanied by food. This was a simple conditioning effect, a simple association which made some people more easily acceptable. In the same way disagreeable experiences can help make other people less acceptable. I myself found that my preferences for various unfamiliar musical selections were shifted up and down in this extremely irrational fashion because of food administered to me, though I had some sophistication in the experiment and would have thought that I could brace myself against so irrational an effect. Let us summarize and say that the acquisition of prejudice through simple conditioning probably occurs. But it is a little too simple to be given weight as a primary factor in the generation of social prejudice.

Sharing the group outlook

A second considerably more important factor might be described under the terms of the group outlook. The little child learns very early to see through the eyes of mother and father, big brother and big sister, and a little later to take over the neighborhood viewpoint, and within the neighborhood learns that he is, let us say, a Baptist and not a Catholic, a Democrat and not a Republican, very much as he learns that he is of Scottish and not Peruvian descent. Long before he has any clear idea of what is involved, he takes over the outlook of those near him. This outlook is not sharply separated as to facts and feelings. One takes over a global outlook involving a certain way of seeing things and a certain feeling tone associated with this way of viewing the world.

Now inevitably, since one must maintain one's stance in a complicated and difficult world, *our* people are *good* people; they tend to be near us, they satisfy our needs, they are on the whole warm and protective, and it is with them that we must stand if we are to make our way. Those who are outside of this little orbit of the personal world are viewed first with considerable caution and sometimes, if life treats us badly, with actual hostility. We early find, then, the formation of a "we" group and a "they" group, a right group and a wrong group from the point of view of our outlook and our hopes for making out of life what we want it to be. If there is actually no marked hostility between the groups involved, if in fact all groups within the community regardless of race, religion, or standards of living participate in the life of the community, take part in trade, interchange of services, appear at school and church without reference to discrimination, take part in the picnics and frolics, the club affairs; in other words, if there is no exclusiveness, no snob value, no bars-up attitude of any group toward any other, the fact of socially definable groups need not by itself create prejudice.

The point is quite fundamental. It is not from the fact of diversity as such that hostility arises. Hostility appears when once the groups have been differentiated, so that one can see where the line of cleavage lies as regards skin color or religious practice or anything else, and then learns that the people who belong in the out group *do not share those values* which are especially precious to us; if, for example, we are Baptists and they happen to be Catholics, their value system contains much that is not immediately real to us and ours contains much which is not immediately real to them. If we care very much about our values, we may be exclusive toward people who do not fully share these. We now move from the region of nonhostile group separation to the region in which group separation begins to involve feelings of rejection.

Interference and exclusion

There is, however, another step to be taken. It may happen that those who do not share our values actually *interfere* in a direct and obvious way with our pursuit of our own values. This will ordinarily not occur on a large scale under conditions which Americans encounter in the matter of religious affiliation. The worship on Sunday morning in many different churches need not involve any opposition, resistance, vituperation by one group with reference to another. They are simply separate groups worshiping in their separate houses of worship. But let the issue be defined, however, in such a way that the pursuit of what is good, necessary, and valuable by one group *interferes* with the similar pursuit of what is good, necessary, and valuable by another group. Take such a very simple illustration as the marked reduction in the number of jobs that can be filled or the area which can be cultivated as a result of such a social catastrophe as a storm damaging the factories and business district of a city or a flood making most of the land incapable of cultivation. Now ill feeling is likely to arise immediately if it turns out that the availability of jobs or of land depends in any way upon group membership. If, for example, there is a lively organization of the Baptists which gets jobs for its boys under this condition of crisis, it is likely that the Catholics, the Methodists, the Jews, in effect every non-Baptist, will express (along with his admiration for the go-getting qualities of the Baptists) a certain amount of hostility for the unfairness of the whole operation. In the same way, if a politically astute leader manages to get boats and farm implements quickly to the region of the land which is still capable of cultivation so that only those of a particular political party have land which they can cultivate before too late in the season, there is likely to be intense feeling on the part of other political groups that a march has been stolen upon them.

We have begun with relatively trivial illustrations. Let us expand this until we have the scene in which only the members of one religious, racial, or ethnic group can obtain special favors or privileges, particularly such as admission to educational institutions or admission to apprenticeships which give them in course of time desirable skilled trades to practice. This kind of exclusiveness does exist all over the civilized world to some extent, and alert groups who care something about democracy are forever fighting such issues; e.g., issues as to whether Jews are to be kept out of certain clubs or Negroes out of certain universities. "Social tension" is obviously present on both sides of the coin, on the side of those who try to break in and on the side of those who try to keep them out.

The sin of being "different"

There is, however, a still higher stage to which this type of development usually leads. Not only do we sense another group as interfering with our own progress; not only do we sense the situation is unjust; we develop from our own sense of immediate and obvious rightness the conviction that members of these other groups chronically and permanently take advantage of us. We thus raise what is a local or temporary hostility into a general and permanent one. Suppose that the Baptists think that the Jews take advantage on a particular occasion, or suppose that the French-Canadians think that the English-speaking Canadians take advantage on another occasion. This could be patched up or even obliterated by disappearance of the issue over which the struggle has taken shape. Actually it does not work that way. Usually a picture of the interfering group becomes standardized during this period of tension. "They are the kind of people who take such advantages." "They are always doing this." "Never trust a Jew." "Hit him again; he's Irish." "The Armenians are like that." And so on, with phrases which could be run to the hundreds, indicating the sense of chronic unfairness, unscrupulousness, and even moral depravity of those whose ways differ from our own.

But it is not only immediate and obvious material advantage which is at stake. Oftentimes subtle matters of feeling play a large part, too. I well remember how savage the denunciation of a certain foreign group became when it had been pointed out that they sat on the lawn and ate watermelons on the Fourth of July. This was undignified, crude, inappropriate, unpatriotic, ultimately subhuman behavior. This is an esthetic rejection; a sense of the boorishness and inadequacy of people who do not practice those ways which we learned in childhood to be the appropriate ways of a gentleman and a lady.

One of the deep stereotypes of Indians (to whom the daily bath has *religious* significance) is that Englishmen don't keep clean. One of the deep stereotypes of Englishmen (who have more water) is that Indians don't keep clean. It is only necessary to remember that the bathing habits of a people in a tropical country vary with all sorts of circumstances, including their pocketbooks, the kind of clothing they wear, the kind of work they do, etc. These are examples of the continuous petty irritations which make the out-group not only an out-group and not only at times a threat to us, but a constant irritation through its want of feeling; that is, the want of the kind of feeling which we regard as natural. We might quote F. H. Allport's phrase regarding the man whose ways constantly run counter to ours and who therefore upsets our expectations: "He breaks our habit." Thus we have, so far, two bases for hostility: first, the direct and obvious interference with our goals which we might perhaps summarize under the word competitiveness, and second, the matter of esthetic annoyance or nonparticipation in our own form of correct conduct.

Formation of stereotypes

But there is still one higher phase in the elaboration of prejudice. Just as we weave together, spiderlike, a beautiful structure of our own essential rightness, decency, and adequacy for living, the capacity of our own people for high ideals, for hard work, for progress, initiative, self-reliance, and nobility, so we can expect any human group to develop its own sense of basic rightness. It may have to kowtow; it may have to apologize for living with reference to others around it who have some sort of superior status; but it has ways of getting even. It has ways of saying to itself in its own heart, "We know our own ways are good." Now let us imagine this sense of the rightness of our own group encountering what we would call boorishness or crudeness in the behavior of others. We come to a time when other people are simply chronically bad. They are chronically lazy, shiftless, dishonest, crooked, dirty, mean, violent, or savage. Compare the words cruel, dirty, and fanatical applied by Hindus in Ahmedabad and Lucknow to Muslims. One speaks in these connections of the prevalence of "stereotypes"; that is, fixed clichés or standardized epithets which are applied by members of one group to members of another group. The fact then that stereotypes are essentially moral and that we end up our sorry story of prejudice by assigning moral inferiority to our competitors should be sufficient to suggest that explanations in terms of single shock experiences or those of conditioned responses are not likely to be altogether adequate as explanations. In particular, the complex structure of the way in which we perceive ourselves in our own rightness and the complex structure of perception of other groups in competition with ourselves and professing ways different from our own should carry us to recognition of the fact that we find prejudice extremely difficult to overcome.

As a matter of fact, when simple conditioning is involved we can usually reverse the process of attitude formation very easily. If you build up a liking for music or a dislike of the Portuguese as a result of conditioning, it is relatively simple to discontinue the process by which the association was formed; relatively simple, for example, to connect the original music with disagreeable things and the pictures or names of the Portuguese with agreeable things, and put an end to prejudice. Actually one encounters no such easy solution.

I know, for example, a very thoughtful social scientist who has worked intelligently and cooperatively with Negroes at all levels from stevedores to professors for a great many years. He has had practically no disagreeable experiences with Negroes in the last twenty years; even in the matter of reading or motion picture portrayals of Negroes the great mass of material has been favorable. His daily associations with Negroes are at a high level of mutual understanding. He nevertheless encounters both in his waking fantasies and in his dreams a great deal which represents Negroes in an unfavorable light; and he finds as he looks over his son's shoulder and sees a comic strip of the Negro that the old infantile stereotypes and hostilities are still there. We are certainly dealing with a very complicated phenomenon.

The psychoanalytic approach

This is one reason why we have often been told that the psychology of the unconscious as utilized by the psychoanalyst is the only adequate way of understanding such responses, particularly understanding the enormous hostilities which often arise when irrational prejudices are involved. There have, in point of fact, been several excellent psychoanalytic approaches to prejudice in recent years, and there can be no doubt whatever that the essential soundness of the psychoanalytic approach to prejudice has been well defined, though documentation of the case is limited to a few points.

We might choose as a single illustration a point which has been made by three different types of psychoanalytic research: (1) by a study of anti-Semitism among patients undergoing psychoanalysis in New York; (2) by a study of students at the University of California with very intense anti-Semitic prejudices; and (3) by a study of Communist Party members in the Eastern Seaboard states who in spite of their philosophical Marxism retain considerable hostility to Jews. In all of these cases it is apparent that two factors are operating unconsciously: first, the group against which prejudice is directed, in this case the Jews, are conceived to be obstacles toward the achievement of goals desired by the individual patients. Members of the middle class who have made their way in economic competition despite great difficulty, and who think of themselves as having a certain position to defend, may be hostile to minority groups and lower economic groups of all sorts who are rising in the social scale as likely to dispossess them from a precarious position. In the second place there is a strong tendency under conditions of guilt (and the sense of inferiority attendant upon the whole middle-class pressure for success, stability, propriety, acceptability) to project upon others their own feeling of inadequacy, guilt, and hostility. Consequently under conditions of stress they are likely to assign to Jews or members of minority groups such traits as aggressiveness, hostility, uncleanness, and all that represents the syndrome in themselves against which they are unconsciously struggling.

It may well be asked whether this reference to the irrational in the field of prejudice does not leave out one essential factor, namely, the possibility that there may be some solid and logical basis for certain prejudices. There may be a "germ of truth" in the stereotype, in the arrogation of sin, dirt, or contemptibility to some group which is rejected. On this point, of course, the data are not all in, but a number of studies such as one by Lapiere at Stanford University have strongly questioned the adequacy of this approach. Lapiere found, for example, that whereas it was "common knowledge" in California that Armenians were financially "irresponsible," the actual arduous job of looking up credit standings and bank accounts indicated that the Armenians were financially a dependable group with a good record. In so far as the stereotype may be factually founded, there are likewise many instances in which a circular relation has been set up between the stereotype and the behavior; the very belief that Negroes are shiftless is likely to be one of the things which drives them into shiftless economic behavior (i.e., they can't get steady jobs). This is by no means an attempt to prove that no factual basis can *ever* exist for group prejudice, a ridiculous proposition on its face. It is rather an attempt to show that the phenomenon of mutual blame, mutual sense of moral responsibility, superiority, the sense of the essential untrustworthiness, boorishness, or moral depravity of other groups may occur *without* a factual core. This is the only point upon which we are at present laying emphasis.

A study by S. K. Mitra at Patna University in India presents us with an interesting comparison between the phenomenon of the prejudiced personality among Hindu boys and the phenomenon of the prejudiced personality as it has been described to us by the University of California study. Mitra's investigation, emphasizing the Rorschach method, appears to indicate that among the boys entertaining the greatest prejudice towards the Muslims there is the greatest tendency to unconscious reaction to guilt and consequent projection of guilt upon members of out-groups. The data appear to be comparable to the California data on anti-Semitism.

Control of prejudice by participation

Over and above all the mechanisms which have been described which tend to show why prejudice is bound to arise under conditions of social identification of contrasting groups, and under conditions of one or another sort of competition between these groups, there arises the question: Can so complex a process be reversed? Can prejudice be controlled? Specifically, is there anything within the reach of the government of India, its universities, its schools, its press and radio, its indirect pressures applied to its officials in the making of local decisions, its guarantee of jobs to all, or anything else in its whole public program which can be consistently depended upon to produce a *marked reduction* in intergroup prejudice?

In attempting an answer, I should like immediately to quote a remark that Kurt Lewin made to me: "It isn't enough that people should know one another; they should know one another on terms of *equal status*." White men and Negroes overcome prejudice to some extent by the removal of misinformation, but the *big* results have come from working together on common projects—like fighting together in the same brigades.

Is this working together in terms of equal status feasible in the Indian scene? Much thinking is being done in India today as to ways in which newspapers and textbooks may be freed of antiminority group expressions. This is all to the good. The primary problem, however, is not to remove unfavorable forms of knowledge or pseudoknowledge, nor even to replace these with factual material of a sort which will encourage genuine understanding, but to implement all this by *personal contact on terms of equal status*. Whatever the textbooks and newspapers can do is trivial compared with what could be done by close interpersonal association.

The minute that one begins to think through this problem, one realizes that Hindus and Muslims who have been physically close to one another (in adjoining houses or on two sides of the same street) may be those who have been inflamed against one another with the greatest passion, just as in the United States many of our most furious brawls have been stimulated by too much closeness, too much acquaintance at the level where people become more and more aware of the basic difference in their values and the basic competitive roles they play with respect to one another. It is *not* sufficient that people should become "well acquainted"; it is essential that they be acquainted in terms of equal status, neither group being able to enjoy a position of snob value or moral superiority with respect to the other.

The only practical way to implement a program like this is therefore in terms of a categorical and uncompromising insistence on the part of government in all its branches that educational, occupational, and other facilities should be available to all simply as citizens of the nation. At the same time, however, a huge task awaits the government in regard to all new steps which are being undertaken. Members of all castes and communities must be brigaded together in common enterprises. In India there are not only Hindu activities and Muslim activities but even Brahmin activities and Kayasth activities for which members of each group put up their money and through which they take care of group benefits (just as we would through fraternal orders or service clubs). This is all the more reason for recognizing that for national unity a redefinition of goals is essential in terms of the participation of all in the pursuit of common goals. It is the sharing of every problem of India, large or small, which will enable members of all communities and castes to respect one another for the individual contribution which each can make.

IV

PROSPECTS OF

SOCIAL HEALTH

I I

India's ways of solving her problems

I hope it has become clear by now that "social tensions" are not minor ripples in some remote little pool aside from the main stream of India's—or any other country's—existence, but are symptomatic of the whole of its national life, an expression of the deepest forces expressive of cleavage and the struggle for unity. Social tensions, then, cannot as a rule be effectively treated "symptomatically"; the only therapy is a therapy which looks deeply at the patient's very life—into the nation's capacity to solve its fundamental problems. Aside, therefore, from the purely symptomatic suggestions offered now and then throughout this report, there seems to be a need for a broader view of three things: (1) the capacity of India to solve her problem (the theme of the present chapter); (2) the help which India requests of the United States (Chapter 12); and (3) the present and future response to this request (Chapter 13).

ABORIGINAL HARDIHOOD

As regards the constructive steps of today, the first question to be asked about the betterment of life in India is whether the people, the basic human stock, is capable of a rapid and fundamental change. We shall attempt to answer this question by looking at the relation of the stock to the culture.

The pre-Aryan population which was conquered by the

Aryan-speaking peoples was a dark-skinned population, with its own rich and complex traditions. Those groups which have not accepted Hinduism and have not been brought within the Hindu system of ideas, and on the other hand have not been incorporated within Islam, are called *aboriginal*. The term "aboriginal" in India is approximately equivalent to the term "preliterate" as it is used in our Western tradition. We think of the American Indians, for example, insofar as they live according to their tradition, as a preliterate people because they never developed written language. We think in the same way of the Fiji Islanders, the Eskimo, the Tanala of Madagascar, and dozens of other preliterate tribes identified and studied by anthropologists. In India, however, there are twenty-five million aboriginals. They are the original raw, sturdy stuff of which the Indian people of today are made, but they are outside the circle of Hinduism.

What sort of people are they? Well, in the first place, most of those whom we met appeared to be rugged and vigorous people, active, competent in the execution of their traditional crafts; also, in the groups we met, warm, humorous, full of zest and *joie de vivre*. In spite of the fact that Hindu society has frequently drawn them into its own caste system, usually at the lowest caste level, and that the British found all sorts of devices for luring them from their forests and extracting taxes from them, most of the aboriginals today have remained quite self-sufficient and are no more excited about becoming Hindus than, let us say, the Indians of the Pueblos are excited about becoming Christians.

They are of so many different subcultural traditions, talk so many tongues, that generalizations about them are likely to be rather absurd. A few cautious ones will, however, be attempted. In the first place, there is enough strength and hardihood in the aboriginals to put to flight at one blow the conception that India is necessarily an unhealthy place in which to live, that its climate or food or vermin or disease constitute some sort of fatal obstacle to effective and joyous living. It also pays tribute to the obvious fact that malnutrition does not have to exist even under the primitive conditions of agriculture practiced in India. In the third place, the aboriginals are often eager to learn what new things Western science and technology have to offer, and their leaders are as keen and sensitive with regard to the contribution of the West as one is likely to find anywhere.

All these are among our reasons for believing that the many types of physical and social disease which characterize Indian life are functions of a historical process and not functions of any biological material of which the Indian stock is made. The Indian stock is essentially the aboriginal stock upon which, however, all the complex forces of migration, conquest, and westernization have done their work. It is a fair guess that insofar as disease and malnutrition appear in India they are functions of historical and cultural processes which are removable or reversible.

LEADERSHIP

The second question is about leadership. Does India have the leaders that can guide her through today's difficulties? Can India solve her own problems?

I believe that a fair acquaintance with the men and women who govern India's affairs, whether at a political, economic, literary, artistic, educational, or cultural level, will convince the observer that India is capable of solving her own problems. I believe that this will be just as evident whether one talks with the Prime Minister, the members of the Cabinet, Speaker of the House, the Prime Ministers or other officials of the various state governments, civil servants, Vice-Chancellors of the universities, heads of secondary schools, or with doctors, lawyers, and businessmen. One finds an educational level which is high, a level of cultivation, clarity of speech, articulateness, and reasonableness of thought which certainly augurs well for India's capacity to work through her amazing new period of trying her wings and achieving essential independence.

One must at the same time recognize, as we tried to indicate briefly in another connection, that many of India's problems require solution at the middle level rather than at the top level. A genius for middle-level leadership, for leadership among the small educational and professional and business enterprises, for example, is a characteristic phase of the family, caste, and village type of group functioning which has so many times been noted. India is no country of wild individualists, each bent upon rocking the boat in his own way. It is true that there is a great deal of tension between caste and caste, family and family. But it is also true that these things have been there a long time, and that Indians know something about these realities and how to cope with them. It is true that India is essentially an orderly, stable, well-structured social organism. The very nature of this external stability is one of the reasons for the wild violence of the breakdown known as riots when once the stable and orderly modes of living are lost, since the young are not trained in controlled, organized forms of expressing aggression. Frontiersmen living as individualists could never be capable of the sort of frenzied chaos of violence which is shown by men in whom order, destiny, and tradition are as deeply ingrained as in the Indian population.

The achievement of working through a feasible Constitution under the conditions of pressure from the British and the Pakistanis in 1947 has been equaled or surpassed in the 1951 national elections in which over half of all the qualified voters took part—city and country, north and south, men and women, old and young, and above all literate and illiterate, taking part largely on the basis of a reasoned and articulate consideration of the issues, particularly their own self-interest

and that of the economic and caste groups which they represented. The whole experiment seems to suggest strongly that
India is capable of effective and rapidly forward-moving governmental activity.

The same is true in the areas of engineering, medicine,
and public health, and above all mass education, including
adult education, to which the central government and the
state governments are working out their own solutions. It
must be remembered that the huge industrial expansion of
India today with its engineering and agricultural developments is primarily financed out of the poverty of India's
village masses. In general, it is from the land that the major
revenue is achieved, and of course this means basically from
the tiller of the soil. Instead of mass protest, one finds in
general an orderly acceptance of this phenomenon, and that
the capital expenditure necessary for these huge enterprises
is in the long run willingly extracted by the devices which
all over the world we call political democracy. Regarding the
primary question, then, whether India is capable of solving
her own problems, I should say categorically yes.

Of course a great deal depends upon the amount and form
of the capital which is to be used. It is true that there is no
way in which India can raise the essential capital except by
heavy taxation, and above all taxation upon land.

It is true that a considerable portion of this revenue is
spent at present upon military items, partly because of the
tension over Kashmir. There is also no doubt whatever that
a great deal is wasted through premature decisions, through
the borrowing of Western techniques before they are fully
understood—for example, by the attempt to use tractors in
regions where they simply cannot be used, by the importation
of machines which cannot be adequately used or serviced in
view of the shortage of adequate Indian personnel. This kind
of waste is to be taken for granted; and the bureaucratic
attitude, which makes possible decisions at headquarters with-

out roaming forth into the field and seeing how things actually work, inevitably adds to the difficulty.

As important as any of these, however, on the basis of our impressions, would be the operations of the black market in India, not only economically serious in itself but a source of profound suspicion and hostility between one group and another, and between each group and the government. Of even greater importance still are the problems of land reform, debt reduction, public health, education—problems unfortunately beyond my competence to discuss. It is my impression, though, that the outsider's opinion as to whether adequate progress is being made on such issues depends largely on the region of India which he has studied and the speed at which he thinks human beings can move.

TOLERANCE

Another factor in our evaluation of constructive possibilities is the almost universal tolerance which goes with the very fact of being an Indian. The nature of Indian life is to "live and let live." Family system and caste system, oppressive though they may be, are in their essence guarantees that people will move within familiar orbits involving no unpredictable interference or coercion from others. There may be severe pressures applied to the individual to change his behavior, but in general such pressures are applied if he does not accept the general way of life to which the community is committed; and there is no pressure upon the individual to adapt his ways to those required by some group other than his own—least of all by a majority. Individuals who are caught in an unfavorable place in the family situation (for example, younger daughters in ill health, of whom much is expected in marriage which would seem to be an infringement of individual liberties), and in the same way groups like the Harijans who are caught in unfavorable social positions, may have no recourse, no escape. The system is impersonal, merciless, objective. At the same time it is free of the compulsion to tinker with or dominate other people and it is almost entirely free of the basic assumption that one has the obligation, the moral burden to impose superior ways on those of other people.

Whatever its limitations, then, tolerance is a force which can be effectively used in Indian life to overcome group hostilities. A hostility which has once developed on the basis of the deep cleavages which exist between groups and the fact that one group seems to another to have perpetrated an act of violence against it, as in the case of the Muslim-Sikh relationship, may take a very long time to heal; but those types of mutual suspicion which are based simply upon the feeling that the culture of others is basically different from or inferior to one's own do not seem in India to be necessarily likely to predispose to hostility as such. At the village level people get to know one another; and, except for gross cases like that of the Harijans, reach to one another across the gulfs that social organization contrives.

We have constantly been asked as to the mode of reconciliation of two primary facts about Indian life: first, its essential passivity, nonviolence, faith in long range, quiet forces of nature and of society without need to resort to the methods of strife and revolution: everything that might be summarized in Gandhi's conception of conquest by spiritual rather than material power; on the other hand, the enormous violence of those outbreaks which have been associated with disturbed relations between caste and communities. Not only are we thinking now of the carnage of the great riots at about the time of the partition of India, but of the smaller riots, the not infrequent killings which have continued here and there against the backdrop of some decades of intermittent, unorganized strife. One thinks also of the frequent hostilities which develop between castes at the village level and of the kinds of village hostility described above in connection with our visit to Sonwarsa.

We are not at all sure of our answer. But our impression is that the violence of physical encounter which expresses itself in the riots themselves is to a considerable extent a function of the fact that nonviolence is a general practice of Indian life. Boys are not in general taught to fight, even with their fists. One can occasionally see the Indian boys of today under the influence of historical teaching going through maneuvers with sticks, pretend-guns, just as they would in the West. But this is sporadic and casual and never comes to grips with the organized problem of hostility of which American gang life is an extreme expression. (Cf. Chapter 4.)

Americans learn how to fight, the males with their fists, the females mainly with their tongues (though with some slapping and hair-pulling). As they get into the elementary school age period they learn highly organized exchanges of violence, whether in the form of boxing or wrestling or in the form of organized competitive group games like football. Then there is all through this a constant preoccupation with sidearms, machine guns, and the make-believe world of cops and robbers, followed frequently by service of actual participation in the National Guard or auxiliary police or some other formalized expression of group force.

Contrast this with Indian life in which there is practically no learning to fight at all. There comes a time now in which the whole bottom has dropped out of life through the loss of land and the destruction of one's future. The pattern of disorganized hostility—savage, distraught, confused, blind striking out against those who are conceivably the aggressors, the obstacles to the fulfillment of one's life—leads by imperceptible gradations into sheer crazy violence. This is often abetted in the critical moment by the organized fighting tactics of the Sikhs, who had a military tradition and knew in the time of crisis how to use weapons. From this point of view we have disorganized Hindu fighting and organized Sikh fighting against organized Muslim fighting, the Hindus very greatly out-numbering the other two groups but representing by far the lowest level of organized aggression. We do not believe therefore that a basic conflict between nonviolence and violence exists, nor that there is any great paradox about the outbreaks of savagery associated with the upheaval of the partition of India.

COLOR

A fourth fundamental factor working to control social cleavages and hostilities in India is the sense that physical type is of no consequence and offers no barrier to good will or effective group action; particularly dramatic is the illustration of color. Despite the fact that the Vedic hymns seem to say that the color of the Dasas, their enemies, is inferior, the fact remains that color, practically speaking, disappeared as a functional value in Indian life until the time of the British. The British, of course, by having their exclusive clubs, hotels, and social centers and by excluding all non-Europeans from many vital functions, succeeded in creating much color consciousness among Indians. In spite of all this, however, it is extraordinary how little attention is given to color as such anywhere today in India, whether at top level or at the bottom. Thus, among university scholars one finds oneself accepted as a person, not as a white man. As far as one can see, one is accepted as a person just as one might be accepted as a Japanese or as an Egyptian, just as the Indians themselves sitting around the table will vary from what we would call very light to what we would call very dark and will ignore the fact. Color just doesn't count among the intellectuals.

Taking this university attitude as one extreme, let me go to the other extreme: Stopping in an aboriginal village in Bihar, I had a little talk through an interpreter with a middle-aged farmer who had helped a little bit in making things easier for the men of the refugee camp nearby. Some of the things in the conversation suggested to me that he did not know that I was from a foreign country, or perhaps even might have thought that I was just a member of the party of university people who had come along to survey the refugee situation. So I said to the interpreter: "Ask him whether I am a Frenchman, a Russian, or a Japanese." He looked kindly at me for a moment, then said to the interpreter, "The color that people have God gives them." He gave a little time for this to sink in, by way of indicating that no conclusions whatever could be drawn from the fact that I was lighter of skin than he was. He ruminated for a moment, and then said, "The man does not come from this immediate neighborhood, not even from Ranchi, twenty miles away. He comes from further away, perhaps from Calcutta." This was enough to show me that one did not easily divide humankind into two types which could be summarized in the words "we Indians" and "those foreigners."

I nevertheless was not quite willing to let the whole matter drop. He went on talking. Some hints were offered that I might be an American; he certainly had some hunches about what Americans were like. Finally he said, with a laugh, "You know there were some Americans camped not far from here. They called us the wild men (jungle men)." Then with a chuckle broadening into a laugh, "But we said to them, 'No, it is you that are the wild men.'" Maybe he was right.

Perhaps we might summarize this general factor negatively as a factor of absence of snobbishness as to color or national pride, and positively in terms of a general tendency to accept people regardless of the divisions and snob values based on physical traits which play so large a part in our own social classification.

RELIGION

The fifth factor which we might stress here as constructive if we are careful in our definitions could be regarded as an aspect of religion. We should be among the first to agree that much that goes under the name of religion is blind and superstitious manipulation of the unseen environment, an attempt by magical means or by threats and invocations to control that which one cannot control by reason, judgment, and foresight. The fact remains that in religion in general and in Indian religion in particular there is an enormous amount which indicates the essential brotherhood of man, the essential dignity of all persons, the essential right of all individuals to receive the same opportunities, educational, economic, political, and social. If it be argued that Indian life before the time of the British was full of arbitrary social exclusiveness, a matter upon which a great deal of scholarly argument has been spent, the fact remains that during the last 150 years, partly by a reinvestigation of the structure of Vedic society and partly by a study of Western liberal and progressive literature, Indian thought has been saturated with humanitarian and progressive values which have frequently assumed in India a highly religious form. The social reform movement initiated about eighty years ago as the Aryasamaj and the earlier reform movement known as Brahmosamaj— both quite conspicuous social, intellectual reform movements —have been movements originating within Hinduism, and have embodied much of the idea of the sacred and the idea of the cosmic and the divine which characterize all Hindu philosophy. When a Harijan woman who has struggled devotedly to make her home clean, attractive, lovely, and a tribute to human dignity says "The dear God should have all our thanks," she is responding in the same spirit of piety which a Pennsylvania Quaker or a Wisconsin Lutheran would express.

It was by no means a political *tour de force* that led Gandhi in his long years of humanitarian struggle in South Africa and then in his own country to emphasize the religious values which bound all humanity together and which, when thus bound together, could serve as a battering ram with which to drive out the British imperial system. A study of Gandhi's *Autobiography* and public addresses as well as the numerous personal acts of devotion, self-control, and pietism will surely convince the reader that it was because he felt very close to the Divine and felt that the Divine was the holding strand which kept all human beings together in brotherhood and aspiration that he was able to lead an effective nonresistance movement, an effective movement toward political self-liberation in the name of human freedom and dignity. Those who look for an emancipation of India in terms of a cold, economically oriented struggle for a higher standard of living will overlook the very rich and deep roots which a religious struggle has in India.

It is true that many, including the Prime Minister, do not talk this language. It is entirely true that he and many others regard these as archaic appeals to irrational formulas. But reporting on our impressions of India, we are ready to say that the use of religion in the sense in which we now use it, to mean a deep cosmically oriented concern for the meaning of human life, is one of the fundamental appeals which drive Indian life forward and integrate it with the humanitarianism and idealism of the Western tradition. We encountered many Indians who had no organized religion. Pars Ram's data from Aligarh revealed some 20 per cent among both the Muslims and the Hindus who reject all formal religion. All of these points and many more like them can be made. It can well be argued that religion as an organizing tendency will fade in India under the impact of science and technology. All of these points do not, however, negate the essential reality which we are trying to stress, namely, the fact that in the India of the next decade or two religion, in the sense of reverence for the cosmic drama represented by human life, the inherent divinity and dignity of human personality, the ultimate spiritual sanctions to be found for everyday ethics, is a fundamental factor in guiding the transition toward the elimination of social hostilities and the integration of a national life.

BASIC EDUCATION

The sixth factor which we would stress in the rehabilitation and unification of India is "basic education." The phrase refers primarily to a system of educational thought and practice associated with the name of the great educator and philosopher, Dr. Zakir Husain. Under the influence of progressive education in the Western world as represented by Pestalozzi and the nineteenth century educational reformers in Germany, and by Horace Mann, and especially by John Dewey and the progressive education of the twentieth century in the United States, Dr. Zakir Husain as a leader in Indian education began to think through the question of developing a curriculum and mode of study really suited to childhood in India. His thinking in this direction during the late twenties and the thirties profoundly influenced Gandhi, who gave his huge support to the conception. At times it is thought of as Gandhi's idea, pure and simple. Actually it had the support not only of Gandhi but of a number of well-trained and far-seeing educators, many of whom served during the thirties to spread and develop the fundamental ideas and to put them into practice. There was a period when all the leaders of basic education were jointly involved in the struggle against the British, and many of them under arrest, with the consequent retardation of the movement until after World War II. Since the partition and independence of India, basic education has been everywhere a prominent feature of Indian thought, notably in the Uttar Pradesh, the Madhya Pradesh, the Bombay state, and Bihar. We were able to observe several basic schools and talk with their leaders, to form some idea as to the variations in attitude and spirit in which this work is carried forward. Therefore we shall give not only a general view of Dr. Zakir Husain's conception of basic education but some idea of the diversity of practice as represented in different schools.

The fundamental thought in basic eduction is that the child, in accordance with his maturity, his understanding, and his strength, should share in all the fundamental enterprises which characterize the group with which he is growing up and within which he hopes ultimately to find a self-sustaining place. The child will therefore learn at a very early age the meaning of seeds and of the process of planting them in the ground, how to water them, how to fertilize them, how to weed; he will learn very early the care of animals, he will come to love them, will protect them against disease and injury, will understand how to prevent their running away, will understand the use of their fleece or their milk and the ways in which human beings make use of their domesticated animals. The child will understand how buildings are made; will from an early age help in preparing or carrying materials which the builders may use.

Especially important, he will understand very early the nature of clothing, the kinds of clothing suitable to the climate in which he lives, the need for preparation of clothing adequate to cover his own body. He will therefore, in a country where cotton is cheap and easily available, learn how to grow and how to card and comb cotton, how to draw it out into thread, how to spin, and how to weave. Using the limited and inexpensive equipment which is feasible in a poor country, he will therefore learn all the processes involved in making for himself the little cotton garments which he wears. This will mean that in many basic schools children will be found not only in the fields and gardens but working a half hour or more per day, in accordance with their age, at the preparation of their own clothing.

Gandhi, of course, is associated with spinning. That aspect of this whole process which Gandhi publicized is an aspect of a revolution against an industrial civilization and an empire built upon the forcing of industrial products upon an impoverished public. This however was not the essential point in the development of basic education. The bare fact is that Indian children cannot afford an education at all unless they themselves are to share in a responsible way in the tasks which make such an education possible. It *is* possible to operate a basic school in which the children do some planting, weeding, watering, ploughing, animal husbandry, cotton weaving and spinning. It is possible for such a school to operate for a year on a few rupees per child, an incredibly small amount of government support, simply because all the other operations are carried out by the teachers and the students.

At the same time, economy is not the sole reason for all this. The primary reason is the belief that if children are to be prepared for a life which they are fully to share, they might as well begin sharing that life when they are little, when they are full of impulses to share. In our own world we find children constantly wanting somehow to share in the big grown-up world but unable to manage the complicated gadgets which grownups have to manage. The children are likely therefore to be given "busy work"; they are likely in a progressive school to make a paper May basket for Aunt Susie; and Aunt Susie will be pleased to be remembered. But this has little functional relation to the child's own basic interests or his own desire to understand and grow into the operations of the group. Basic education means learning participation in the group.

At the same time, of course, the basic school gives the child the linguistic, literary, scientific, mathematical, musical, and other materials of the culture to which he belongs. Typically there is integration between the practical values and the scientific values as one finds them meaningful at the village level. For example, a science teacher at one great basic education center has been working on the chemistry of cow dung (a generally used fuel) to find out to what extent fuel values and fertilizing values can be chemically separated into two different products. One finds that the study of plants, animals, and the stars are all brought into relation to the child's eager questions and in relation to the larger, more philosophical interests of adolescents or adults. One finds that the sharp separation between pure science learned today and applied science carried into execution tomorrow is largely nonexistent. Children's questions are answered as they come up, answered by the science teacher or whoever is capable of answering them, and practical applications for the life of the farm and school are immediately evident insofar as an answer can really be found.

It is fundamental in the conception of basic education that one uses one's eyes and ears and sense of touch, that one manipulates, gives one's intelligence to the understanding, the discovery, the application of the laws and principles inherent in the material that nature gives us. Consequently one is preparing all the time for the village life from which one comes and to which one returns. One of the great tragedies of Indian life over the centuries has been the disappearance of her best village boys (more recently, both boys and girls) into the world of the universities through the funnel which leads into scientific, professional, technical, or business activity in the cities, to the permanent loss of the village. This is one of the primary reasons why the village population is frequently hostile to the education of the young. One has good reason to be hostile, having seen over the generations what this means in loss of human material—often the best human material. An essential aim of basic education is to guarantee that boys and girls become effective leaders in the village life from which they spring.

The educational process is conceived partly in individual, partly in group terms. Individuals learn no competitive relations one to another in the course of their basic education. They need not be given gold stars nor names on the blackboard. They need not strive to outdo others. Their task day by day, year by year, is to learn and to be glad in what they learn. There is plenty of room for individualizing of experience at times in a child's development. One little boy at one of the Ashrams hidden away in a tiny village on the west coast simply *painted*, day after day, because that was the thing most fulfilling to him—mostly he painted the animals of the forest. It would not follow that inevitably he would continue year after year to do this, be a painter and nothing more. On the contrary, the whole idea of experimentation, the whole idea of trying one thing and another to see what is best, is a part of the essence of this whole flexible approach. It appears to a Western observer that perhaps the approach, instead of being "competitive" or, on the other hand, "cooperative," is really neither the one nor the other but, rather, "individualistic" in a sense; that is, the child undergoing such education is simply preparing for his own future life in his own village rather than developing habits of outdoing his competitor or of group action with his fellows. There seems in fact to be some reason for doubt whether group thinking in the solution of problems is a primary aim.

When the educational work has been carried through the whole period represented by elementary and intermediate education, one goes forward into what is called "post-basic education," at the college level. There is now active discussion of the establishment of a basic university using the same essential methods and including not only arts but sciences and even a medical school. At a level of such boldness of thinking it is clear that the leaders hope for a process of group discovery through which India may be enabled to find completely new solutions for her problems, and that training in group thinking will have to become paramount.

Even without training in group discovery, an essential part of the whole basic approach has been the acceptance of all human beings in one fellowship. One sees on the walls of an Ashram portraits of Moses, Zoroaster, Mohammed, Jesus, Confucius, along with Buddha and Gandhi; in the early morning services one hears the literature, the hymns, and the prayers of many great faiths. Gandhi himself and all those who have expressed the spirit of basic education have been ardent believers in the oneness of the human family. Basic education therefore is profoundly concerned with intergroup tolerance and with an ideal which is broadly human.

ADULT EDUCATION

Seventh in our list of constructive forces is "adult education." In some parts of India, notably in the Delhi province just outside of Delhi, every village receives the benefit of modern techniques to convey a knowledge of reading and writing to every adult citizen. The 300 villages in the Delhi province, for example, all receive periodic visits from a sound truck together with an eager team which sets up a sort of county fair and field day with competitive sports and other displays of children's painting and creative work and typical agricultural prize-winning products. It then goes on to put on a play which in the place of the traditional plays from the Indian epics shows the struggle between wisdom and foolishness in the agricultural and educational problems of today. Adult education, learning to read and write Hindi, is a normal part of the circuit-riding activity of these adult education caravans. They are not *limited* solely to the reading program, but it is reading which is the core of the whole endeavor. In many other parts of India these adult education caravans are similarly effective, some of them under the state governments, some in private hands.

Hindi is not a difficult language to learn to read and write, and progress is rapid. In general, all castes work together and although for the most part it is a matter of the men and older boys, there are sometimes some women included in the program. As in everything else, adult education is held back by the lack of facilities. One encounters for example a single lantern hanging to a hook on the side of a barn, illuminating the Hindi characters on a large chart for twenty-five men and boys who wearily and sleepily struggle to make out a few letters with their accompanying sounds while the jackals in the field beyond howl in competition with the voice of the teacher.

Everywhere in India, as in most parts of the world, learning in school is conceived rather largely as a process of pumping information into the accepting mind of the learner. The children usually sit in rows, or, if a visitor comes in, they stand in rows to greet him; they sit down again and go on patiently with the task, reading and droning in the traditional fashion, learning by rote. It is hardly fair to expect adult education to produce very effective learning when inadequately trained teachers who are themselves tired at night work with a tired and uncomfortable crowd who ought to be in bed after their heavy work. The more remarkable is the rapid spread of the adult education pattern and the rapid increase in the number of adults learning to read Hindi or other tongues.

Some estimates indicate that it will be fifteen years before India will have the force of teachers and the system of school buildings adequate to provide the universal education which the new Constitution envisages.

THE UNIVERSITIES

The eighth factor in the strength of India, as we view the matter, is her universities. I spent a large part of my time in the Indian land in visiting one university after another, and whatever biases and limitations I suffer as an observer are likely to be made peculiarly acute by the fact that my own affiliations and outlooks are university affiliations and outlooks.

The first point that I would stress is that I always felt just as I feel in a university anywhere else in the world. University atmospheres, as far as I am concerned—American, British, or Indian—are essentially alike. Indian universities, then, have many of the strengths which we expect universities to have. Among the first and the most obvious of these strengths is a sense of the continuity and the oneness of human culture, including its literary, esthetic, and scientific aspects. In Indian life one finds universally, I should say, a sense of deep respect both for Indian and for other traditions, a sense that things are to be compared, appreciated, enjoyed, developed, and above all understood, rather than praised or blamed, exalted or maligned. The Indian university system seems to me to be fully worthy of the university tradition as far as this catholicity of knowledge and this universality of appreciation is concerned.

As to her scholars, her professors, and her university teachers of lower academic grades, my impression is that the selection has for the most part been rigorous and that the men are the ones who would be expected to be chosen by the competitive intellectual system as it operates. This means that they are avidly concerned with fundamental theoretical issues; they are skillful in discussion; they are quick to encounter weaknesses and difficulties in arguments; they have, so far as I could observe, a genuine interest in understanding and in communication.

The fact that men such as these have been chosen for their posts is *prima facie* evidence, I think, for the essential integrity of the selective system, indicating that no very gross distortion in the selection process has been at work. Women are entering the system, too; our impression is that the demand for qualified women is greater than the supply.

Now it is necessary to look at the obstacles with which the universities are confronted. First and most obvious, one has to do with the grossly inadequate facilities for instruction by way of libraries and laboratories. The Lucknow University, which is exceptionally good in every respect in which I could gauge it, has slightly over a hundred thousand books—a pitiful fraction of the number needed. Such a huge and powerful university cannot possibly do a modern educational job with this number of books in circulation. And of course the deficiency in technical material, and above all in the technical *journals*, is of enormous weight.

Even more serious, however, is the shortage in laboratory and other facilities. Laboratory equipment can be adequate under only one or the other of two sets of conditions: First, there may be a very large budget for the purchase of new material required for essential experiments; second, there may be highly skilled technicians competent to work in wood, metal, and other material and competent also as electricians, to follow professors' directions in setting up the requisite apparatus for teaching and for research investigations. India does not have the resources for the first of these methods, and has not the personnel for the second. The result is that Indian laboratories are very far indeed from what they need to be.

The academic standards demanded of students appear to be almost everywhere very low; the point is universally deplored. The fact is due in part to political pressures exerted by students and their families—pressures greatly increased by the mass movement toward the universities in recent years.

Add to this last point an extraordinary failure at educational integration which has come down from the British system: The student elects as he goes to college whether he is to become an arts student or a science student. An arts student is of course primarily concerned with languages, literatures, philosophy. The science student is concerned with mathematics, with the physical and biological sciences. Never the twain shall meet. The arts student studies no science; the science student studies no arts. The result is that each goes out into the world a half-trained individual. It is true that the West does much the same thing in some of its engineering colleges and in many of its arts colleges but in a less clear-cut way and with a somewhat less perfect "justification" for narrowness than that which is conveniently offered to the Indian student.

One can immediately see how the social sciences are likely to fare from such a point of view. The social sciences ordinarily are not regarded as sciences. The laboratory facilities which are required in economics, for example (by way of tabulating equipment, map-making, and the like) and the laboratory apparatus required for experimental psychology are likely to be penalized by this very system. More serious than this, however, is the point of view encouraged regarding the social sciences. One learns the "talking methods" in the arts training and the "doing methods" in the science training. The result is that one thinks one can solve problems at a verbal level if one goes through the arts course, and since the social science student gets no training in science, and has no exposure at all to scientific methods, he develops almost no research outlook, no conception of research methods, relevant to the discovery by Indians of answers to Indian problems.

There are social science techniques which in some degree are capable of being mobilized in the West for the solution of social science problems; for example, the methods developed recently in Great Britain for getting groups of coal miners to understand and to cooperate very much better with one another, with a huge improvement in tons per man per year. It would certainly be important for India to have the benefit of scientific techniques of the same sort in relation to her social problems. Thus, while her scientists frequently fail to find jobs in the scientific and technological world of today, the social scientists almost inevitably become social scientists who talk and go on talking to younger social scientists about things that "ought to be done," with no conception of *how*. The awareness of social issues on the part of science-trained young students is likely to be at the general popular level of the newspaper reader rather than an understanding in terms of science as such, and the understanding of scientific methods by the arts students is likely to be at least three removes from reality.

This difficulty involves even the men at the top of their profession. It was our experience everywhere that Indian psychologists and sociologists and cultural anthropologists and economists talk the common social science language known all over the world, but that whenever biological concepts, whenever concepts about heredity, growth, the learning process, adaptation to physical conditions of life were concerned, the social science groups showed a lack of exposure to science training. We made as a matter of fact one vigorous plea (in a public lecture at Lucknow) for the injection of science into the arts course and arts into the science course, and found that there were some who were feeling as we do; but the problem is very far from ripening for solution at this time.

As far as the work of creating national unity is concerned in India, it may therefore be said that not a great deal is to be expected very soon from the social sciences as such. This is a regrettable admission to have to make. There is not only the inadequacy of the university training; there is in general the resulting feeling that problems can be solved by exhortation and political action without a thorough grounding in facts. Professor Vakil points out that the response of administrators to the work of the Planning Commission shows a gross unconcern for the science of economics and the facts which it already makes available for public action.

And most serious of all, there is still the feeling among young people that the lucky ones get away from the village, get a university training, can equip themselves for cushy jobs in civil service and other administrative positions, or in the professions or sometimes in business; and one is up against such serious difficulties today for oneself and one's family that one pursues the safest and most lucrative position rather than thinking about global problems. Part of this is a familiar pattern everywhere in the world, but the universities under various pressures have in the West become centers where research on national economic and social problems is sometimes conducted as a scientific problem, and so far as we are aware, the Indian universities, by and large, have not as yet assumed this conception of their role.

But the point is that they are willing to see this as their role if they are given work to do and means to do it. It was very extraordinary to see how rapidly some members of each university assumed the new orientation when post-war conditions gave them encouragement. We believe that the great response given to the work of UNESCO is an augury of what may be expected of the universities if they are given a job to do; and that the Indian universities will be responsive indeed to the appeal that they give intellectual and scientific leadership, if they are more and more called upon both by state and central government to participate in research and in the training of scientists and technicians which the country needs.

It must of course be remembered that for the most part the universities represent the various states rather than the central government. They are financed mainly by the taxes which are administered by the state governments, and as a rule each university has been drawing its pupils almost exclusively from the region within which the university is situated. In spite of these divisive forces it is impressive that an all-India conception of education at the postgraduate level has been developing, that more and more students make their way outside their own provincial boundaries. The obstacles are, however, huge. The "Universities' Report," to which a large number of scholars gave a great deal of time, involving the investigation of staffs, facilities, curricula, student bodies, the whole educational process in the Indian university system, a 600-page document, has had, we were everywhere informed, very little influence.

Perhaps one expects too much too soon. Our evaluation at this time would be to say that there is great readiness of many *individuals* within the university system to respond to a conception of national service, a conception of using scholarship and science to advance the welfare of the people, but that this is not as yet an organically recognized part of the university's activities; that it is not a part of the express program of the Vice-Chancellors or the senates of most universities; and that it is largely through the stimulation of outside agencies that Indian university personnel have begun to think in terms of national service through university research and application as a part of their job. Their traditional task has been the training of individuals, mostly for administrative and professional jobs. Included in this has been the preparation of many excellent doctoral and masters' essays. The time is coming when these problems for masters' and doctoral essays will be chosen in terms of the welfare of India and in terms of possibilities for collaboration of many universities in the solution of some urgent question. This time is not in the immediate future but it is coming.

In the social tensions problem, nothing is more important than the mobilization of the universities.

TRADE UNIONS

Eighth in our list of assets would come the trade unions. Trade unionism began in India as an effective force late in the nineteenth century and in a few industries such as textiles unions have made considerable gains. In general the unions have a political orientation; this is true in general of European unions also. That is, a particular union will be Socialist, another will be Communist, another will be affiliated with the Congress Party, etc. The result is to interfere considerably with the economic power of the union in the sense that economic action is limited by the political outlook; and at the same time the effect of such a clear political ideology is likely to be the exclusion of those whose economic interests are rather similar to those who are members of the union, but whose political orientation is different. The unions are not, from a Western point of view, strong; and they have, from a Western point of view, a tendency to seek tests of strength before they are really ready for them. The number of disastrous strikes has been considerable and the advance of the trade union movement has not been clear-cut.

Take, for example, the textile industry. Here in the late twenties a rather effective union was organized in Ahmedabad partly under the influence of Gandhi, and here the union has done fairly effective work in creating a solidarity among all groups including the various castes and the Muslims as well. Here the various communities are represented by their effective leaders and here systematic and orderly presentation of complaints week by week is made and processed throughout the year, so that the worker has some real means of putting on pressure; and if his grievances are serious he can make a good deal of noise and is likely to get some result. The Ahmedabad textile union is not, however, strong enough to force any great increases in wages over the wage that would be determined by individualistic rather than collective bargaining. In fact the rate of compensation is not appreciably different from what is available for similar workers in other Indian cities with less adequate unions. It is very hard to see how under the present conditions an effective type of collective bargaining could be established. Some of the highly skilled male workers do make over three rupees a day, but they are separated not only by technical skill but also as a rule by caste from other workers, and the atmosphere has never developed for what we should call "vertical organization," in which all elements would stand together in a collective bargaining effort to force improvement in wages and hours. In other words, even a rather good trade union has not proved very effective with relation to basic economic problems.

During the last few years, the Bombay textile industry has been riven with great strife including a calamitous strike and an attempt to call a general strike of Bombay workers during the fall of 1950 which led to rather humiliating disaster and the impoverishment of the workers. In another huge industrial city, Kanpur, the intercaste struggles and other hostilities have helped to keep the union relatively impotent. It is to be very much doubted whether effective trade unionization in the European or American sense of the term can be regarded as imminent in the near future. People just do not have either enough capital, enough savings, or enough education to take chances. They take what they can get.

The same doubts can be expressed regarding the cooperative movement. Cooperatives have long been attempted in India. Those who have a little margin are not willing to commit themselves to a common fate with those who have no margin. If one is going to get people to work together in cooperative buying or cooperative selling, they must all have some margin to work with, and there must be no great likelihood that two or three consecutive bad years will destroy the more successful as well as the less successful; for if there is such a likelihood, the more successful have no motivation to join the cooperative.

VILLAGE DEVELOPMENT PROJECTS

Far more realistic from our present point of view is the attempt to combine the ordinary self-interest motive with the enormous capacity for learning by experience which is evident in every village. Whereas under the industrial conditions of the city one takes a long time to learn group action and learns actually only by very costly mistakes how to develop a powerful bargaining position with regard to wages, one can learn rather quickly and easily in the village how to better one's lot at the same time that one learns to cooperate with others in joint problems. India is studded all over with agricultural development projects, devices for a quick elevation of the standard of living of the village population through improvement in care of crops and animals, through irrigation, through road-building, and countless other improvement plans. We were ourselves especially impressed with the Etawah project in the Uttar Pradesh and think that a few words about its success may have some broad relevance in regard to the whole problem of tension and unity in Indian life.

During 1946 the Prime Minister in a series of conversations with Mr. Albert Mayer, a New York architect and town planner, developed a scheme for a project in village agricultural and educational development. This was talked over with Premier Pant of the United Provinces who, together with the legislature, worked on the problem, and finally some hundreds of thousands of rupees were appropriated for a "pilot development project" operated out from Etawah through a hundred villages.

The ideas were very simple. A number of Indian-trained

agricultural workers known as "village level workers" were to give ocular demonstrations day by day of the ways in which new seed, new ways of irrigation, fertilization, etc. were to be used. New crops were to be brought in and made to succeed; it should be clearly shown that the yield would be very much larger than had traditionally been assumed to be possible. The aim was not to teach anyone anything out of the book, but solely to give simple and direct demonstration that things could be done which never had been done before, and to answer each villager's questions as clearly and simply as possible. Within a few months it became evident through these hundred villages that much information was being conveyed which was gratefully received and quickly and effectively applied. As a matter of fact, the yield was so greatly increased in these villages that it was possible to take on shortly thereafter a second group of a hundred villages and then a third and then a fourth group.

These 400 villages have been developing according to a more or less uniform scheme through the spread of village level workers and higher Indian technical service. The essence of the whole method was to answer questions, to show people the answers to things they needed to know. An essential feature of the whole plan was to *set definite short-range goals*, so that one could tell month by month, year by year, whether one was actually *achieving* in terms of production what one had undertaken to achieve—and learn thereby what sorts of things were practical.

In visiting the Etawah project, one of the most impressive things was to see the rapidity with which initiative was developing, with which people had gotten the idea that they could do things in new ways without needing to be shown how, or even without being told that there were new things to do. We saw, for example, a wide, straight, and well-constructed roadway which had just been finished for the use of bullock carts between one village and another a mile away. Previously these villages had been connected only by a narrow footpath and it had been impossible to convey goods in any quantity back and forth. Whose idea was this? Not at all the idea of Mr. Mayer or even the idea of the village level workers. It was an idea which had occurred to a number of the villagers as they began to think that they could do things for themselves, that they could be self-starting. In the same way we saw nearby a new school which had just been erected by a group of villagers who determined that there should be better educational facilities for their children. They made their own levy of taxation; they went to work, hired the builders, did much of the heavy work themselves, and came through with a school of which they could be proud.

It has been a normal process in this whole "Pilot Development Project" to encourage group discussion, to work through the caste and village panchayats and to cultivate the notion that the villagers were to make their own decisions as to what they wanted next and how they were to obtain these many things. The project therefore automatically encourages the democratic processes, including intercaste communication. An example of an intercaste squabble connected with the refusal of Harijans to participate in the village panchayat, and to remove animal carcasses, was mentioned previously. The Pilot Development Project, by focusing people's minds on the problem of finding a solution for group goals, has by now notably reduced caste tension in the village in which this quarrel had occurred.

The Ford Foundation determined in the fall of 1951 to make an investment in the agricultural and educational development of India, based upon the model of the Etawah project. At this writing at least fifteen Etawah-like training projects have been established by the Indians with Ford support in various parts of India. How far they will parallel the Etawah development is not clear. It is however clear that full social science research techniques are to be included as part of the project; there is to be a sociological study of the changes in village life as a consequence of these new developments and a systematic testing of various hypotheses as to the types of social change which are likely to occur, including studies of village leadership, changes in family, caste, and other social structures.

This sociological approach, while not apparently the primary center of interest from the point of view of the Ford Foundation, would become from the point of view of our present analysis a primary factor in spreading the utilization of social science techniques in India. It will mean, for one thing, the recruitment of a large number of young social scientists who are to work with the fifteen projects and should do a great deal to give administrators a sense of the importance of systematic sociological research in effecting social change and, even more important, a sense of the possibility of factual evaluation month by month of the degree to which hopes can actually be fulfilled. As the Pilot Development Project showed, it is one thing to make a grandiose plan, another thing to determine in advance how to find out where one's expectations are realistic, where one's hopes are unsound. In a country doing all sorts of new planning, with all sorts of high aspirations, nothing could be more important than the disciplined enterprise of checking up on oneself to find out month by month where success is achieved and where a change in direction is required.

12

Help—acceptable and unacceptable

As we study this series of constructive steps ahead being taken by Indians to meet India's needs, the question arises whether other nations, and specifically the United States, can help. To this there may be a strong temptation to reply at once: "But look at what we are already doing; look at the work of American millionaires, American educators, American scientists and engineers, and today look at technical assistance and the beginnings of large-scale economic aid!"

Before replying, it might be worth while to ask: "Are we thinking of what *we* believe to be India's need, or what *Indians* consider to be their needs? Are we in a position to give what India wants? Specifically, what does India want that the West can give?" The answer is fairly complex and we shall attempt several facets of the answer.

INDIAN EAGERNESS FOR CONTACT

It has been our experience that wherever human beings go over the face of the earth they enjoy sharing their ways with other human beings; they enjoy looking, listening, feeling, exploring the ways of other folks. There is much more than exploitation here; there is much more than the need to acquire a stance from which one may master the new environment. There is much that reminds us of the little child so eagerly drinking in with eyes and ears and skin the new experiences in this strange world. The interest of the traveler everywhere is in part an interest in learning to see through

264

the eyes of others. One mingles the sense of the quaint and the bizarre with the sense of discovery—the electrical thrill of sensing beneath another costume, another skin, behind another façade of gestures or of sounds, a kindred spirit.

The Indians have this sense of joy in sharing their own ways of life with others even more keenly than most other human beings whom it has been our good fortune to encounter. Everywhere in India and at all levels one discovers eager joy in learning the ways, the outlook, the values of life from those who come to meet them. Whether it be the women in Purdah who fall upon a sister visitor from across the seas with a torrent of questions as to the activities of women and children in faraway lands, or the forest aboriginals who want to know who these wild men are who come from cities of stone and iron, or the students who love to learn to sing with us: "I've been working on the railroad," or the governors and high ministers who prod one with endless questions regarding the real meaning of the American way, one finds in India a very genuine and intense desire to understand us.

There is no need whatever that we create a bad intercultural situation by pushing ourselves into Indian life. It is not we ourselves or our intrusion as such that is resented. They are not only eager to tell us about their lives and to hear about our strange country and to compare notes back and forth; they are perfectly willing to tell you the weaknesses of their own civilization provided they are not put on the spot by endless "Mother India" types of odious comparison. They regret much that is intrinsic in their tradition, and much that has happened as a result of British rule, such as the loss of many of the democratic institutions of the Vedic period. At the same time they are eager to learn, and eager to make the most of the solid and substantial features of their own national esthetic, cultural, religious, philosophical tradition.

"RESISTANCE" TO AMERICAN IDEAS

What, then, is to be said about the supposed resistance to American ideas; the "mounting anti-American feeling" about which the papers tell us? The answer is quite simple: India wants to be let alone politically to develop in her own way. Though there are all kinds of Indians, and this may seem oversimple, I believe it is true that 99 per cent or more of the people of India are convinced that they have learned a great deal and can continue to learn a great deal from the West but that they want to be free to sift and choose and integrate in their own way. They are not particularly eager to ape the peculiar combination of economic competitiveness, political democracy, salesmanship, universal education, freedom of worship, radio advertising, televised baseball, mysteries for juniors, et cetera, et cetera, which make up present phases of American civilization. They want to study, to think and to choose. They resent very much being told what position they should take on either economic or political matters, whether at home or in the international tribunals of today. For the most part literate Indians are familiar with Marxism and familar with the Soviet applications and deviations from Marxist theory. For the most part they are willing to think experimentally and are very averse to the application of the techniques which the Kremlin has developed. They want their own chance to think and experiment. They do not want to be constantly told that they have to make an all-or-none decision between the white ways of the West and the black ways of the Soviet Union or China. That is not the way they see the issue, and the more effort is made to push them into an alignment the more skepticism, unrest, bitterness, confusion and failure of communication is likely to arise.

THE RESPONSE TO WESTERN LIBERALISM

How, then, do they view us? What do they take us to be? What is it that they want from us? To all these questions we believe the answers are really very simple: India has since the sixteenth century been the "discovered" rather than the discovering nation, in the sense that ships and men at arms came their way, while they struggled ineffectively to resist. Learning that one had to submit, they learned the techniques of acquiescence. In the case of bright young men with family backing, this meant learning the ways of the West well enough to be able to assume positions of prestige and power in the administration, and in the case of most of the rest of the population it meant learning minor devices for evading or giving surface adaptation to the requirements of an alien regime. Basically the British, unlike previous conquerors, remained socially aloof from the people of India, so that in general there was a two-way agreement of Indians and British to remain culturally isolated from one another.

On the other hand, during the nineteenth century, partly as a result of British pressure as represented by Macaulay, who wanted to modernize education essentially by Anglicizing it, and partly as a result of the growing awareness of the Indian that life could be made healthier, more rational, more just by the study and use of Western liberal ideas, young Indians began in increasing number and with growing energy to study the thought of Western humanitarians, liberals, reformers, men of the stature of John Stuart Mill, John Ruskin, William Morris, Henry David Thoreau, Walt Whitman, to conceive an overwhelming enthusiasm for the ideas of emancipation from the shackles of superstition and a case-hardened social system. Beginning with the great social reformer, Rajah Ram Mohan Roy, at the beginning of the nineteenth century and proceeding through a long series of

Indian leaders, one finds the Indian scene of humanitarian thinking and social action closely following the British and American scene. A widespread demand arose to put an end to an ancient aristocracy based upon arbitrary family power and wealth and to make real through education and social legislation a universal concern for the dignity of individual personality regardless of caste.

These liberal ideas sank deep into the structure of the Indian intellectual world. One reason why this was possible was that the ancient Indian tradition was itself full of open-mindedness toward new ideas, possessed certain kinds of democratic institutions, and in many ways respected personal dignity. The later development of sharp caste lines, the inferior and frequently degrading position of woman, and what might be called the snob value of great wealth have been repudiated by the many humanitarian and reformist Indian teachers throughout the centuries, and especially in the last hundred and fifty years, just as the student of early Christianity may today say, "Let us go back to the simplicity, the dignity, the humanity of the early church as against the growing incrustations of an authoritarian, greedy, and frequently superstitious leadership which forgot the simplicity and purity of the tradition." All this is by way of suggesting that Indian thinkers insofar as they acquired education —and this was mostly Western education and had to be Western if the recipients were to be leaders in the political movement of India in the nineteenth and twentieth centuries—turned eagerly to the West for the keynote to the thought of their own reconstructive nationalism, anti-Western though it was. They had to use Western ideas, for indeed nationalism itself was a Western idea.

THE CRAVING FOR SCIENCE AND TECHNOLOGY

Along with the hailing of the great light from Western liberalism came an equally enthusiastic salutation to the sun of science: science as a way of understanding and clarifying the structure of the universe; science as a way of seeing behind the façade of illusion, through the use of instruments like microscope and telescope which make evident the ultimate order and beauty of the world. Science, moreover, when turned to human use can put an end to smallpox, diphtheria, vitamin deficiencies and a thousand preventable diseases of the body, and at the same time can turn to human use the enormous natural storehouse of energies which lies unutilized about us. The response of Indians to the West was just as intensely appreciative in the realm of science and technology as it had been in the realm of humanism and liberalism.

So far we might conclude that the only attitude of India to the West was one of acceptance of her leadership. "If once the British will get out and let us have our own country, we shall be a modern state in the Western tradition." Actually this is a ridiculously one-sided approach. India cannot possibly take simply a Western point of view regarding those Indian institutions which are challenged or supplanted by Western institutions. India cannot possibly regard her own rich way of life as a fabric of superstition and human debasement. By way of the Middle East and by way of the endless caravans by land and sea which kept India in touch with the West, India has always been well aware that the Western tradition is itself based in large part upon the selection and development of clues from all over the world. It is not easy for an Indian to ignore the fact that it was an intended route to India which led Christopher Columbus to stumble upon the New World. Indian scholars are moreover aware of the enormous subtlety and complexity of the philosophical tradition, the literary arts, the magnificent handicrafts and work of the anvil and the loom which made India appear to Western observers of the sixteenth century to be a true "Paradise," as Vasco da Gama called it.

THE "INDIAN WAY"

Moreover, if one sinks a little deeper into reality one begins to realize that Indians are deeply devoted to their great tradition as expressed in epic and lyric poetry, music, folklore, philosophy; perhaps first of all in a sense of cosmic meanings in religious and ceremonial symbols. Very deep is their sense of the cyclical continuity, the dignity, the persistent resonance of life expressed magnificently in the great epic poem of the *Ramayana* and in countless gems of religious meditation and aspiration, in such religious poems as the *Gita*, with its reminder of the ultimate unchangeableness, beauty, strength of cosmic process of which human life is a momentary expression. Against this sense of resonance and reverence, the Indian comes full tilt into direct contact with the industrial technological successes of Western empire building.

He saw these processes in the railroads and mills established by the British in the nineteenth century. He saw the exploitative aspect of science and technology. He saw inevitably the process by which the blood, sweat, and tears of the coolies of Bengal were converted into wealth as they cut the jute into the stream of shipladen wealth that went to Dundee and came back in the gay costumes worn at the great hotels in Calcutta or in the even more curious form of the acid Calvinism which the Dundee owners of the jute mills expressed. However sympathetic, however warm and wise the individual Scot or Englishman might be in relation to his Indian workers, one could never forget the enormous gulf which separated the two, a gulf reinforced by the hotels and clubs for Europeans only, the formal isolation of Christian groups (even converted Indians being to a considerable extent Westernized and living in enclaves separated in large part from the great caste and family structure which is Hindu life).

The West therefore was essentially alien, though its science and technology had much that was good. The question therefore was not the question of an essentially good Western world with incidental derelictions; rather, it was a question of an essentially threatening world in which the more educated Indians might discover much which they could adapt to Indian life *provided they could do it in their own way*. It was not a question of taking over the whole of the Western approach and adapting it to Indian needs; it was rather a question of a highly critical sifting and assorting of those particular things in the Western world which could actually be used.

It must be remembered after all that the material prosperity—the Cadillacs, skyscrapers, ten-dollar dinners, fashion resorts and bathing beauties on Florida beaches, motion pictures of excitement, sex experimentation and violence—and behind it all the slums, the juvenile delinquency, the neglect of the weak and the old—are things which seem to Indians to characterize the "individualism" of the West, of American life. Americans wince when the word "materialism" is used and are likely to sidestep the issue by saying, "Well, we might as well be comfortable, we might as well develop a high standard of living." From the Indian point of view there is a very serious question whether the degree of preoccupation with food, physical comfort, the insulation of oneself from labor and from the primitive contact with the soil, the elements, and physical reality cannot actually sap the vitality and sap the spiritual vision of those who are "blessed with a high standard of living."

The beauty of simplicity

It is generally agreed today in India that Gandhi overstressed the conception of simplicity and that his idea of a system of home industries based upon the spinning wheel could not possibly elevate India's standard of living to a point where men and women could live in any kind of adequate standard of health and nutrition. Basically, however, most Indians of all levels are responsive to Gandhi's appeal for simplicity. They themselves, though they be mill owners, landlords, engineers, or administrators, almost invariably dress very simply and usually live in simple though beautiful surroundings. They protect themselves indeed against actual physical distress, but most of them decline to indulge in that continuous process of expenditure upon sheer physical things which for men of the West, and particularly for Americans, represent proof of progress in civilization.

The Indians then have a very real reason from their own point of view in rejecting Western materialism. They are not in the least disposed to reject science, but many are disposed to be cautious regarding the technology which has spread "black satanic mills" over the landscape of much of the industrial world; they are aware also of the attendant impersonality which has grown between employer and worker and the exploitation which has been considered a normal part of the industrial expansion of the last two centuries.

Without retracing any of the historical background discussed earlier, we may grant that the squeezing of the landless by the landed and of the impoverished by the wealthy is characteristic also of the economic life of India, as of much of the rest of the world. It is true, as we noted in another connection, that the expropriation of land and the process of squeezing the largest possible rent out of the borrower, together with the dispossession of all that one owns, are a normal part of the process of landlordism and of moneylending as seen in India. These malpractices are, however, regarded as archaic in the modern world; they are morally on the defensive.

Now one cannot say that the sense of moral wrong is attached by the West also to the *industrial system as such*, because it often oversteps the rules relating to ordinary competitive profit and loss and begins to become morally calloused. Indeed, the essence of the whole industrial expansion, like the commercial expansion which preceded it, is sometimes conceived to be the completely impersonal operation of economic motives of an "economic man" concerned only with gains and losses. But the system itself appears to many Indians to be corrupt and incapable of salvage. Whereas the system of landlordism and of usury are regarded as something to be abolished as soon as the opportunity permits, no such easy suggestion can be offered as to what is to be done about the inequities associated with industrialism and imperialism as the Indian sees it. For the most part, however, Indians today are inclined to experiment along various lines which we of the West would call the "middle way." They are concerned with the attempt to regulate large and small business in the common interest, preserving such businesses as can be carried on without gross social damage and liquidating those which cannot.

Any attempt to generalize here is ridiculous in view of the infinite variety, the infinite subtlety of the shades of thought and feeling. Nevertheless, we may in general say that a noncommittal and experimental attitude characterizes the approach of the Indian to Western economic institutions and that the same experimental attitude attaches to the various sorts of socialism which are to be found on the European continent and in Australasia, and even toward the type of experimentation now going on in the Soviet Union and in China, although a very marked reluctance is everywhere evident to embark upon totalitarian and authoritarian methods of control from the top which characterize these revolutionary movements. The Indian, in other words, is skeptical of us, even more skeptical of the Communist, and determined to have his own opportunity to experiment.

INDIAN QUESTIONS AND AMERICAN ANSWERS

While this book is not primarily concerned with the questions which Indians ask of the United States, a few words must be noted, because otherwise one would give the impression of a complete evasion of certain central issues which everywhere confront us. The fact is that Indians do have questions to ask of the United States. They have questions which they would like to ask boldly and publicly, to which they would like to have bold and public answers. Since they cannot get internationally public answers through the United Nations or any other tribunal of world affairs, they can ask the individual Americans to come to terms with their problems.

We regarded ourselves as perfectly fair game in relation to such inquiries. On one occasion, for example, after a public lecture on the UNESCO studies of social tensions at one of the colleges in the City of Aligarh, a request was made by a group of graduate students to have a group interview with me. This was arranged in the home of the Vice-Chancellor. They arrived twenty men strong to submit me to a series of very pointed questions. They began, as had happened before, with a very simple question which can be couched approximately as follows: "America is a country of inconceivable wealth, ready to do things in terms of tens of billions of dollars; the standards of living are incredibly high. She can appropriate in this year something of the order of sixty billion dollars for defense alone. India is a poor country struggling to free herself from medievalism and from the effects of two centuries of imperialism. A half a billion dollars a year would certainly get us on our feet, would prime the pump, would get us started, would make it possible for us to take care of essential health and nutrition needs. Why does it have to be always a question of loans or long-range credit? Why cannot Uncle Sam simply give us a half-billion dollars so fundamental for us, so trivial for himself?"

This question is partly a factual question, partly a rhetorical question, of course. The interviewers did not actually expect a detailed analysis of the reasons why. They were in part asking a question, but in part protesting against a situation regarding which they had relatively little hope.

I do not know whether what I did in this case was right or wrong. What I said was along these lines: "All right, let's imagine that you are the President of the United States. How would you get this through Congress?" They looked blank, stalled, could not think of anything to say, because of course they had not thought in terms of political realities, ways and means. Then I went on to find out whether they understood something about the way in which money is raised by taxation, and whether they grasped the feeling of most Americans that they are taxed to death, frequently for purposes very remote from those which they can immediately understand. I tried to find out whether they understood the procedure by which Representatives and Senators are elected, and the fact that representation in Congress necessarily (although of course very crudely) represents the self-interest and what makes sense to the majority of the voters; that democracy inevitably involves this kind of expression, this kind of joining of conflicting wills and that in the nature of the case America could not know very much about the needs of people all over the earth. From this, as the questioning went on back and forth, I tried to develop the theme that just as Indians know very little about the United States, so the people of the United States know very little about India, and that inevitably there is a gross failure to understand the nature of Indian poverty (let alone the fact of famine) and that there is no very easy device by which the American government could make clear to the people through press or radio the actual extent and form of Indian suffering. "Inevitably it is the threat to the United States which is going to be important in the minds of common men and women when they appropriate what is to them a very large part of their livelihood for the sake of tasks to be done far away at the other end of the earth."

I think this may have made a little impression; at least the questioning became less hostile. On this occasion and on other occasions the gentlemen of the far left then naturally took over and began to talk about the collapse of capitalism, the huge amount of unemployment in the United States, and other familiar themes. I do not at all mean to imply that the majority of my interlocutors were of Communist persuasion. I mean however to point out that the Communists are among the ones who have sharply phrased, definite, challenging questions to which the person interviewed must make some sort of coherent reply. For the most part those who stand somewhere not very far from center to right or left are not equipped to follow up in such discussions. Everywhere over the world the Communist has his organized outlook, his series of questions, his presumed answers, and he can pretty well force the interviewee into a position of answering in terms which are likely to give him a chance to pursue his questions along his own line. One has to have an extremely aggressive and well-thought-out line of counterattack in order to avoid being put in a corner by this procedure.

There is however one sort of attack upon Western ideas and upon American ideas which must be fully understood. There is the very natural feeling after these 200 years of British control that those of white skin may remain in India to dominate Indian institutions; and there is today a fairly widespread feeling that the United Nations, UNESCO, the

World Health Organization, and other instrumentalities are to a considerable extent Western agencies which are in India to do something. After all, were not the missionaries for 200 years secondary adjuncts to the imperial system which was there in India to do something, something in the long run for the interest, or at least expressing the outlook, of men of Western faith? This feeling that "You foreigners are here to do something to us" is a feeling which runs very deep. When now one visualizes the present writer as a designate of UNESCO sent as an American from the Paris office of that organization to study social tensions in India, nothing can be more natural than the Indians' assumption that they were on the spot, that there was something wrong with them, that their country's institutions were in some way in need of correction, that social tensions were a bad thing which the Western world would like to eradicate, and that there was no real escape from the surgery destined to be carried out.

Twice in public addresses this took the pointblank form: "Why with your social tensions in the United States, your maltreatment of minority groups, and so on, do you come to India to tell us what to do about the problem of our minorities here?" In both cases all I could do was to say, "I come here because the Government of India asked me to come." In both cases the inquiry came abruptly to an end with what appeared to be good grace and no renewal of the attack. Whatever went on in terms of veiled feelings is primarily of interest insofar as one remembers that whether the question is explicitly framed or not, there is always in the background the feeling, "Why do Europeans and Americans have to tinker with our national life, try to make us like themselves?"

It would really not be extreme oversimplification to say that from the Indian point of view what India wants is all that is good from the West and nothing that is bad. This is a rather formless response, but is, I think, not very far from what many Indians would actually say. They would be willing to spell out what is good, I think, by specifying first of all science and the scientific way of thinking, working, and applying knowledge; and second, political democracy and the equalitarianism and respect for individuals which goes with it. Personally I doubt whether there is very much else that they want from us in long-range terms. In short-range terms they want to be helped to their feet economically and to be able to trade and to interchange discoveries and ideas, thoughts, books with us in perpetuity. They do not want permanent dependency upon us in any form, and they do not even regard science and political democracy as a loan or gift from us to them. They regard these ideas as ideas which have been discovered by men all over the world in many different periods in which a temporary advantage was won by the men of the West in the recent centuries and to which they are willing to give their obeisance today in recognition of the backwardness, the imbalance to which their national life has fallen prey.

From such a viewpoint very grave questions arise regarding the "uplift" role which we of the West conceive ourselves to be carrying out. Under the guise of Point 4 economic assistance and the whole system of the Mutual Security Agency, pressed forward by our fear of the Soviet Union and our fear of the influence of China upon India, we have developed more and more the feeling that we must "save India," that we must step briskly into that benighted land, offer strength of all sorts, put a gun into the hands of our Indian ally, stand behind him, teach him how to shoot it, and gloriously share with him and with all the others the task of free world defense in which we continue to be the leaders.

This outlook is rather well understood by the Indians and they simply don't want it. In fact, many of them would rather give up the short-range economic help and the long-range scientific and ideological help and work things out as well as they can for themselves[1] rather than submit to so complete a renunciation of their national destiny. Will Americans wake up rapidly enough to the fact that this kind of reconstruction, this kind of salvaging of India, will simply not work? For Americans are slowly beginning to realize that India will have to decide what she will take and on what terms. If these terms are unfavorable to American aspirations, these aspirations will have to be given up and new ones developed.

. . . .

[1] It should be remembered that, for instance, the Etawah project was already running and being supported by the Government of the Uttar Pradesh before American assistance under Point 4 and the Ford Foundation support began to emphasize similar ideas and proliferate them on a broader scale.

13

An American opportunity

Perhaps I have already expressed a bias. A bias to the effect that it is not a very good habit for an American to picture himself in the guise of a knight in gleaming armor riding off in all directions to save the world while making it acquiesce in his personal outlook. This bias of mine hopelessly colors the present concluding chapter. But I think there is a very great deal that America can *share* with India, and with the world.

As I have already hinted, one basic question has to do with the exchange of *persons* and of *ideas* between India and the United States. Let us deal very concretely with what is being done and what might be done under this head.

AMERICAN OPPORTUNITIES FOR INDIANS

First, what about Indian personnel trained in the United States? The opportunities for America to teach Indian students in American universities would seem at first sight to be altogether extraordinary. It would seem that we have so much in the way of science and technology, medicine and public health, educational administration and practice, the philosophy of democracy, that certainly we ought in this way to be very useful to so backward a country as India.

Let us look at the various steps already being taken to implement such aid to India. First, the question is, what opportunities do we provide for Indian students to learn our ways by coming to the United States? There are about 2,000

Indian students in this country, largely financed out of their own resources. How about official United States aid? Despite the care and attention given to the program an average of less than 200 students per year have received United States Government assistance.

I turn to the question of Americans traveling and working in India. We encountered a fairly large proportion of the Americans other than missionaries who were functioning in professional capacities at the time we were there; but the total number is still very small. A few work in the Embassy or in the various Consulates; a few are studying on their own power; a few are studying with fellowships from the United States, such as Social Science Research Council fellowships. Not many appear to be functioning as professors in Indian institutions with or without Fulbright assistance. To say that this is a drop in the bucket would be a considerable exaggeration. It would hardly be a molecule in the drop. (I cannot evaluate the influence of the missionaries except for the note on page 271. But liberal and humanitarian ideas and impulses, emphasized above in discussing the role of education in India, have often been a prominent and vital part of missionary endeavor.)

MUTUAL COMMUNICATIONS

I turn next to the media of communication. In general, news about the United States appears in the English language press in India on the front page and it is likely to be half a column or a column long, dealing rather largely with Washington political news or with major economic or political news elsewhere, or of course with dramatic events such as scientific discoveries, train wrecks, or the deaths of celebrities. Considering that the Indian newspaper is short, the amount of space given to American affairs is relatively adequate. It gives, of course, a primarily political and secondarily economic picture, and hardly to any extent an educational or cultural picture.

Again let us change our point of view. What is the American source of daily information about India? Except for the *New York Times*, no American newspaper considers it worth while to have itself represented in India by a full-time general news reporter. The *Christian Science Monitor*, the *New York Herald Tribune*, and a few newspaper syndicates are represented by part-time and feature writers. One large class of items which are regarded as interesting enough to make the American press is the activity of those who are regarded as expressions of other-worldliness, including ascetics, wisemen, snake-charmers, fire-walkers, and fakirs, adepts with the rope trick and the miraculous mango tree.

It is in this context of the feeling that India is a land both of religion and of the exotic that one must understand what is often offered as political news by American reporters. It is interesting and important that a humble prophet in the Gandhian tradition goes about begging those who have land to give it up for the common good; the question, however, is whether the newspaper reporter can count upon an American public which is willing to listen to the whole complex economic background in which an event which is both religious and economic can be understood. The American public seems not to have time to understand plain ordinary men and women of today's India among whom these things that may seem strange to us are not strange, because the religious and the economic are not as sharply separated as we may wish to believe.

Of course the picture may be altered somewhat if one emphasizes magazines such as *The Nation*, with their regular stories on India, and the rather extraordinary series of interesting full-length books about India from people such as Vincent Sheehan, E. M. Forster, Louis Fischer and Margaret Bourke-White. These books, while not best-sellers, are actually indications that there is a public of a few tens of thousands in this country which is eager to find out about India not solely for political or exploitative reasons.

Perhaps the outstanding event in intercultural communication is the film *The River*, based upon the novel by Rumer Godden and magnificently produced by Jean Renoir. This film, while a story of a British family in India, does nevertheless manage in its background shots to indicate something of the charm and dignity of Indian life. Unfortunately, we must close our brief account by noting that *The River* is not the kind of film which gives an understanding of what India passes through today; nor is it a film likely to reach either Senators or local leaders of American small-town life, both of which groups may possibly benefit from some awareness of qualities other than the picturesque and the charming. We should be grateful, however, that the picturesque and the charming can have some place in competition with the grotesque and the exotic.

But it may be felt that we are postponing too long the discussion of the primary medium of communication from the United States to India, namely, our own motion picture industry available for export to the Indian cities. No more harrowing story could be told than the story of the way in which grandiose extravagance and big-shot brutality, as represented in American films, can at times color their conception of what life in America must inevitably be. The less said, the better.

But what of other ventures? What, for example, of the book business? Well, the serious book business which was operated by British firms has inevitably distintegrated. Now there is a huge scheme for flooding the Indian market with American 25- or 35-cent books, probably on sale for a rupee, that is, 21 cents, in the Indian market, in the cities. This would presumably give some sort of a cross-section of what American literature is like. The whole question arises as to what one means by literature. Probably 50 per cent nowadays of this kind of literature in American bookstands, drugstores, railway stations, and so on, is simply crime; most of it is in the form of what we quaintly call mysteries, with pictures of strangled or bloody heroines pitched down staircases on every lurid front cover as a continuous testimony as to where our preoccupations in the literary realm have led us. If our classic crime preoccupations, as for example in the case of Edgar Allan Poe, could be crystallized as a small dose of what American crime-makers and crime-analysts have undertaken to purvey, a little good and not very much harm might well ensue. The question is immediately thrown into the open, whether we wish simply to have ourselves stand as the naked and the dead before the mind of the Indian public, which is capable today of buying practically any quantity of serious high-grade literature from the Soviet Union and even a fair amount of it from China; whether we actually wish to enter this competition; and what we think the outcome for international understanding might be. Certainly some more thinking about the nature of book interchanges with India might be carried out.

If, then, we recapitulate (1) exchange of persons in two directions, (2) exchange of ideas through the press in two directions, (3) exchange, mostly on a one-way basis, by way of motion pictures and books, we do not seem at present to find that the basic tooling-up, the basic thinking-out of American policy about communications with India has been seriously undertaken. If we are going to "teach" India, we must have a medium by which India can be taught. We shall have to decide what it is that we want to teach, what kind of people shall do the teaching, and what the content of the message shall be. It is rather late in the day to decide these matters. In the meantime, pumping economic aid into India is going to be associated with some kind of *ideas;* ideas are the wrapping in which any such techniques are to be shipped. Whose ideas, what kind of ideas shall they be? We know from the story of the American occupation forces over the world that wherever Americans go they are judged to a considerable extent by the kind of literature, the kind of comics, the kind of conversation they represent. If America is to do anything on a large scale in India, she will be judged by the content and form of communication which exist today or by something which we have already begun to plan. It looks as if we should be teaching a little bit of science and technology through Point 4 and various private enterprises, and that we have no real plan for anything more. As usual, the Soviet Union, and perhaps the Chinese, too, will fill the gap.

WHAT COULD WE "TEACH" INDIA?

What is it, then, that we could teach? How about beginning with what we generally agree is good education for our own children or adolescents? How about supplying India with the standard materials of literature, mathematics, science, art, business, technology representing the pabulum of instruction given at various levels in our educational system? In other words, why not make available on very reasonable terms standard educational material at rates which are feasible in India? So far, discussions with American publishers have not given me very much cofidence that any such step is being planned. The gap between what Indians can pay and Americans can accept in terms of the ordinary imagination of the ordinary American publisher has not been bridged. Actually this is not very surprising. Most American publishers when it became evident in the early depression period that there was a time coming when inexpensive paperbound books would be widely sold in the United States, as they are in France and Britain, expressed great skepticism. The tens of millions of such books sold today are a tribute to the imagination of a very small number of publishers, not to the mass. In the same way, a small number of publishers and people with ideas working in combination may well contrive to get the best American material, which would certainly be in demand in India, into a form which Indians could afford to buy. That Indians would buy a great deal of sound educational material is reasonably certain, and perhaps this simple economic fact will ultimately prove to be a large part of the solution of our problems. In the meantime, it must be acknowledged very frankly that we are not teaching India very much and that in many areas we are not capable of teaching India very much.

WHAT CAN INDIA TEACH US?

The question arises, then, what we can *learn* from India. One of the things that is most apparent is that we have already learned something from the life and work of Gandhi, from the life and work of Nehru, and from the books and utterances of many other modern figures who have voiced India's outlook in literature, the arts, music, science, and education. One thinks of the world influence of Tagore long before the special problem of American-Indian relationships arose; one thinks of the influence of the dancer Shankar, and other great dancers of today, who are beginning to make their American tours. It is likely that as we come to know India we shall learn things that are much less easy to specify and much deeper in the bone. It is likely that we shall learn a great deal more about simplicity and generosity, warmth, reverence, and perhaps above all, reverence for the child.

Observation of the skill and subtlety of interpersonal relations in India may perhaps lead some to feel that the Indians are ready to develop their own social sciences, their own ways of viewing social problems, in objective and even in experimental terms. Our own impressions would not warrant such confidence at this time. The social sciences as we think of them today, with their orderly disciplined search for facts, their systematic attempts to test hypotheses, as in the best work in economics, political science, sociology, and social psychology, are represented in India only by a handful of men, mostly trained in the West and all of them heavily dependent upon Western sources. It will certainly take a tooling-up process of many years to enable the students of today to catch the best of what the West can offer and adapt it to Indian conditions. Relatively few Indians will be able to travel to the West under present conditions, and those who do travel will stay only a short time and hardly be able to establish themselves fully in modern modes of thinking and research. International social science, the dream of all those who attempt to formulate scientific problems in a manner independent of the prejudice of any particular national group, will inevitably depend largely for a long time on those national groups which have been so lucky as to experience in their own bodies and their own training the development of the social science ways of thinking and acting.

It must be frankly recognized that this is something which America can give if America is willing to accept two conditions: First, such things must be given not to India but to the whole world, forgetting the relation of polarity which makes a single nation a giver and a single nation a receiver, accepting in other words the conception that this is a common human enterprise to which we individual Americans will give what we can along with all other individuals of other nationalities. Second, American participation in international social science will have to be premised on the assumption that Americans take part in the investigation of social pathologies *wherever* they exist, including those in their own country, sharing on equal terms with specialists from other lands who are concerned with these issues as common human issues.

AN "AMERICAN DILEMMA"

It is quite characteristic of our inability to make up our minds in this matter that we encourage social science through universities and through foundation-sponsored projects, but hesitate to look for any "political" consequences, in other words, refrain from any real pressure upon legislative or executive bodies to put into action the facts which have been discovered. It is quite characteristic of our American situation that a Foundation should supply the funds to bring a specialist, Gunnar Myrdal, from Sweden to study the race problem in the United States and quite characteristic that this study of "the American dilemma" was hailed as a masterful probing of the contradictions and social waste involved in racial discrimination. It is equally characteristic of American life that no governmental implementation of the findings is made; that in spite of local and state gains we have just lived through a period of loss of federal action in the protection of economic opportunities for Negroes, in that the Fair Employment Practices Commission has gone by the board. We usually tend to separate as sharply as we can what is socially ideal and what is politically expedient.

This means that for the time being international social science will have to be essentially a private matter as far as *action* is concerned, and that when basic fact-finding, aside from action, is involved, it can count on genuine international collaboration insofar as there is no threat that political consequences will ensue. Let us take what we can get; let us have a National Science Foundation in the United States, including the social sciences, and an international social science laboratory and research program sponsored if possible by UNESCO. Let us not, however, deceive ourselves into the belief that public instrumentalities, that is, political instrumentalities, can automatically achieve the goals which social science points out. To use facts which Congress may use is good, but self-deception as to what this may accomplish is evil. Both in educating the public and in providing data for the use of Congress the research investigator can expect to work hard for very limited results, and run the large risk that every careful documentation of fact will lead to suspicion and even penalization, if the facts are disagreeable.

It is common today to hope that the contact between India and the United States will be a pacemaker for a world-wide exchange between occidental and oriental ideas. In Northrup's significant phrase, this should serve "the meeting of East and West." Several similar attempts such as the December, 1949, meeting of representative Indian and American leaders in New Delhi and the 1951 conference of philosophical leaders under the auspices of UNESCO may serve perhaps as a beginning. It was our feeling, however, in India, that to expect a real meeting of minds is to impose too much of a burden on both sides. We are not competent—none of us are—to represent the West or to represent the United States; nor is anyone in India competent to represent India. Least of all is this atmosphere of a meeting of East and West likely to bring out the simple sharing and group quest of ideas upon which world unity must depend. One senses in the agenda of such meetings the ways of making clear the nobility of one's own tradition and present aims; the desire not only to be understood but to be understood as wise and good. At the same time not only can no one represent India or the United States, but India can in no way represent the East and America can in no way represent the West. It is true that many Indian ideas, notably religious and philosophical ideas, have spread through Indonesia, China, Japan, and many other parts of the world, and that American ideas, especially in science, technology, and economic organization, have permeated almost every fastness in the Western world. This does not, however, mean that good mental health can attend this conception of America like Horatius at the bridge, "holding the line" against all dangers. In a certain sense France is much more typical of the West, though relatively weak economically and politically today. Italy, custodian in many respects of Roman civilization and of the magnificent arts of the Renaissance, is capable of representing us in other respects. The West can also be represented in respect to architecture and drama by the Scandinavian countries and in respect to music by Germany and in respect to the dance and the arts of conversation and gracious living by the men and women of Latin America. It is sheer snobbishness for Americans to go forth alone as representatives because they happen at the moment to be economically, politically, and militarily the strongest of the Western peoples. The self-consciousness and the posing which come from this sort of interchange can more healthily be replaced by a sense that we of the United States and they of India can serve to some extent to probe and understand one another's minds and hearts in the hope that every community may spread ultimately to merge in a world community.

LEARNING TO GIVE

The end of the British regime may be thought to offer a foreboding of a catastrophe which may similarly overcome our American adventure in India. It is my own thought that this is not to be taken too lightly, for there is a very real danger that we may proceed now in the next century or two to commit very similar errors. We are already talking about helping India almost in the manner of the white man's burden. Some of us are already talking about pouring aid into India on the assumption that India will gobble up all that is offered. We could in this way literally kill much that is vital in India; we could literally put an end to much that is precious in India's civilization. It is true that India is too big for us. The British neither would nor could destroy Indian civilization as a whole and neither could the United States. But we could easily carry out a process both infernally stupid and barbarically cruel; we could easily impose a sense of shame and a sense of helplessness by favoring some in India and leaving others to suspicion and hostility because they are not among the favored few. Many will experience what Pars Ram has referred to as the guardian angel complex. We with our money to spend may help a few here and there to their feet, and these few, becoming dependent on us, fawn upon us, pray to us, and turn with a backward glance over their shoulders at the wretched mass who are not allowed to enter into this largesse. Whatever indigenous roots of strength, faith, continuity exist in Indian life could be crushed in so far as we had the money and the manpower to do the job.

There is another way to look at the whole issue. This is in terms not of the next few years nor even the next few decades but the panorama of history as a whole. It is certainly true that we must be intensely on our guard with reference to the maintenance of our own institutions in the next few years. The main problem, however, is not the next few years; the main problem is the establishment now in this critical time of a relationship with India which may flower over centuries into a strong, sound, mutually beneficial and constructive experience, something like the relations which have obtained between France and the United States in the last hundred and seventy-five years, or between Sweden and the United States in the last hundred years, with much exchange of persons and ideas, with mutual respect, with eagerness to follow the cultural and scientific and educational developments which each national group represents. Actually we have never had any such relation with any oriental country. Today China is out of touch with the West. Japan is momentarily close, insofar as she accepts or appears to accept the American political and other institutions which have been supported by an army of occupation, and insofar as she now expects, through American science and technology, to be able to find her way to the position of a great power again. The United States has never as yet lived on the kind of basis of brotherly exchange with China or Japan which has characterized the relations with France or with Sweden. American relations with the Philippines were again relations between conquerors and conquered; from the point of view of Filipinos who had successfully thrown off the Spaniards under the leadership of Aguinaldo, Americans came as despots and remained as patrons. With Thailand and Indonesia the United States has had scant contact. The great opportunity is India. What Americans do in India is not only by far the largest chunk of the immediate plan of action in the Orient, but will be the pacemaker for the rest.

Sensitive Americans will experience their relations to India not only as giving but as receiving and they will, in the process, be learning as well as teaching. India and America can develop a happy relationship and not just a sense of duty and sacrifice on one side and a sense of dependency on the other. From a broad historical point of view the conception of a recently established Western civilization as capable of giving something to, and receiving nothing from the age old and infinitely rich civilization of India becomes grotesque.

While it is "later than you think," it is also much, much earlier. It is the beginning of a period of perhaps decades, perhaps centuries in which sound relations with one of the great peoples, one of the great civilizations can be established; something better than technical aid, something better than a military-economic alliance against some third party can be pursued by the more imaginative. India will remain in the world quite a little while yet. Perhaps the West will, too. As long as we both remain, it is worth while to plan more than a few years at a time.

Appendix

INTERVIEW FORM USED IN BOMBAY

Excerpt from Questionnaire for Refugees, Hindus, and Muslims

15 (a) (For Refugees and Hindus only)

A group of people comes to associate definite qualities with other groups, rightly or wrongly. For example:

1. Some say the Muslims are loyal to their friends; others say they are disloyal. What do you think? Loyal ? Disloyal

2. Some say the Muslims are clean; others say they are dirty. What do you think? Clean ? Dirty

3. Some say the Muslims are frank; others say they are not. What do you think? Frank ? Not frank

4. Some say the Muslims are fanatical; others say they are not. What do you think? Fanatic ? Not fanatic

5. Some say the Muslims are carefree; others say they are not. What do you think? Carefree ? Not carefree

6. Some say the Muslims are cruel; others say they are not. What do you think? Cruel ? Not cruel

7. Some say the Muslims are generous; others say they are not. What do you think? Generous ? Not generous

8. Some say the Muslims are moral; others say they are not. What do you think? Moral ? Immoral

9. Some say the Muslims are courageous; others say they

293

are not. What do you think? Courageous ? Not courageous

10. Some say the Muslims are treacherous; others say they are not. What do you think? Treacherous ? Not treacherous

11. Are there any other qualities which you associate with the Muslims?

12. Of the qualities described so far, which one do you associate most with the Muslims?

(b) (For Hindus only)

1. Some people say the Refugees are clean; others say they are dirty. What do you think? Clean ? Dirty

2. Some say the Refugees are moral; others say they are not. What do you think? Moral ? Immoral

3. Some say the Refugees are appreciative of local help; others say they are ungrateful. What do you think? Appreciative ? Ungrateful

4. Some say the Refugees are behaving in a very difficult situation admirably; others say that they take undue advantage of their situation. What do you think? Behaving admirably ? Taking undue advantage

5. Some people say that the Refugees are very industrious; others say they are idlers. What do you think? Industrious ? Idlers

6. Are there any other qualities which you associate with the Refugees?

7. Of the qualities described so far, which one do you associate most with the Refugees?

(c) (For Refugees only)

1. Are you satisfied with the treatment that you receive at the hands of the local Hindus? If no, please indicate why. Yes ? No

2. Do they extend a helping hand to you? Yes ? No

3. Do you feel they treat you as unwanted? Yes ? No

Excerpt from Questionnaire on Hindu-Muslim group tensions

24. Arrange the following   Congress   Jamiat-ul-Ulema
    political parties in order   Muslim League   Communist
    of your preference: Maha Sabha R.S.S. Socialist

25. Which of the above organizations would
    you like to be banned?

26. Do you agree/disagree with the
    following?

    i   Hindus and Muslims are two nations   Yes   No   ?
    ii   They have separate culture   Yes   No   ?
    iii Hindus are discriminated against in
         Pakistan   Yes   No   ?
    iv   Life and property of Hindus are
         insecure in Pakistan   Yes   No   ?
    v   Hindus have no freedom of speech
         in Pakistan   Yes   No   ?
    vi   Congress has ceased to represent
         all the communities in India   Yes   No   ?
    vii There are strong pro-Hindu mem-
         bers in the centre and the state
         cabinets   Yes   No   ?
    viii Secular state is far from being a
         reality   Yes   No   ?
    ix   Muslims in Pakistan have brighter
         future than in India   Yes   No   ?
    x   Muslims have no right to stay in
         India   Yes   No   ?

42. When you hear that a communal riot
    has broken out in your town what will

you do? Place a check mark ($\sqrt{}$) against what you would do.

   i   Report to police
   ii Ascertain facts
   iii Believe those who carry the news
   iv Organize peace parties
   v   Organize groups of neighbors of both communities for defense
   vi Organize parties of both communities to fight mischief makers
   vii Stay at home and mind your own business

43. When there is a rumour of a disturbance would you pass through

   (a) Hindu locality   Yes No
   (b) Muslim locality   Yes No
   (c) Refugee colony   Yes No

44. Should the refugees get the following:

   i   Preference in services   Yes No
   ii Preference in the allotment of houses, shops and in grant of licenses and permits   Yes No
   iii Free monetary grant   Yes No
   iv Loans without interest for business, etc.   Yes No

45. Should a capital levy be paid in India to pay compensation to the refugees?   Yes No

46. Should India, if peaceful solution is not found, wage war with Pakistan for the settlement of evacuee property issue? Yes No

47. Should the refugees be settled

    i   in separate colonies   Yes No

    ii inside the cities (Lucknow etc.)   Yes No

48. Would you welcome more refugees in
Lucknow?   Yes No

49. Do you think that a considerable section of
the refugees consists of anti-social elements
which are ever ready to quarrel?   Yes No

50. Has the presence of refugees affected communal relations in Lucknow?   Yes No
How?

51. Do you agree that the refugees are

    i   Hard working   Yes No

    ii   Rude   Yes No

    iii Clean   Yes No

    iv Selfish   Yes No

    v   Honest   Yes No

    vi Quarrelsome   Yes No

    vii Unreliable   Yes No

36. To which of the follow-   Brahmins
ing communities would   High-Caste Non-Brahmins
you let your house, if it   Lower Caste Non-Brahmins
falls vacant?   Harijans
   Muslims
   Christians

37. Which of the above groups is hindering your progress?

38. Which of the above groups is helping you?

39. Between Northern Indians and Southern Indians whom do you prefer as

		North Ind.		South Ind.	
(a)	Employer	North Ind.		South Ind.	
(b)	Employee	"	"	"	"
(c)	Co-worker	"	"	"	"
(d)	Neighbor	"	"	"	"
(e)	Co-tenant	"	"	"	"
(f)	Kinsman by marriage	"	"	"	"

40. The Government is do-
ing some things badly and
some things well; what is
it that you *like* most in
the policy of

   (a)   Central Government
   (b)   State Government

What is it that you *dislike*
most in the policy of

   (a)   Central Government
   (b)   State Government

41.[1] I would like to know your feelings towards some of the groups of people arranged in alphabetical order. To which of the six categories mentioned below would you like to admit them? Please note that I want your reactions about each group as a whole and not with reference to any particular individual or individuals of that group whom you may know.

Write 'yes' or 'no' at the appropriate place for *each group*.

Brah-mins	Chris-tians	Hari-jans	High Caste Non-Brah-mins	Lower Caste Non-Brah-mins	Muslims	Parsis	Sikhs
___	___	___	___	___	___	___	___

1. To kinship by Marriage
2. To take food in your dining room
3. As an intimate personal friend
4. As a guest in your house
5. As your neighbor
6. As an acquaintance

[1] Referred to in text as Social Distance Test.

Index

301